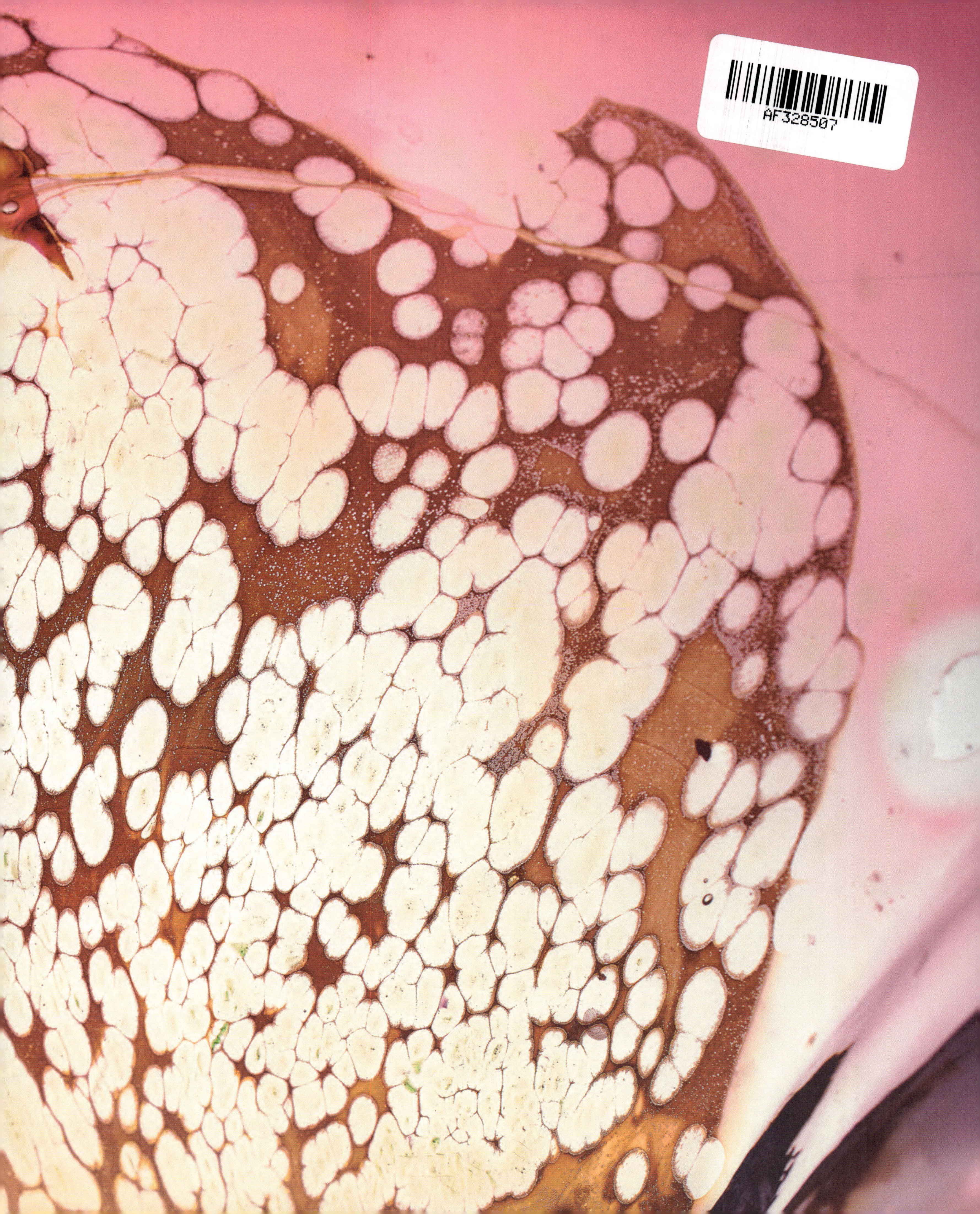
AF328507

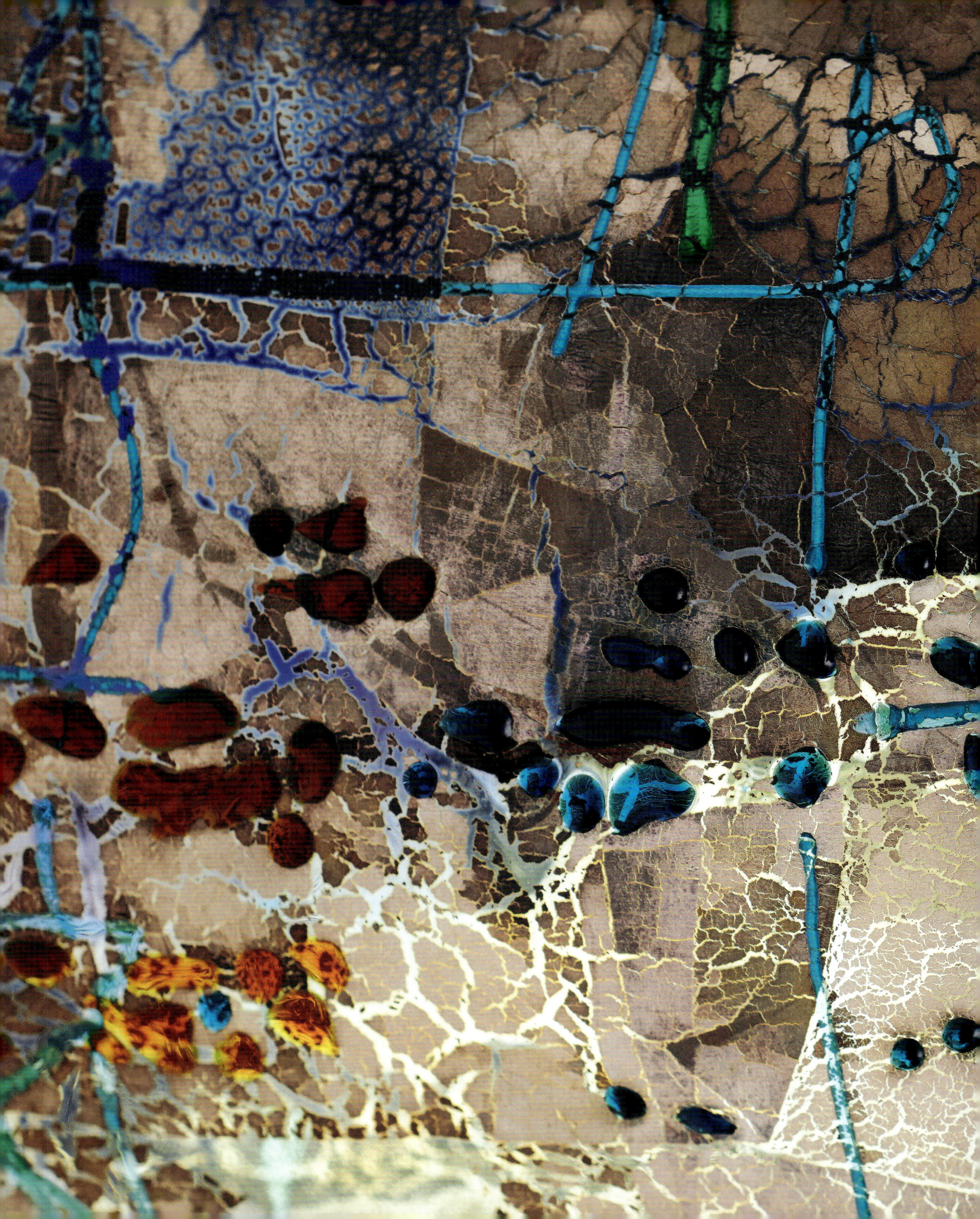

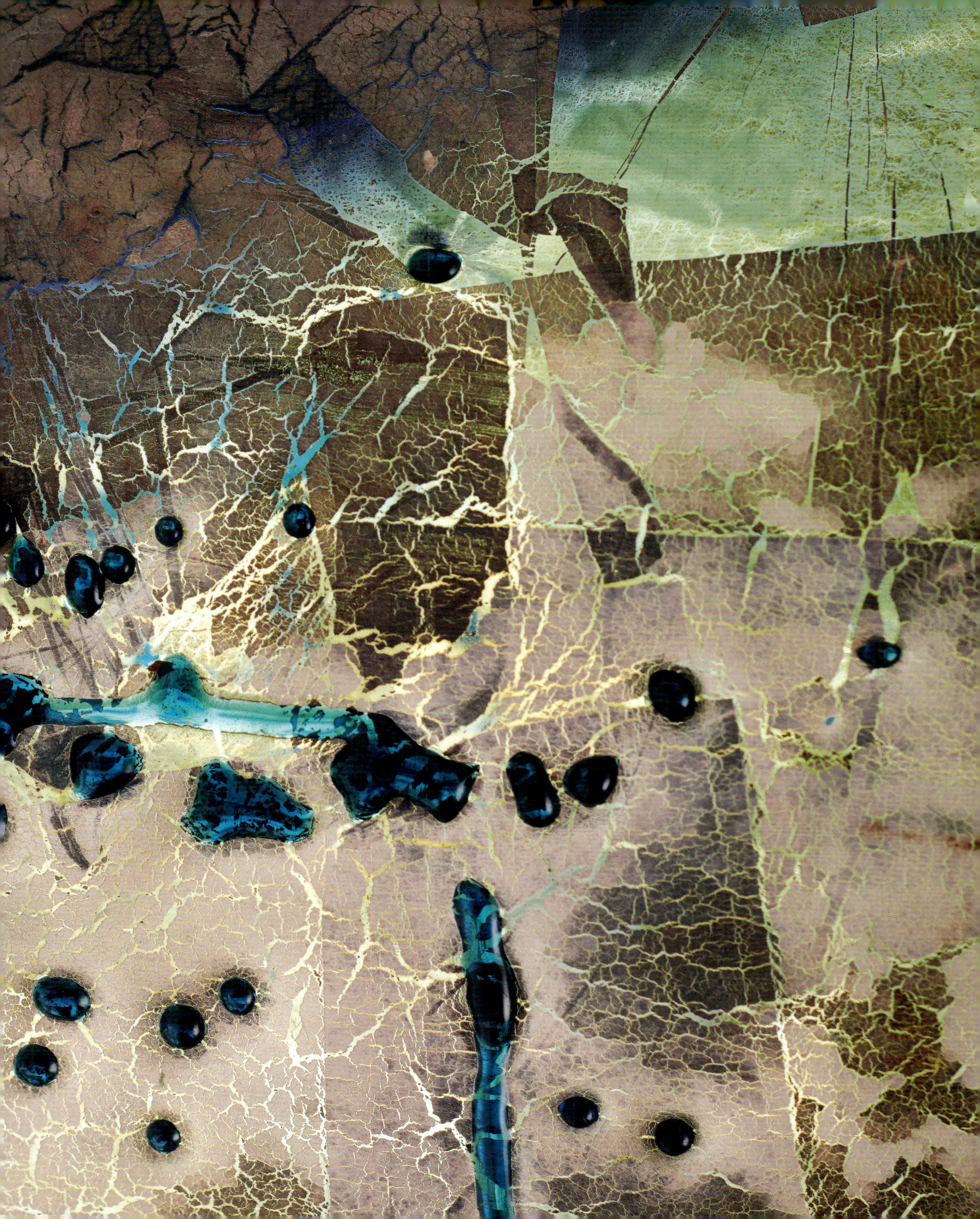

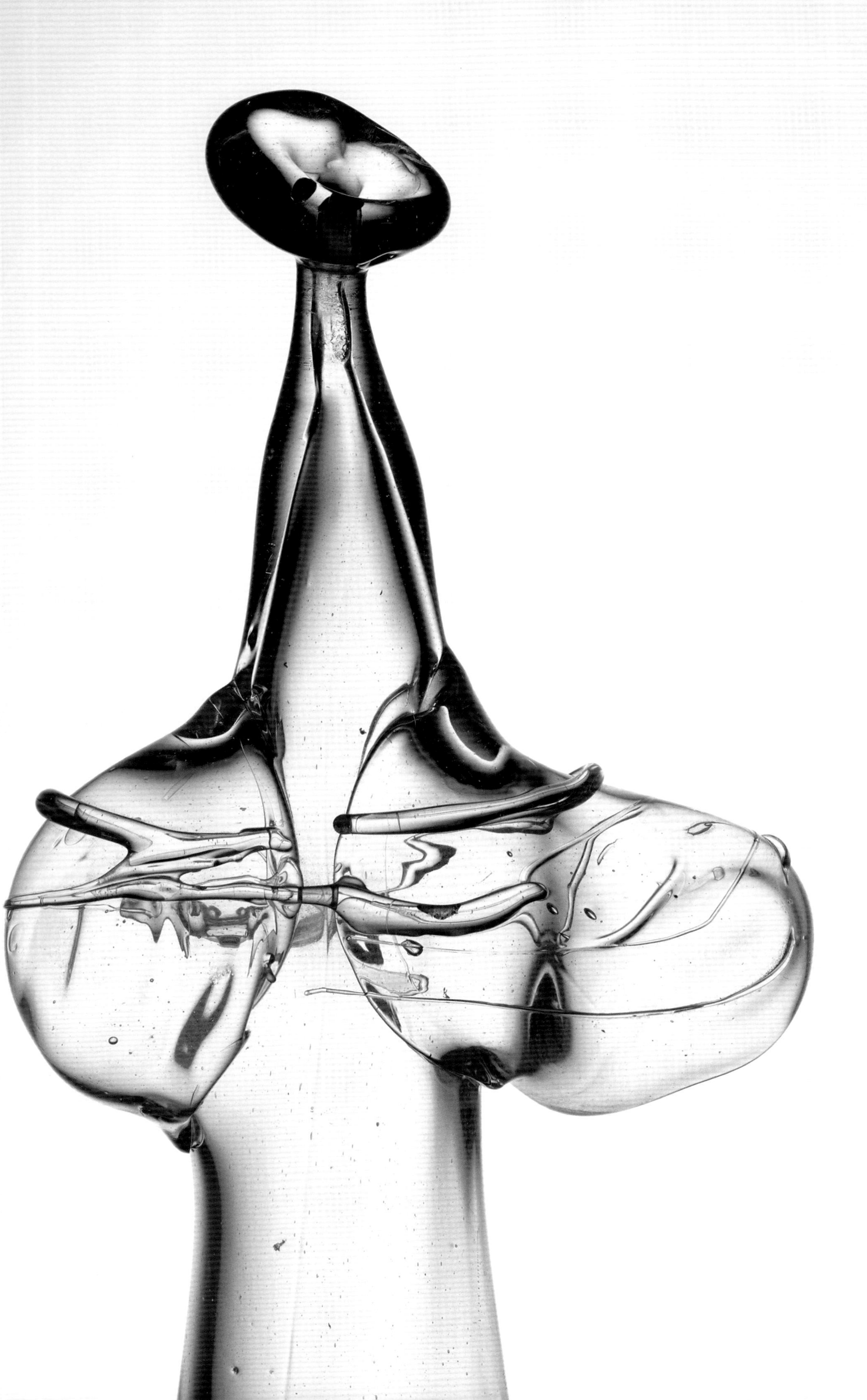

Sam Herman

Edited by Rollo Campbell

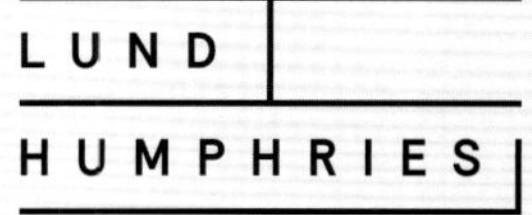

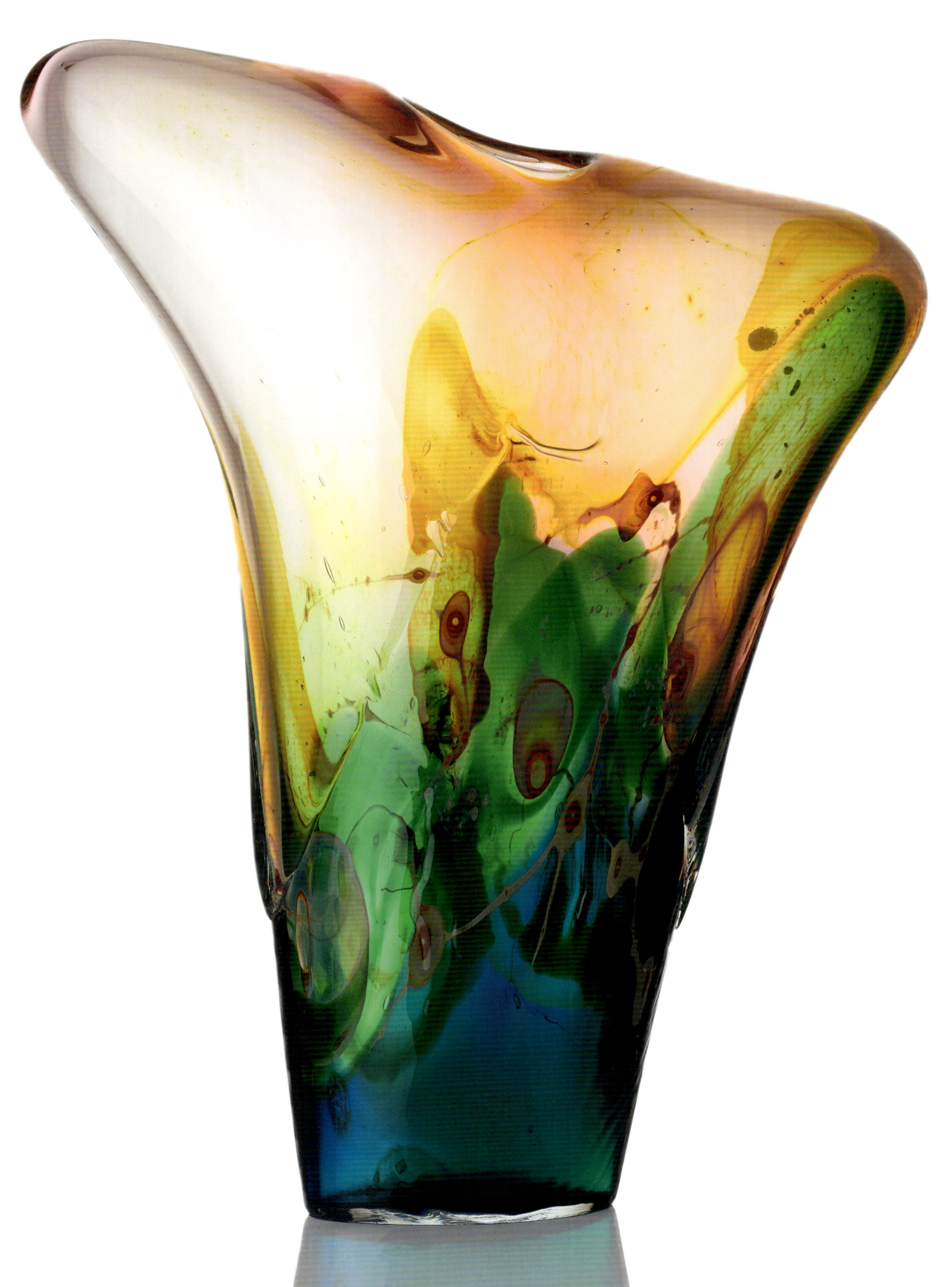

Contents

10 **Foreword**
The Marquess of Queensberry

15 **Introduction**
Rollo Campbell

19 **The Early Years**
Lucy Abel Smith

27 **The Birth of Studio Glass, 1963–65**
Michael Boylen

33 **The Studio Glass Pioneer, 1965–84**
Mark Hill

53 **The Glass Artist**
Mark Hill

127 **The Educator**
Greg Votolato

133 **The Sculptor and Painter**
Michael Regan

166 Notes
167 Chronology
168 Selected exhibitions since 1966
169 Selected works in public collections
169 Selected bibliography
170 The making, signing and numbering of glass pieces
171 The authors
172 Index

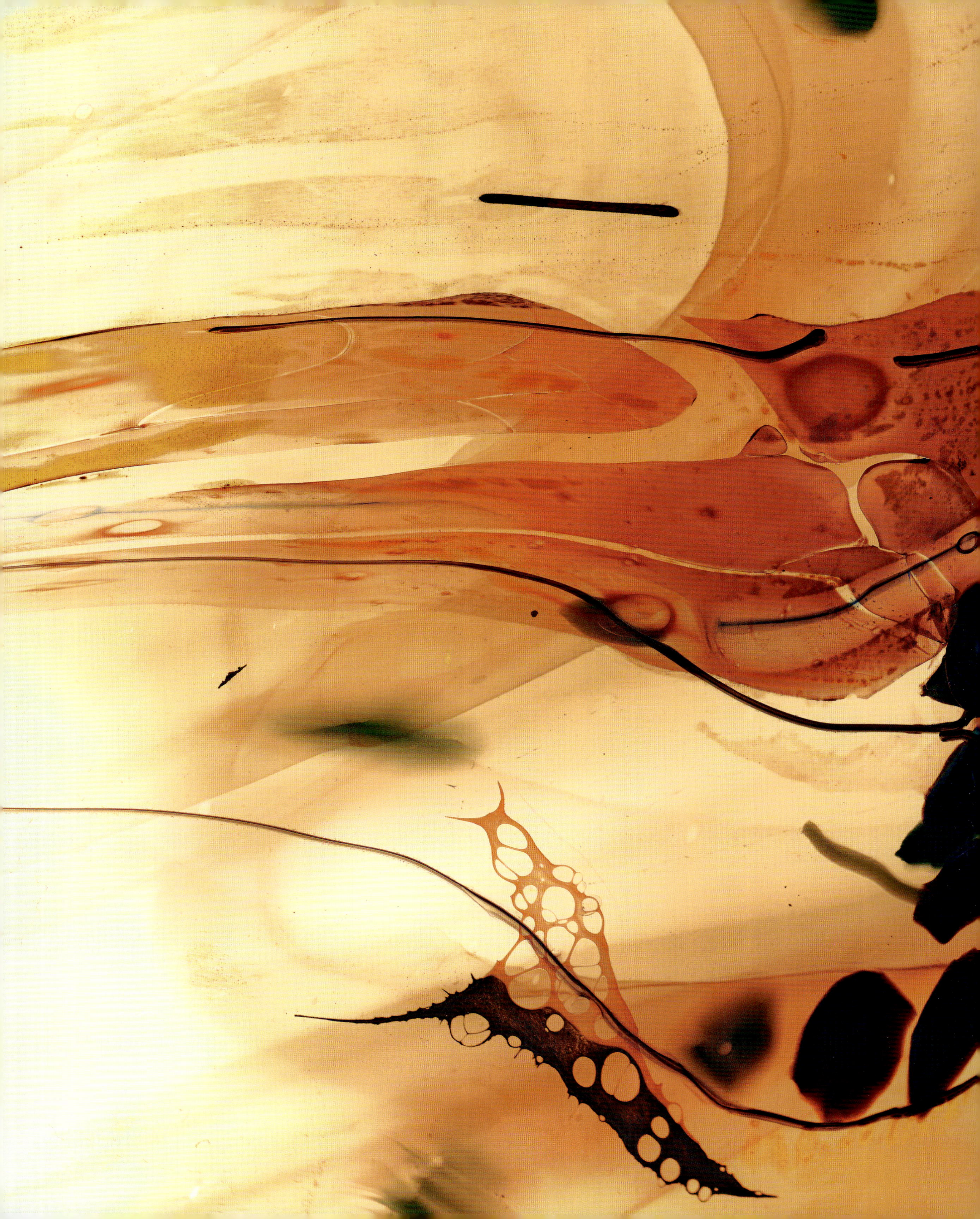

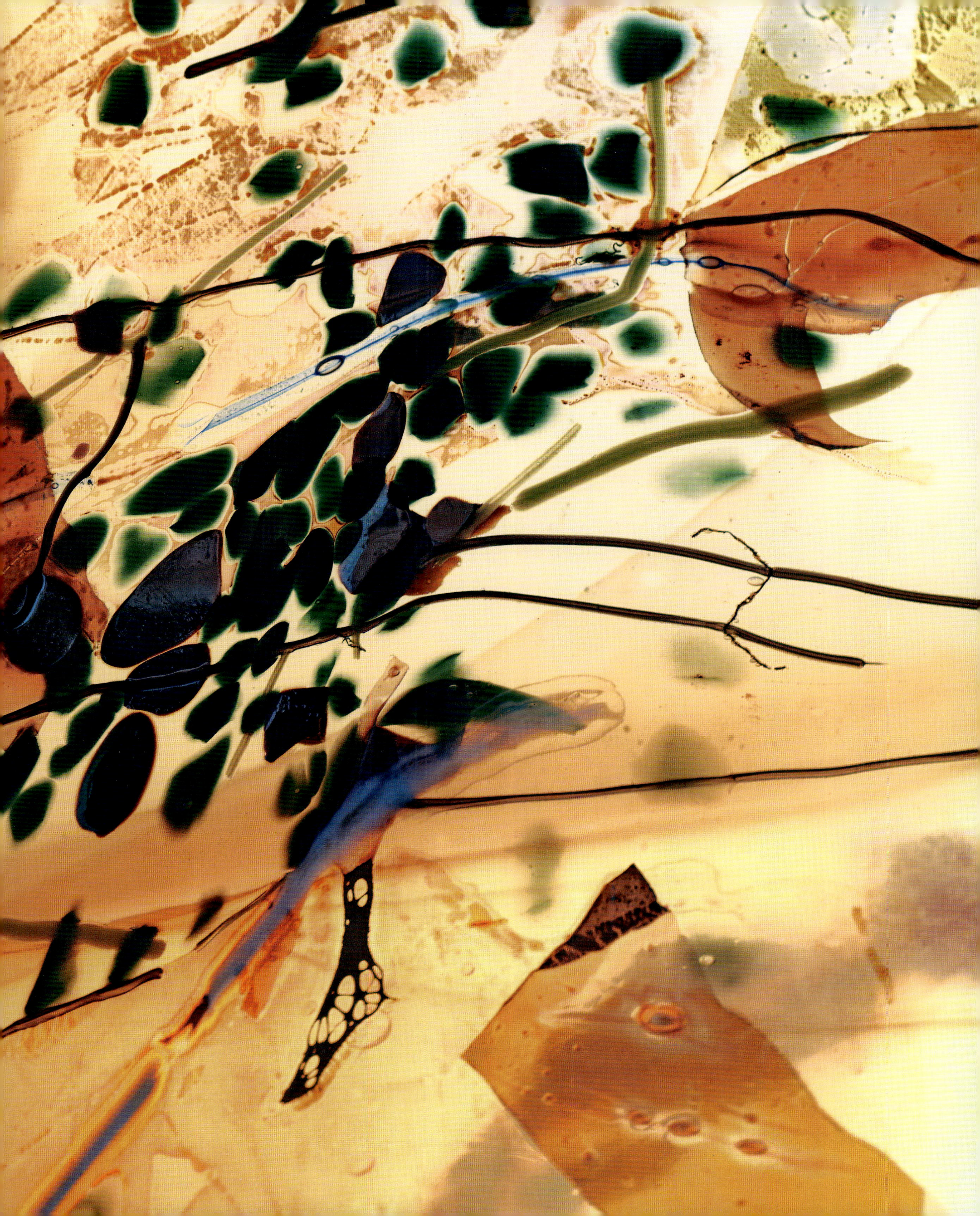

Foreword

The Marquess of Queensberry

I first met Sam Herman in 1966, which was to be the beginning of rethinking the 'Glass' Department at the Royal College of Art, London, and the start of a friendship that has lasted for more than 50 years.

I was appointed Professor of Ceramics at the Royal College of Art in 1959. Sir Robin Darwin (1910–74), Rector of the College, decided that glass had an affinity with ceramics, and a decision was made that it should be linked with the Ceramics Department. The students of ceramics were experimenting with materials and techniques, and we had a wide-spectrum approach to the subject. By contrast, in glass at that time the students hardly touched the material: designs were developed at drawing boards and, if approved by the head of department, were handed to the glass-blower Bill Heaton to make.

The Industrial Glass Department was primarily aimed at producing designers for the glass industry in Stourbridge, West Midlands, where glass had been made since the 18th century. The Stourbridge glass factories, with a few exceptions, had a pedestrian and traditional approach to design, which contributed to the demise of the industry. In contrast, the Scandinavian glass industry's approach to design has resulted in its survival to the present day – the prosperity of an industry is closely linked to an enlightened approach to design.

Sam came to the UK in 1965 to study cold glass techniques with Helen Monro Turner (1901–77) at Edinburgh College of Art. Before that, he had been one of Harvey Littleton's first students at the University of Wisconsin, from 1963 to 1965, where the Studio Glass Movement famously originated.

In the spring of 1966, Sam arranged for a travelling exhibition of studio glass by Littleton's students to come to the UK. Littleton (1922–2013) visited the exhibition and I invited him to give a lecture about his work and approach to glass making, which he had pioneered at the University of Wisconsin. I found his talk and Sam's exhibition inspirational. It was immediately obvious to me that our boring and uncreative approach to the subject had to be changed: we had to follow in Littleton's footsteps. Littleton had great respect for Sam and suggested that I talk to him about the possibility of working with us and introducing his studio glass concept to the Royal College of Art. The College agreed that I could offer Sam a research fellowship of two days a week to teach the students how to build small and inexpensive furnaces that were suitable

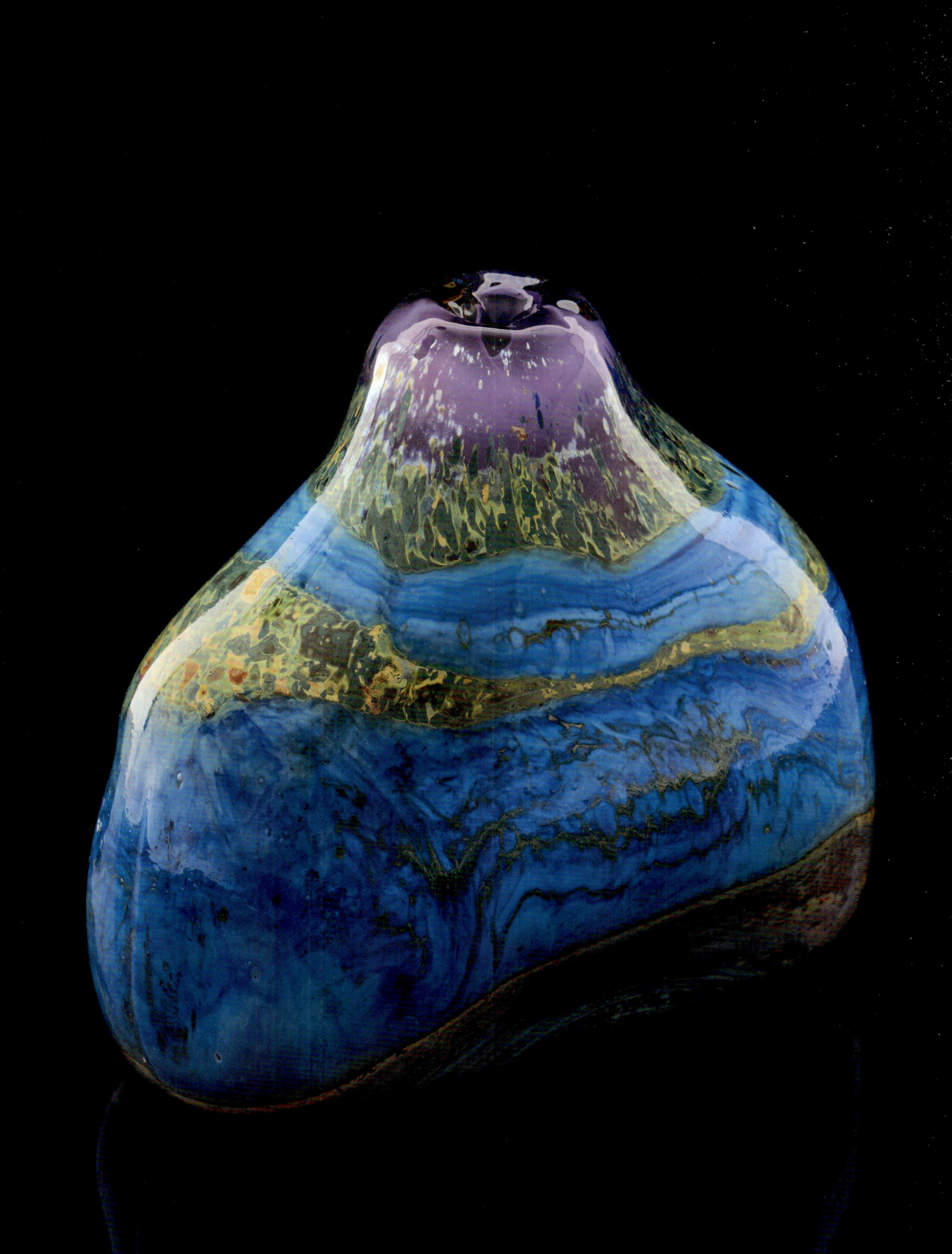

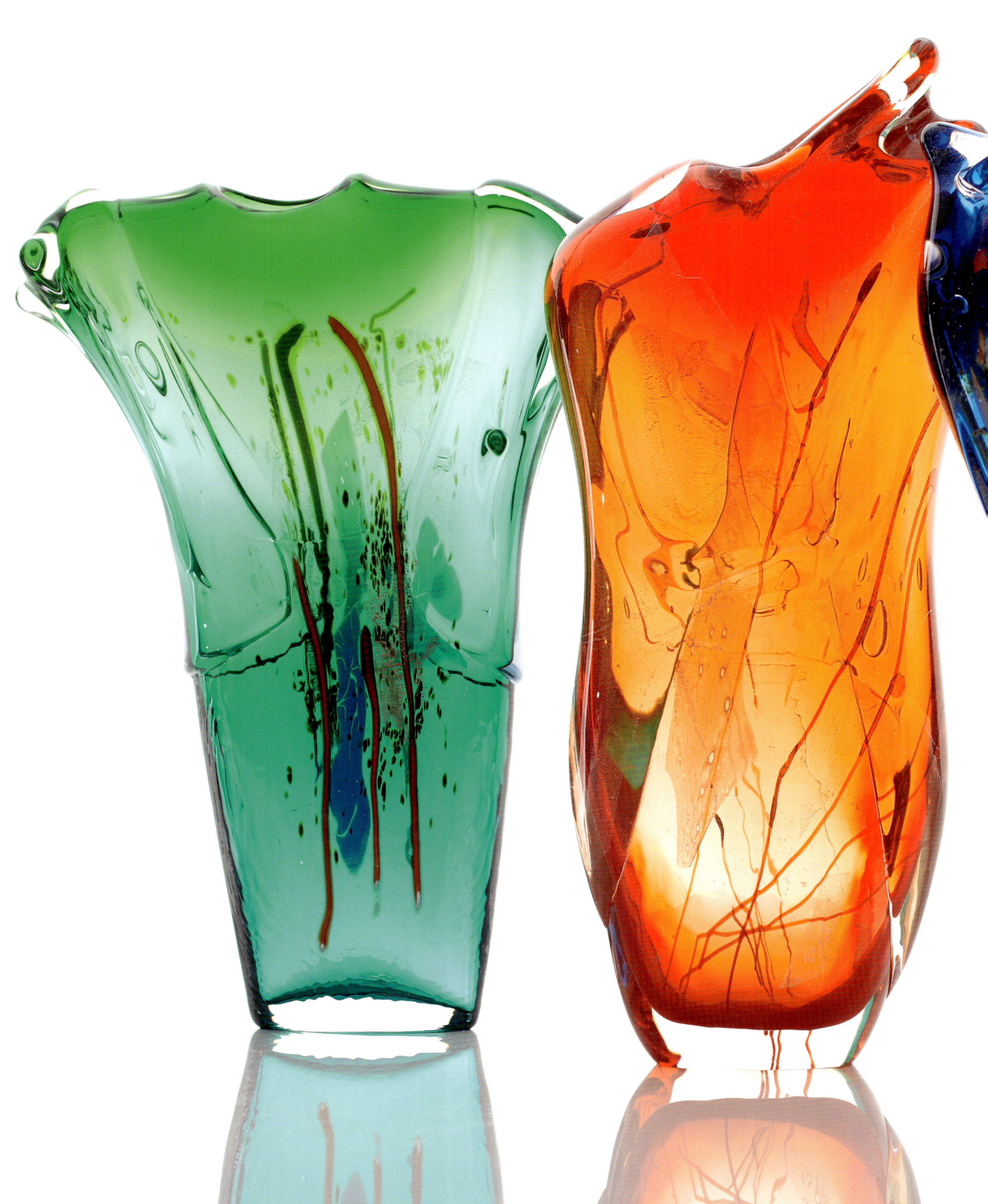

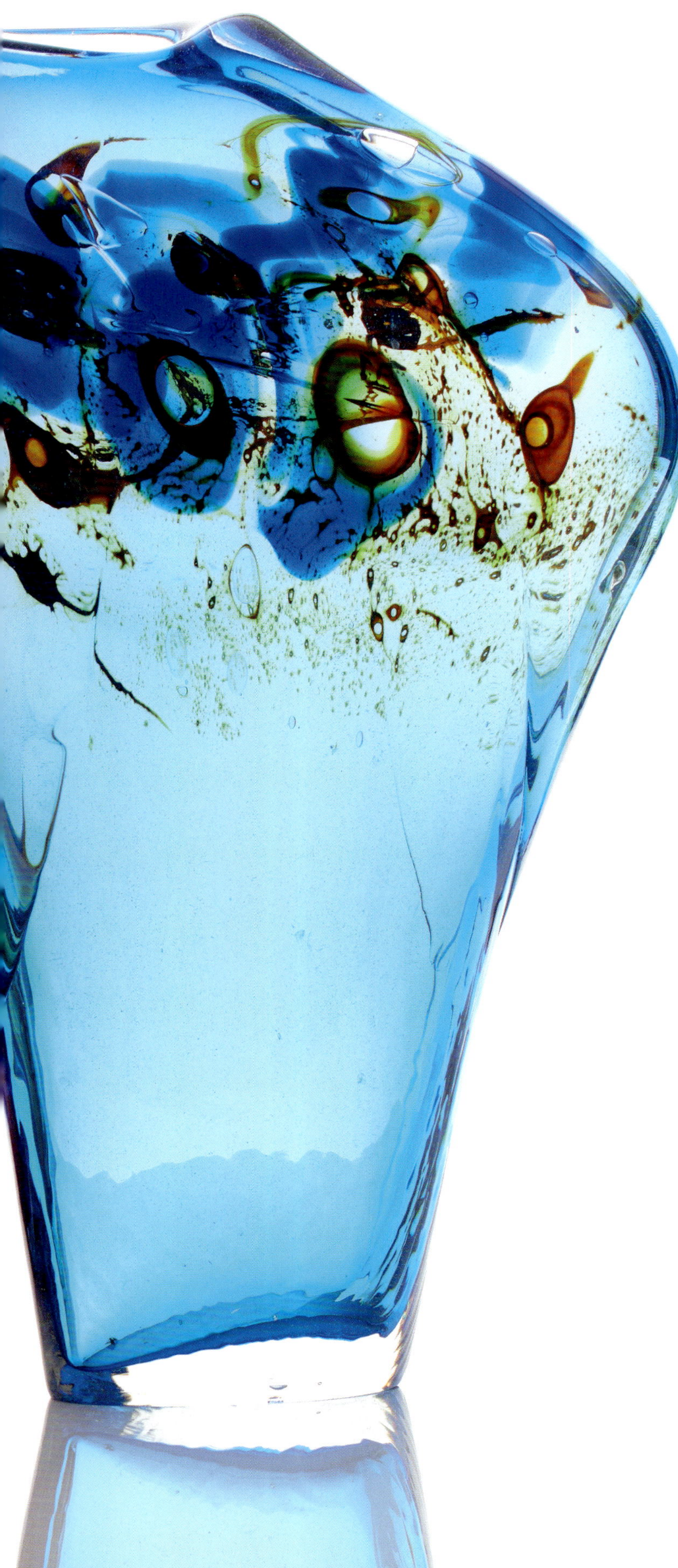

for studio use, and the techniques developed by Littleton at Wisconsin.

The departure of the Head of the Industrial Glass Department, Michael Harris (1933–94), who, inspired by the studio glass techniques, decided to set up a glass-making studio called Mdina Glass in Malta, gave me the opportunity to invite Sam to take the position, which he accepted in the autumn of 1967. The days of students sitting at drawing boards and never touching the material were over. Looking back on it now, I think that appointing Sam to work at the College was the most important event in the study and teaching of glass in this country in the last 50 years.

Perhaps the best way of evaluating a college of art is to look at the achievements of its graduates. Many of Sam's students went on to become internationally known artists and designers, whose work is represented in many of the world's great museums and their collections, not least the Victoria and Albert Museum in London where Sam himself was rightly honoured with an exhibition in 1971.

Sam also had a wonderful influence on the Ceramics and Glass Department, not just glass, and I found his opinion on applicants at the entrance exam particularly valuable. Elizabeth Fritsch (b.1940), who has become one of the UK's most famous ceramicists, had been a student of music and applied to our department with practically no ceramic work, which normally would have resulted in a rejection. Sam, however, thought differently and argued that there was something about Liz and her work that was very special, and that we should give her a chance. How right he was.

Sam has always been an innovator, pushing boundaries in his glass work, sculpture and, more recently, painting. A book about his work and many achievements is long overdue and I am delighted and honoured to be writing the foreword.

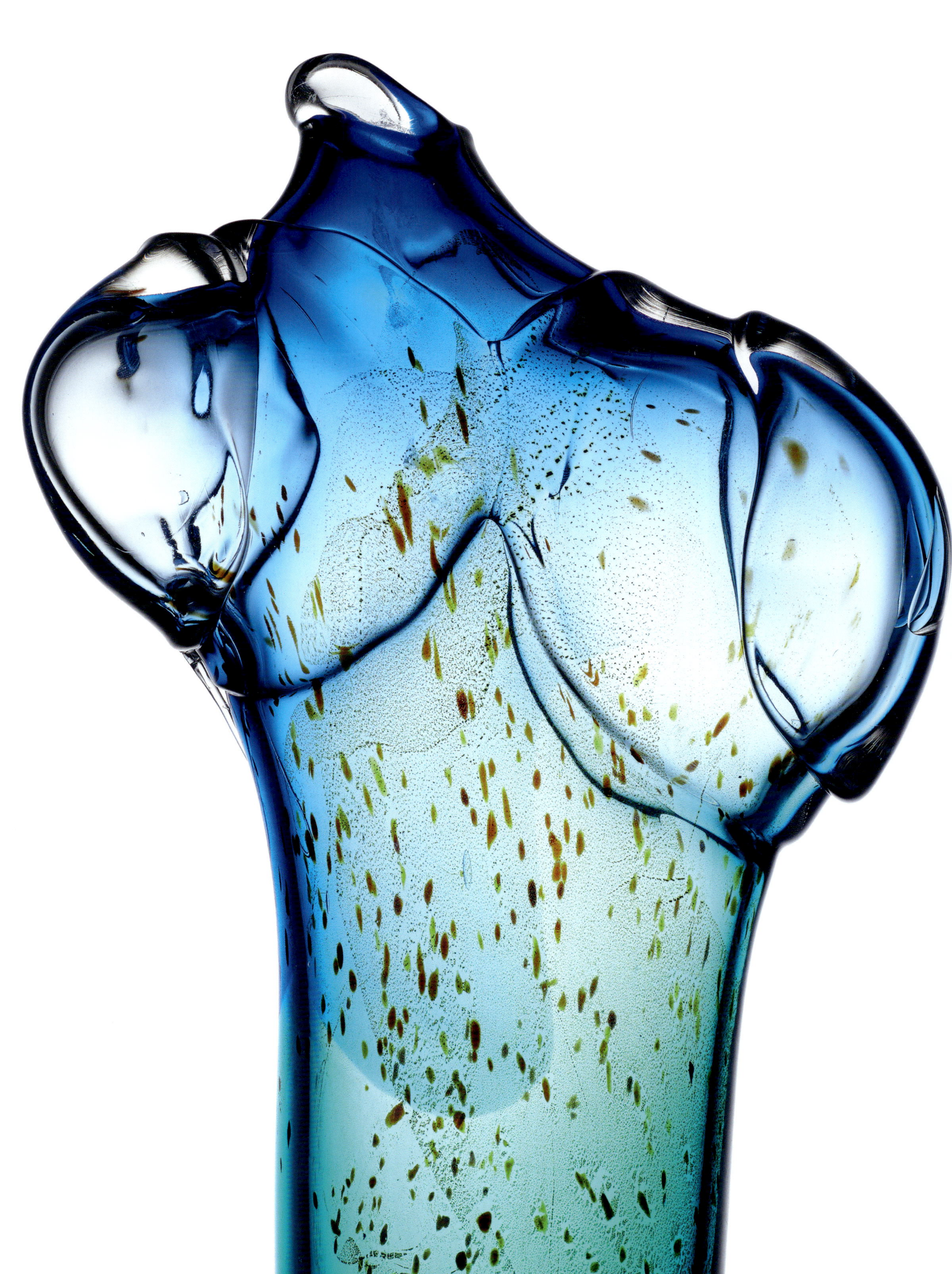

Preface

Rollo Campbell

It is over 50 years since Sam Herman (b.1936) arrived at the Royal College of Art (RCA) in London and famously built the first small glass furnace in the UK. This was the moment that marked the start of the British Studio Glass Movement, and provoked a revolution in glass art.

Just a few years later in 1971, and still in his early 30s, Herman became the first contemporary glass artist to have a major exhibition at the Victoria and Albert Museum in London. It is this rapid rise and sudden blossoming within the context of British and international modernism that has always intrigued me. How had this young Mexican-American Polish émigré, brought up in the tougher boroughs of New York, managed to spark a new artistic movement from within the surrounds of one of the UK's most esteemed arts institutions?

This first major monograph on Herman answers this question, throwing new light on his early years growing up in Mexico City and New York, as well as his time in Washington State, Wisconsin, Edinburgh, London, Stourbridge (UK), Adelaide and, later, in Mallorca and Gloucestershire. It shows the influence that he had on his students, his colleagues and his contemporaries. More than any of this, though, it is an illustrated history of the work that he has produced over the last five decades. When all is said and done, it is the work that most eloquently tells the story of this remarkable, pioneering man and his unwavering thirst to push hard at the boundaries of technique and creativity.

Acknowledgements

This book has been the sum of the efforts of many brilliant individuals and their formidable minds, energies and skills, all of whom deserve our immense gratitude.

First and foremost, thanks must go to Sam Herman himself. As a private man, he has graciously accepted being prodded and pushed throughout this project – often taking him away from his beloved work – and has been nothing but welcoming, helpful and encouraging to all contributors.

Thanks also to the Marquess of Queensberry for his foreword, and to all our authors and contributors: Lucy Abel Smith, Michael Boylen, Mark Hill, Greg Votolato and Michael Regan. All were a pleasure to work with, and we are extremely grateful to them for their expertise, insightful questioning, razor-sharp thinking and elegant words.

Alongside the authors we would like to thank those who assisted them by writing down their thoughts on Sam Herman's impact on their lives, in particular, the family of

Erwin Eisch, as well as Dick Richards, Clifford Rainey, Peter Aldridge and Pauline Solven.

An enormous thank you to our brilliant photographer Sylvain Deleu. Glass is notoriously challenging to photograph, and each work could have been taken in a multiplicity of ways. Sylvain's creative eye, supreme skill, work ethic and generosity of time have been at the centre of the success of this publication. We are also very grateful to others who have supplied photographs, not least the extremely talented Ester Segarra.

Thank you also to the team at Lund Humphries and Frestonian Gallery, particularly Lucy Clark for recognising the importance of this project, as well as Sarah Thorowgood, Tom Furness, Matt Incledon, Catherine Hooper and Myfanwy Vernon-Hunt.

Thanks must go to some of the key players in Sam's life who have given him the support, care, advice, grounding and encouragement that have helped create the environment for him to carry out his life's work so far: Sam's children, David and Sarah, Jonathan Stone, John and Sarah Campbell, David Queensberry, Suzanna Robins, Gilbert Weynans, Paul Woods and the late Harvey Littleton, Dominick Labino, Leo Steppat, Helen Monro Turner, Graham Hughes, Dan Klein, Gilbert Meurrens and Fred Daden. Thanks also to the teams, artists and technicians that he has worked with in Wisconsin and Stourbridge, and at the RCA, Val St Lambert, The Jam Factory, Lots Road, Aaronson Noon, London Glassblowing and Loco Glass.

Most of all, thanks go to Sam's wife Joanna, who has been the rock in his life for the last 40 years, not only in assisting him with the practical side of his work, but also as counsel and support in all areas of his life. Jo has played an integral part in pulling together and coordinating major aspects of this publication. This book would not have been possible without her.

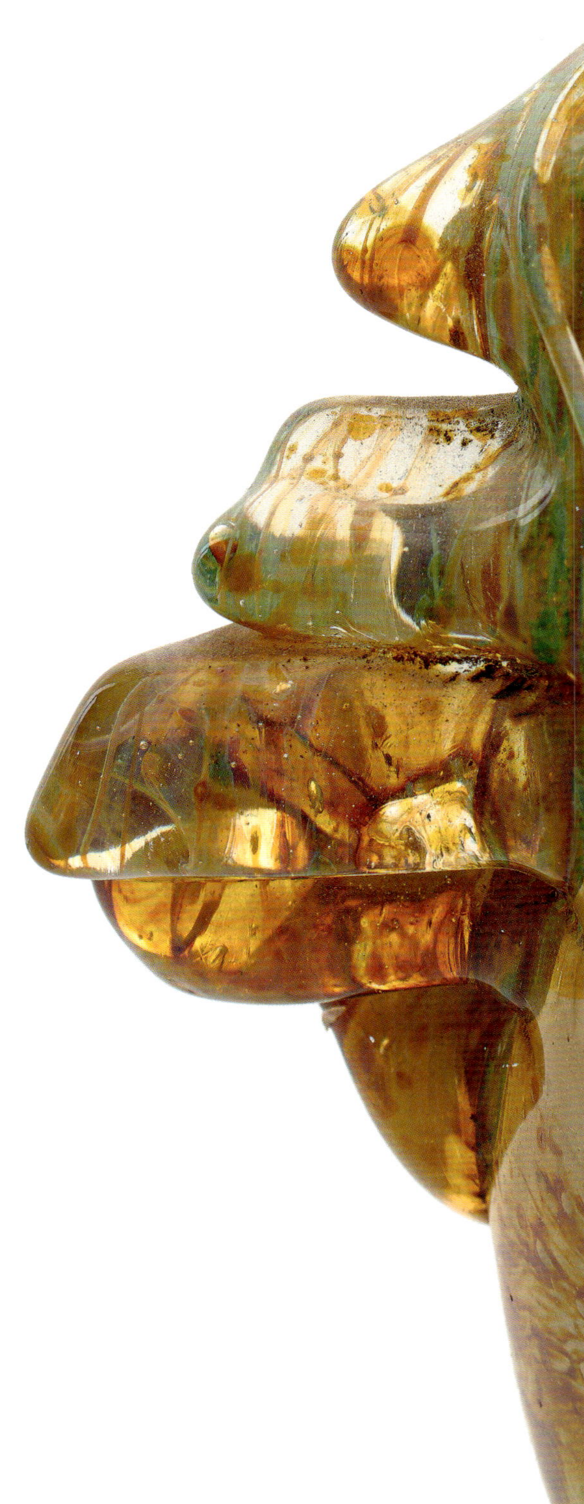

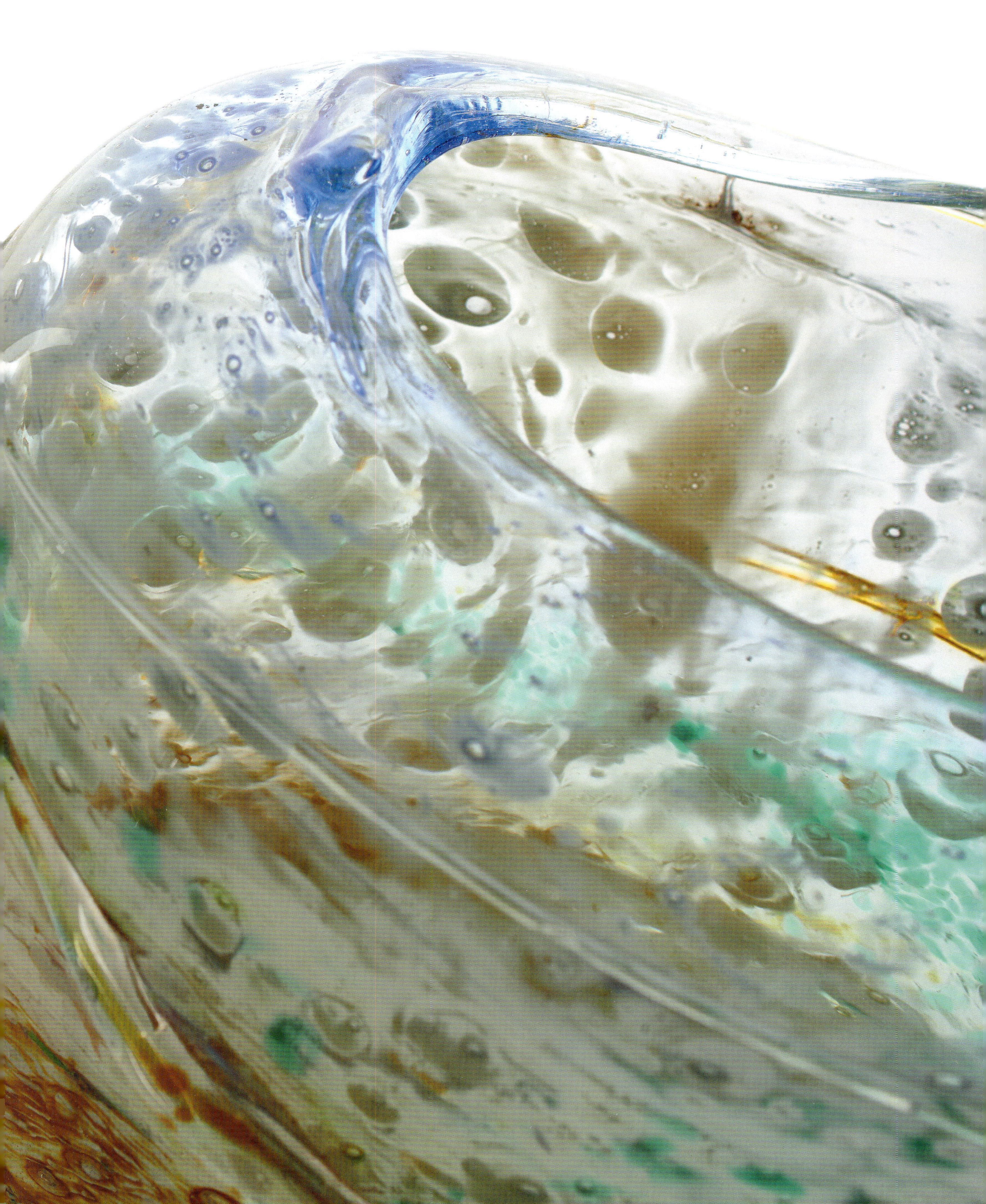

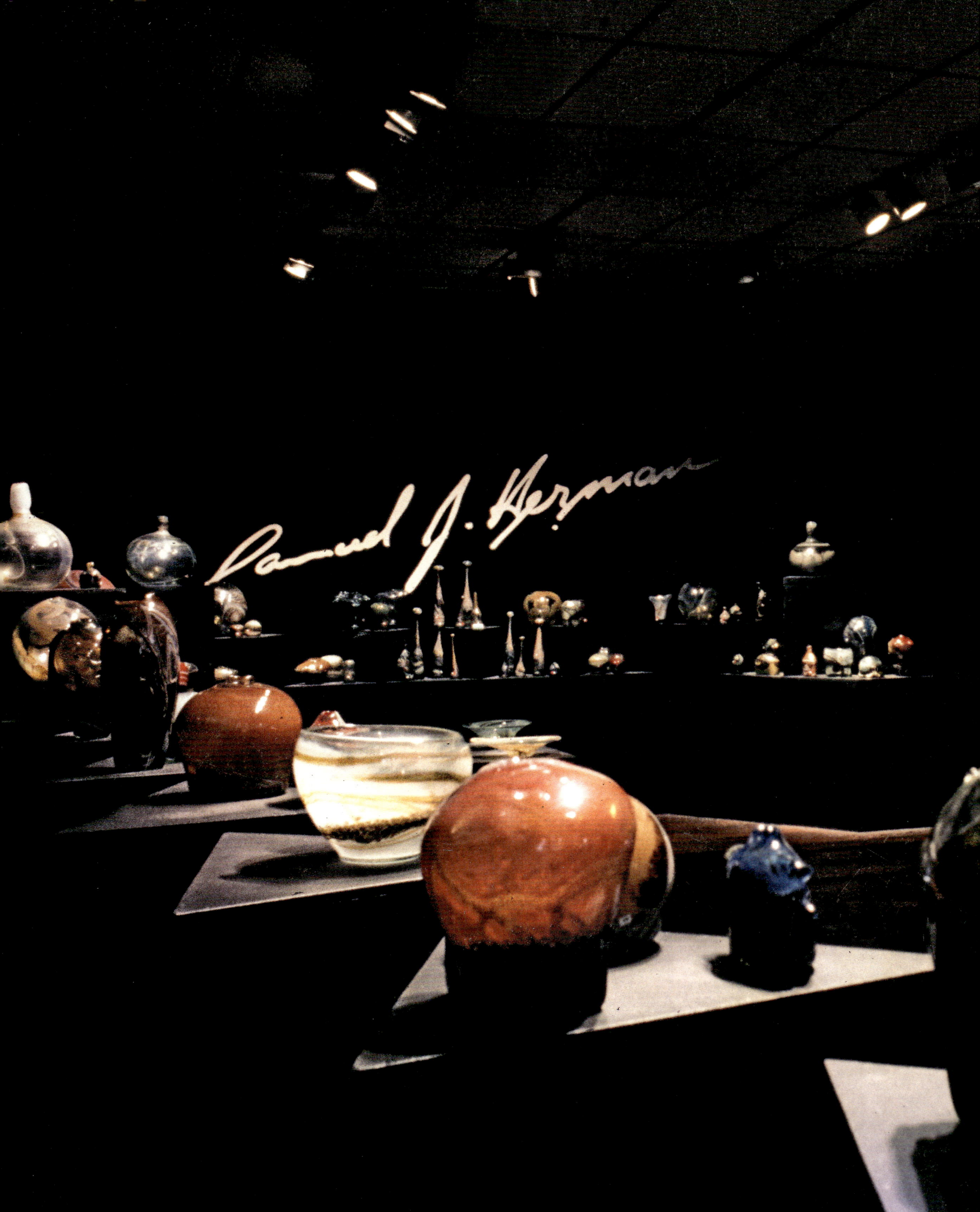

Daniel J. Herman

The Early Years

Lucy Abel Smith

In the spring of 1971, the Victoria and Albert Museum (V&A), London, world class in terms of the applied arts, mounted a joint exhibition of new work by American glass artist Sam Herman and British jewellery designer and maker Gerda Flöckinger (b.1927). The exhibition was a sensual and thrilling experience. Nothing had prepared me for the aggressive elegance of Herman's glass. With its lustre, swirling colours and control, I was instantly converted to contemporary glass.

At 21, I was an habituée of the V&A. I had studied there, using the library extensively, and had led gallery talks as a volunteer. So I had handled and seen much more artwork than many of my contemporaries. Since that time I have been to more than a thousand exhibitions, but still the Flöckinger/Herman exhibition is the one that stands out most in my visual memory.

I remember the graphics by Dennis Bailey (1931–2016), clear and measured. I remember walking into the large exhibition space that was Room 45. There, in the words of Alan Irvine (b.1926), master architect turned exhibition designer: 'The gallery was completely darkened by being lined-out with an opaque black fabric with grey carpet tiles on the floor. The glass was displayed on stepped blocks on each of the long walls and lit from crown silvered spotlamps at high level . . . being a low source brightness which would not destroy the illusion of a black void.'[1] The objects became like dancers on a Degas stage. With the hush of the carpeted floor and the drama of the work, Room 45 became half inner sanctum, half nightclub. Bounded by this theatre, the smaller jewels of Flöckinger had the same impact as the larger glass pieces by Herman.

For those involved in the exhibition, including Irvine and research assistant and glass specialist Betty O'Looney, the glass of Herman was revolutionary. They had never seen anything like it. In the foreword to the 1971 catalogue, Hugh Wakefield, Keeper of the Circulation Department, writes, 'we have sought craftsmen whose work is mature but fully alive to change and development'.[2] These two craftspeople wished to concentrate upon the full expression of their present concepts rather than upon their past development. Most of the work had been made in 1970, and Herman showed 69 pieces.

After the exhibition, I bought a piece from the Fine Art Society, which I still have. I shook as I wrote the cheque, but I had longed for one of the remarkable lustred sculptural pieces that had so captivated me in the exhibition. These were out of my league.

What is so remarkable about Herman and his skills as a designer, maker and teacher is that so soon after coming to the UK on a Fulbright scholarship from the USA he was teaching new techniques with exciting outcomes at the Royal College of Art, one of the country's top art colleges, and had landed a major exhibition in a major museum with his glass – a material that since the Renaissance had barely been given a second thought in the UK as anything other than utilitarian. Perhaps, as Margot Coatts, research assistant in the Circulation Department at the time, suggested 'because he was not afraid of anyone'.[3]

Who was this Sam Herman, what was his background and how did he come to be living and working in the UK?

Herman is as disciplined, yet fluid, and as innovative as his glass. However, little of his future success as teacher, artist and trailblazer in the Studio Glass Movement can be discovered in his family background. Equally, the brief résumé of the first three decades of his life, which follows, reveals little in artistic terms of the man who was to achieve so much. 'I was always just me', he insists when questioned. Herman is the perfect example of late development, finding his way not only by his natural skills and curiosity but also sometimes by pure chance.

Herman's roots are Polish, prosperous Jewish upper-middle class, totally assimilated into society. The family owned property and businesses in Szczuczyn, Podlasie Province, Poland. But, the German invasion and the Second World War changed all that. Apart from his mother and her three sisters, who had left Poland earlier, all the rest of the family were killed in the Nazi death camps. Of the four sisters two settled in the USA and two in Mexico City (the quota for North America was full). Herman's mother, Rose Dorf (1914–2001), ended up in Mexico City.

Rose was pivotal for Herman, but her own life was not easy. Her circumstances changed hugely from her privileged upbringing in Poland and her comfortable life in Mexico City to her very modest lifestyle working for a furrier in New York. It was not an uncommon scenario for Central Europeans escaping the Nazis and/or communists during the first half of the 20th century.

Samuel Jacob Herman was born in Mexico City in 1936. His father disappeared from the scene when Sam was just

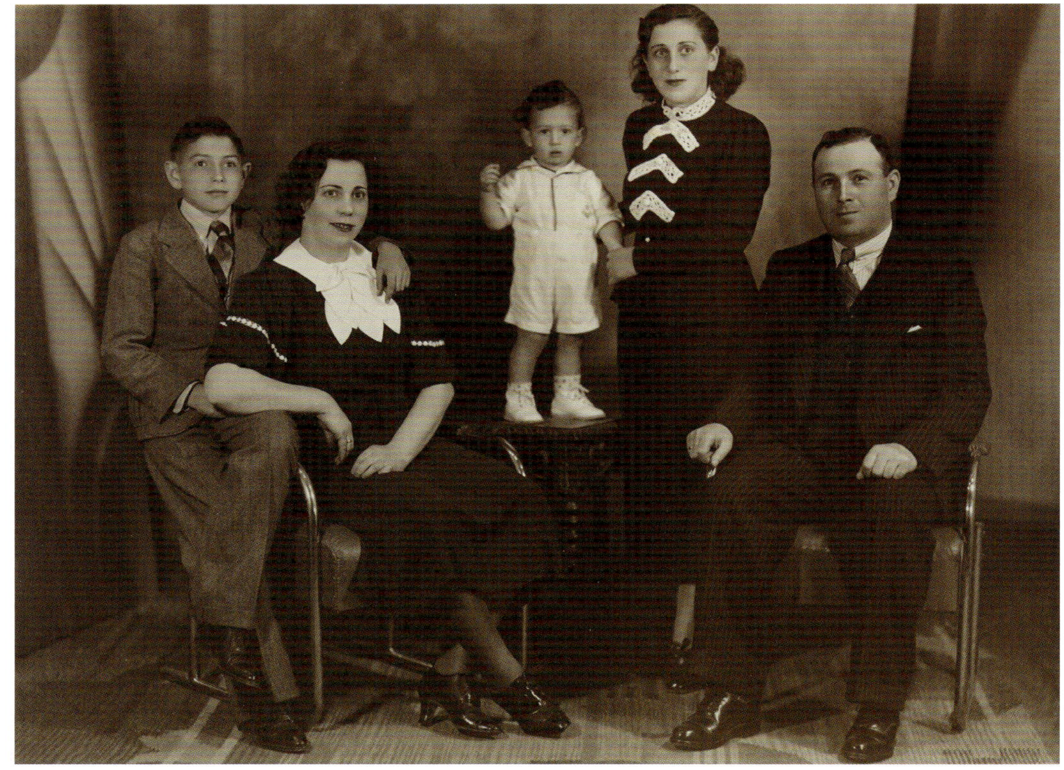

Page 18
Entrance to Sam Herman's show at the Victoria and Albert Museum, London, 1971

Left
Mexican family portrait, from left to right: cousin Efrain, aunt Miriam Fishbein, Sam Herman, mother Rose Dorf, uncle Abrahm Fishbein, 1938

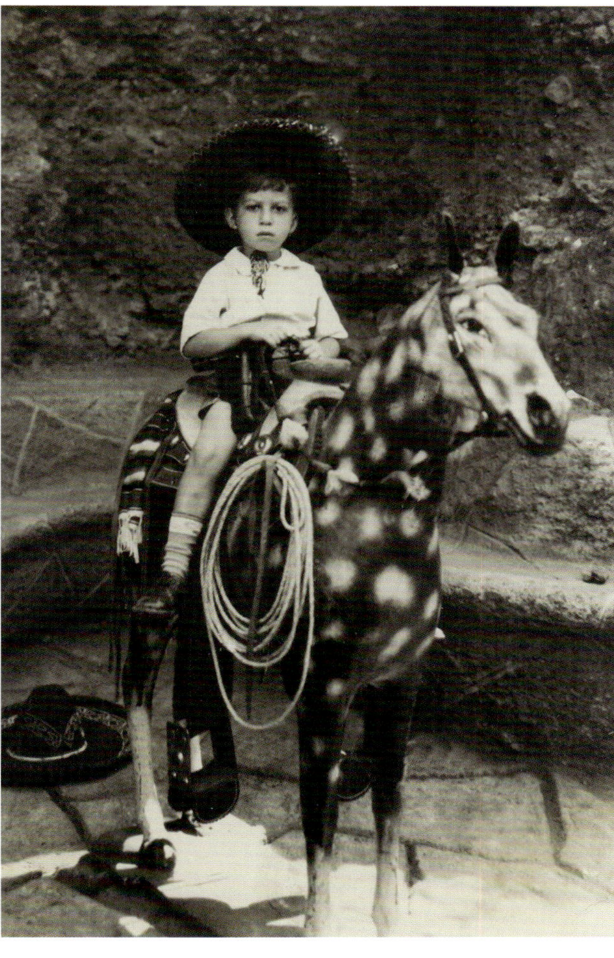

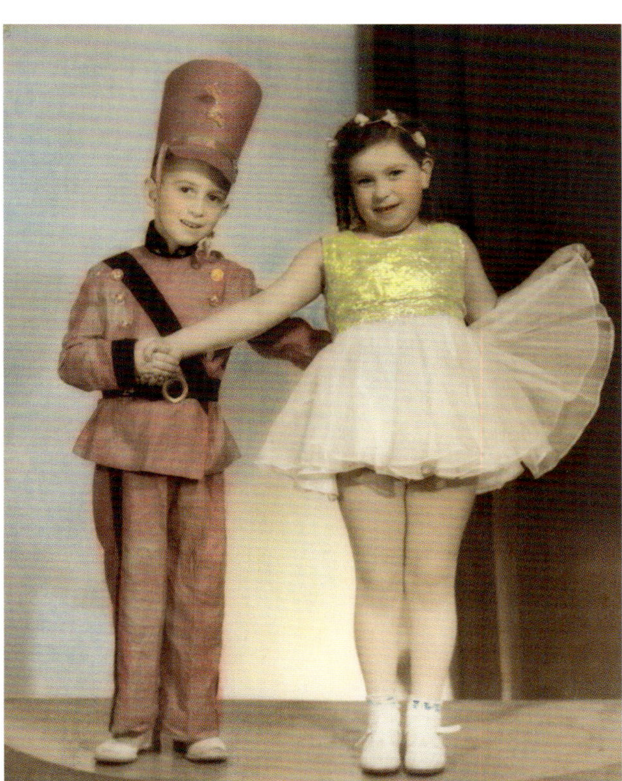

three months old, and his mother steadfastly refused to reveal his identity to her son. However, Herman's early life was happy and home life was very loving. The languages spoken in the house (for years he considered himself Mexican) were Yiddish, Polish and Spanish. Home was comfortable and shared with his Uncle Abrahm, Aunt Miriam and cousin, Efrain. There were staff, music and books, as was common in an educated household. A major influence on his childhood was his Mexican nanny Felicity. There was a flourishing Polish population in Mexico City in those pre-Second World War years, which centred around a 'country club' where Herman remembers spending many happy times. Mexican society would have frowned on Rose taking up work, but as a single mother she had to support herself and her son. Herman's description of his mother as sociable and someone who loved to dress up were characteristics she put to good use when visiting her sisters in the USA. Her Polish-Mexican friends put in orders for designer clothes and she smuggled them back to Mexico. This sort of life, however, could not go on indefinitely; Rose needed to make a proper living.

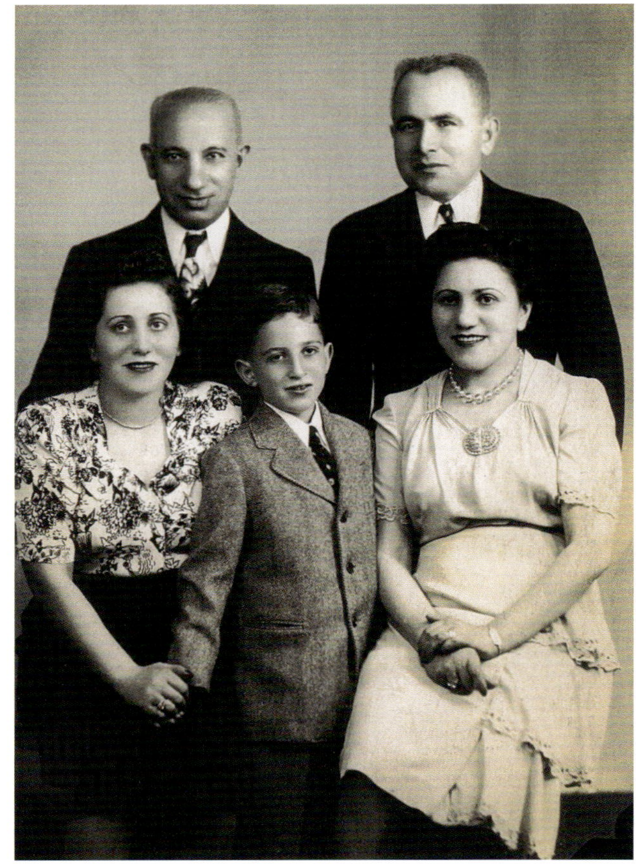

New York family portrait,
back row: stepfather Philip
Farber and Uncle Nathan
Wiseman; front row: mother
Rose Farber, Sam Herman,
Aunt Bella Wiseman, 1945

At the age of seven, Herman was asked if he would
rather stay with his family in Mexico or go with his mother to
start a new life in the USA. He chose to travel with Rose and
leave the comfort and security of his extended family. As
immigration records show, on 14 February 1944, he and his
mother crossed the border at Laredo, Texas. He remembers
well the journey by train from Mexico to Texas, during which
they lived on a diet of cheese sandwiches as they were
the only things his mother could request in English. They
continued by train to Baltimore to stay with another aunt
and uncle, where Herman began to learn English.

In 1945 mother and son then moved to New York. They
lived very modestly in Queens with Rose's sister, Bella, and
her husband, Nathan. Nathan worked nights and often took
Herman to the cinema during the day. Herman maintains
that it was watching the great Hollywood films that really
improved his English. His mother found employment in the
clothing trade where she could, and was eventually able
to afford the rent on an apartment in the same block as
her sister. Herman attended Public School 70 in New York,
where, being small in stature, he had to learn to fight or run
fast in order to survive. The world was in the depths of the
Second World War by this point and Herman remembers

The graduating class from the US Navy AEA School in Jacksonville, Florida, 1956. Sam Herman in the back row, second from the left.

Sam Herman in the US Navy, visiting Nara Park, Japan, 1957

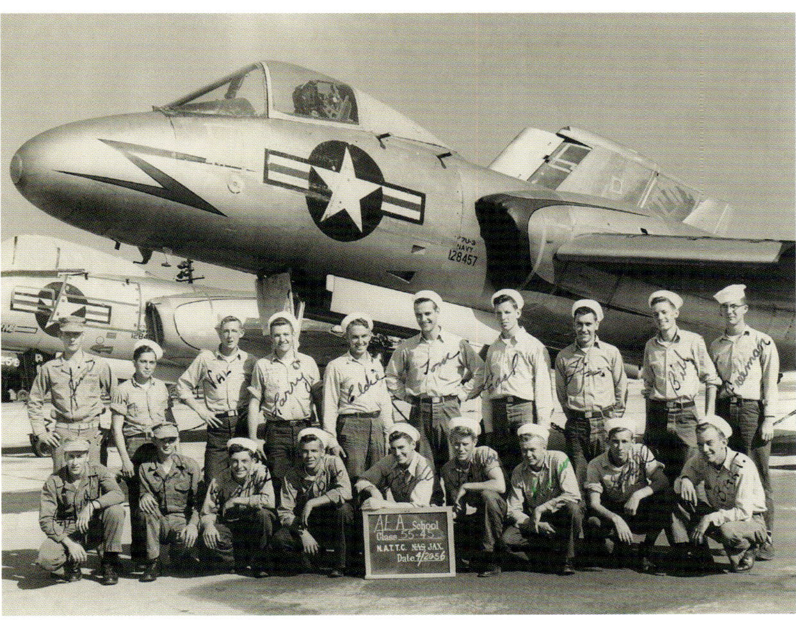

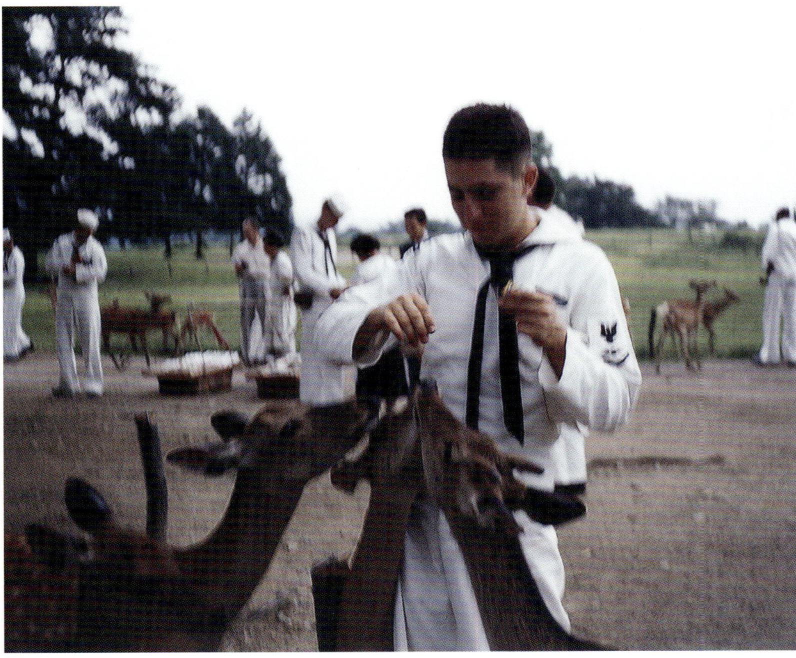

being told to 'think of the starving children in Europe' when he did not wish to eat the meal put in front of him. The rest of the world, though, seemed very far away to him.

Eventually Rose remarried, a White Russian, Philip Farber, also in the clothing trade, and they moved to the Bronx in *c*.1948. Herman's stepfather was kind and intelligent if not totally engaged with children. Admitting to being a menace at school and a troublemaker, Herman only found two teachers who encouraged and inspired him: one in literature and one in algebra. Conversely, he read avidly anything he could lay his hands on. He disliked all sport except cycling, through which he made many friends, becoming a member of the Italian cycling club and competing at an amateur level. Herman returned to New York in the late 1960s to discover that many of his fellow students had ended up in the Sing Sing Correctional Facility, a maximum security prison in New York State. He was one of the lucky ones.

Herman felt much loved even if this love was at times claustrophobic, describing his mother as 'typically Jewish'. Discipline was firm but he regards himself as having been 'a spoilt brat'. In 1955, at the age of 18, with little chance of going to university (financially, things were too tight, and his school grades were not good enough) Herman joined the US Navy as he considered this a better option than being drafted into the Army. He realised as soon as he arrived at boot camp that intellectually and emotionally it was going to be a disaster for him. However, he worked hard and was given the opportunity to undertake officer training, but, given that this would have resulted in an extension of his time in service, he opted instead to enter naval aviation as an electronics technician. He was in the Navy for a further four long years. He found living at close quarters and with very few kindred spirits difficult. However, the study of electronics within naval aviation and the ability to work as a team was useful to him. 'Discipline is a tool',[4] and Herman believes to this day that you either let these sorts of experiences get you down or you use them to your advantage. Those four years were some discipline.

To have any sort of fulfilling future, Herman had to go back into education. His age and service made him eligible for the veterans' GI Bill, which paid for fees, books and provided living expenses. He was accepted at Western Washington State College, Bellingham, Washington, almost on the border with Canada and as far from New York and home as it was possible to be. He read Anthropology and Sociology, graduating in

1963, and, for the first time in his life, he found that he had no problem with the academic work. It was also at Bellingham that he became interested in sculpture as a minor subject. Here, too, as a city boy, he fell in love with the landscape and took up mountaineering, which became a passion.

At Bellingham, he met and married Judith Christiansen, a fellow student. Herman wanted to do a Masters degree, and his tutors suggested that he apply for a Master of Fine Arts as he showed such promise. He was offered places at two universities. He dropped out of the first, Seattle, as the professor would not let him work in the abstract. Searching for a focus and an income, he had a go at being a managerial trainee for a retail chain. That was not a success. In autumn 1963, Herman re-applied to the University of Wisconsin, where Leo Steppat (1910–65), professor and head of the Sculpture Department, offered him and Judith graduate accommodation plus a teaching job while studying. Here was a real opportunity. However, by now he had not only a wife but also his first child, David, to support. He turned his hand to anything, supporting his studying, teaching and fathering by cleaning offices and doughnut machines, often having to accept very low wages. The teaching at Wisconsin was excellent, allowing for experimental work in sculpture, from welding to papier mâché, and also offering a course in art history.

Then came another break. About to join a course on ceramics, he met fellow student Rodger Lang who was enrolling on a glass course. Herman thought this sounded interesting. The course was taught by a man called Harvey Littleton (1922–2013).

Herman's curiosity coupled with his fine art training fired his interest in this new way of working an ancient material. It was risk-taking, experimental yet disciplined. It is no accident that the two great glass artists that Herman admires most are Erwin Eisch (b.1927) and Stanislav Libenský (1921–2002), the two men in Europe whose glass work is closest to sculpture both intellectually and aesthetically. Herman found both concept and material exciting. The idea of studio glass was new. The maker was the designer: each object the work of a single individual, not a team with designer and gaffer (glass-blower) as separate entities. There were few ground rules and no teachers. Everyone learned from each other. Littleton accepted Herman on his course, and this was the start of the path that led to my entering the doors of Room 45 in 1971 and more than four decades of collecting glass.

Sam Herman hiking in the mountains near Bellingham, Washington State, 1962

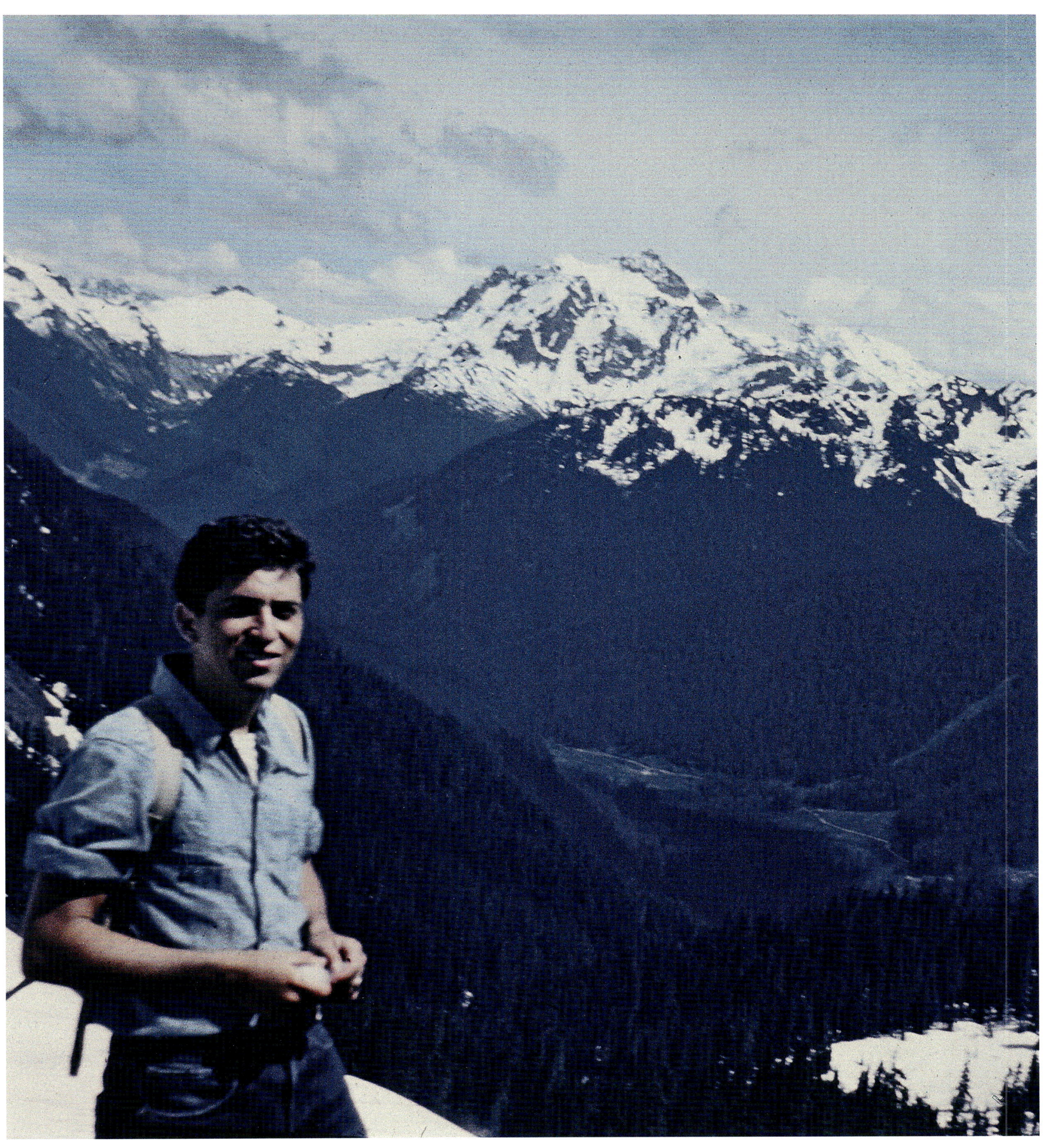

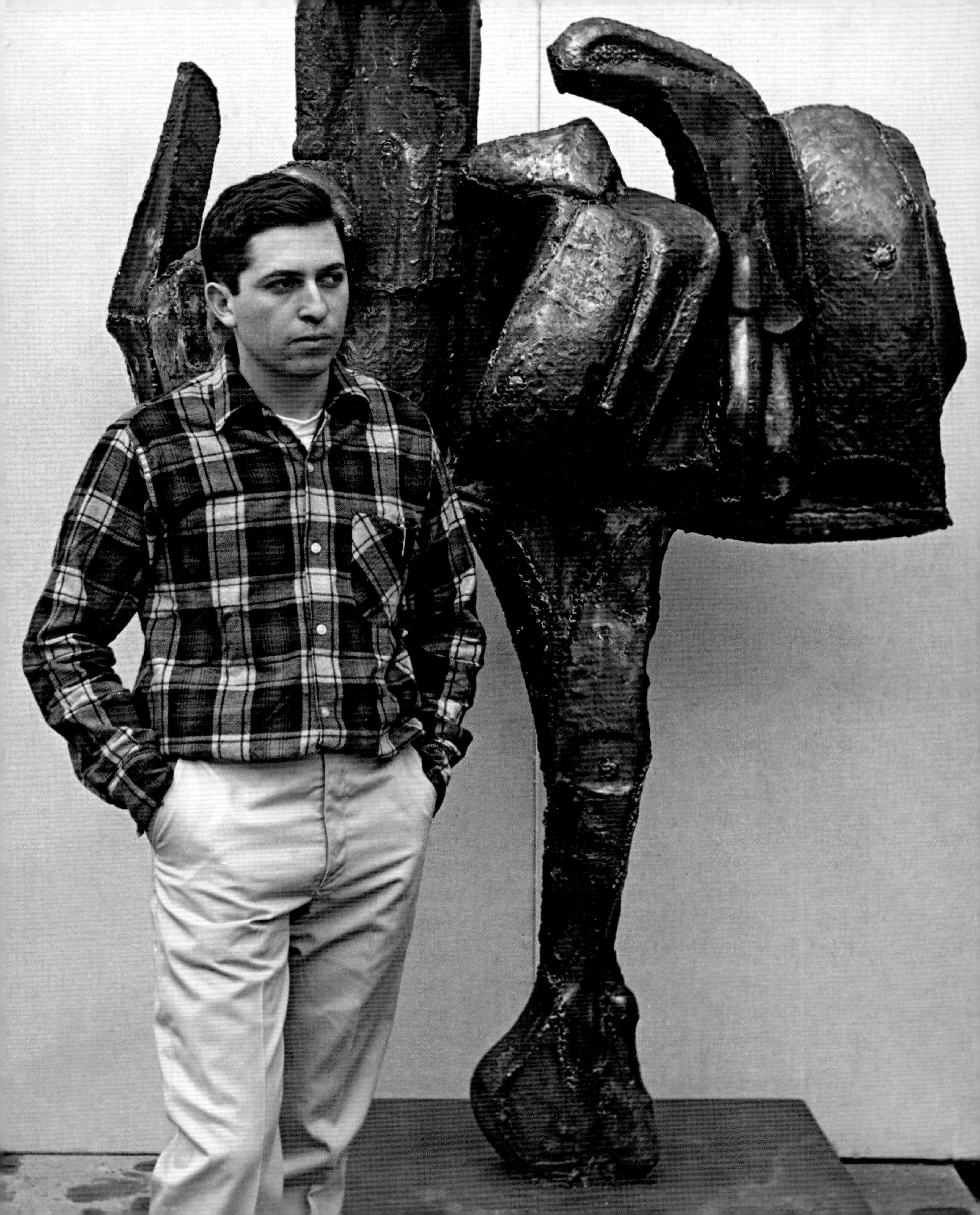

The Birth of Studio Glass, 1963–65

Michael Boylen

The graduate students in the first studio glass class at the University of Wisconsin were not quite sure what they were getting into. However, we shared Littleton's excitement and enthusiasm in being at the beginning of something really interesting. Very few students came with a specific interest in glass. Most of us, like Sam Herman, were there to learn other disciplines. I had come to Madison to study ceramics and Herman to study sculpture under Leo Steppat. We were all required to do some work in an additional medium, and some of us gravitated to the new glass project. We were looking at a blank slate, in an empty, high-ceilinged, Nissen/Quonset-style metal building in an out-of-the-way corner near the university football stadium. Our starting point was based on Littleton's long-time interest in glass, his historical research, personal studio trials and the two experimental glass-blowing workshop sessions he initiated at the Toledo Museum School of Design in Ohio in 1962.

The early months were devoted to putting in as much time as possible, more or less around the clock, to figure out the basics and to get things going. We had a general idea of what it took to blow and finish molten glass but no one trained in basic skills to show us how to do it. Littleton had collected some hand tools, and we found a commercial source for more. We had no examples of small-scale equipment for glass melting, reheating or annealing beyond the experiments of the Toledo workshops. We were learning by doing, learning from each other, pretty much on our own. Free to come and go every day at all hours with no one bothering us, searching for information everywhere we could, we were figuring out equipment and technique as we went along.

As we got going, we learned how to work individually or in pairs with a material and process that, for good reason, was historically a team activity. But that was part of the goal: to work as individual artist-craftspeople as distinct from traditional factory production. Eventually we settled into a regular schedule of work periods and took turns at maintaining and monitoring the studio. We met as a group at least weekly with Littleton to compare notes and critique each other's work, in a process that was more cooperative than competitive. As our knowledge and skill grew, we discovered the incredible possibilities of the material's fluidity and the relationship between glass and light.

The technical challenges were many. Fortunately, the basic question of what to use for glass had already been addressed at the 1962 Toledo workshop, when Dominick

Page 26
**Sam Herman with sculpture
made for his degree show,
1965**

Below
**Sam Herman working in the
studio at Wisconsin, 1964**

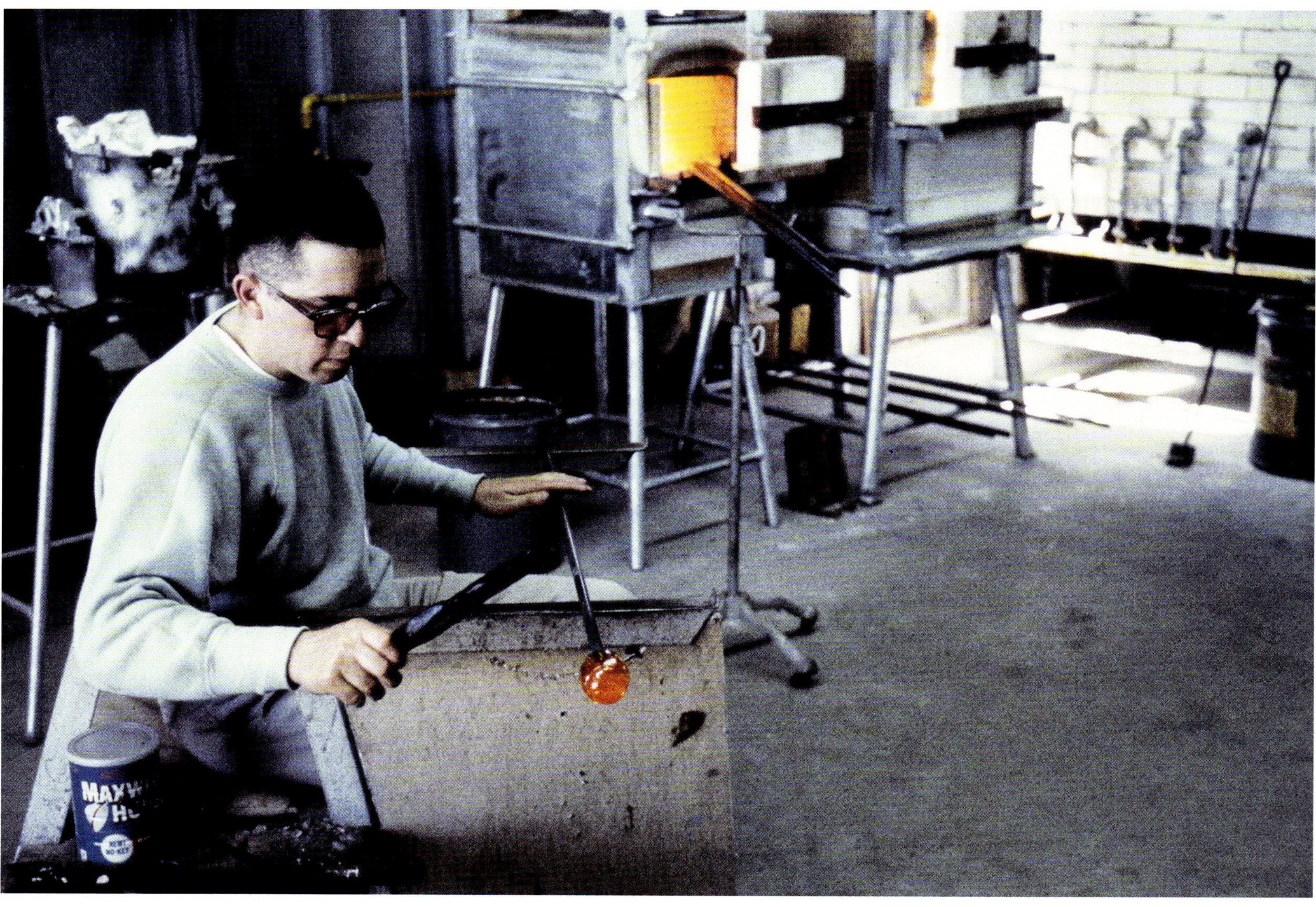

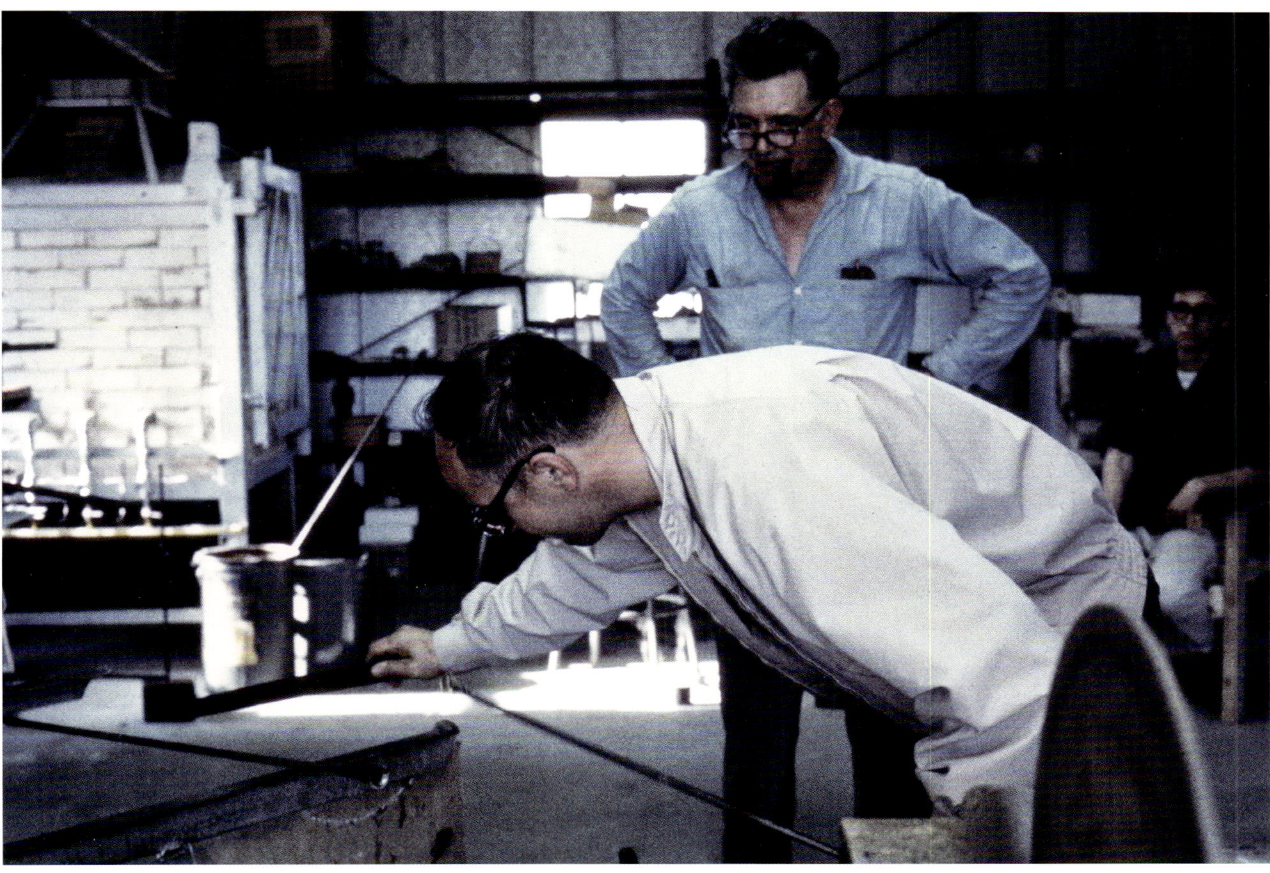

('Nick') Labino (1910–87), then Director of Research for Johns Manville Glass Fiber Division, made the first of his invaluable contributions to the evolution of studio glass. He offered his #475 glass, in the industrial commodity form of marbles, as a practical start-up material. Developed for glass fibre production, it was less than ideal for glass-blowing, but it worked well enough and avoided the issues involved in producing batch glass with raw materials. He also recommended using a tank-type furnace instead of a pot furnace to melt the glass.

In our new studio, the first attempt at a melting tank, an impressive brick and steel structure with a side-mounted blower burner, did not work very well. It was too big and did not get the glass hot enough, so blowing was hard work. Eventually we got it right, building a tank based on a specific Labino design with a top-mounted burner.

Sometime during that first year we piled into Littleton's little Ford van and more or less flew east to visit Labino at his personal research lab and machine shop near Grand Rapids, Ohio. We knew Labino had much experience as a glass-industry scientist and engineer, but we were still amazed to see the impressive and efficient glass-blowing set-up he had built and his growing glass-blowing skill. There was a table covered with blown forms in many shapes, sizes and colours made from various glass batches he had formulated. His melting tanks, like all his equipment designs, elegant in their compact simplicity, were a revelation. They became the model for the early stage of small studio equipment.

Later on, in 1964, Herman and I took a road trip to visit Joel Myers (b.1934), then resident designer at Blenko Glass Company in Milton, West Virginia. Myers had a background in studio ceramics and industrial design. He also was 'learning by doing' in a somewhat different way, fitting in around his factory design job as much personal study and glass-blowing practice as possible. He had visited the University of Wisconsin studio, and we had a mutually beneficial connection.

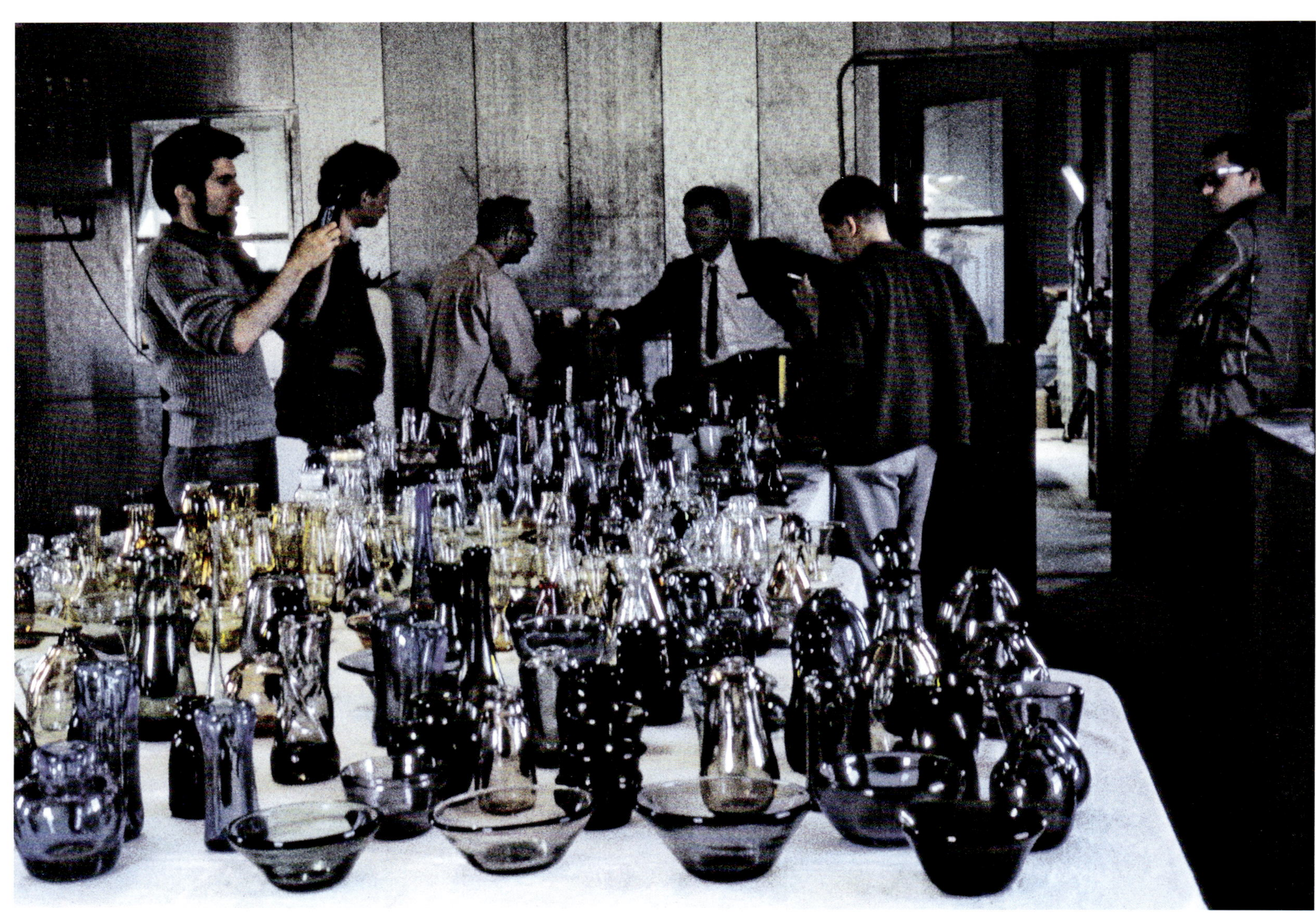

A visit to Dominick Labino's
studio in Toledo, Ohio, 1964.
From left to right: Michael
Boylen, Rodger Lang, Harvey
Littleton, Dominick Labino,
Sam Herman, Marvin Lipofsky

As a result of Littleton's initiatives, Labino's technical contributions and student accomplishments during that first year at the University of Wisconsin, studio glass began its rapid expansion and spread in the summer of 1964. The main event came in June at the first World Congress of Craftsmen, convened at Columbia University in New York City. Sponsored by the World Crafts Council and the American Craft Council, the event was the first of its kind on such a large scale. Participants from 46 countries included industrial designers, teachers, writers, government officials and some working craftspeople.

Littleton had promoted a demonstration glass workshop in the conference programme. He found a location for it in a small courtyard at Columbia Teachers College, where we set up the equipment brought from Wisconsin and Ohio. Labino contributed the #475 glass, one of his glass melting tanks and the use of his personal annealing oven. With Littleton presiding and joined by Norman Shulman (1924–2014), Erwin Eisch from Germany and several graduate students from Wisconsin, the glass workshop was kept running throughout the conference, providing basic instruction for anyone wanting to try blowing.

The demonstration workshop, a constant centre of activity and attention, was a revelation. It highlighted the practicality of this new approach to blowing molten glass as an individual art form on a studio scale. It also implied an alternative to the long-established glass industry practice of rigidly separating the roles of designer and maker. It marked the start of a broad ripple effect that initiated the worldwide Studio Glass Movement.

Immediately following the New York conference, I transported the glass-blowing equipment to Haystack Mountain School of Crafts in Deer Isle, Maine. Labino had donated the melting tank to Haystack, and I set up the studio and got it running. Herman came later to Haystack to give some workshops, as did Littleton.

After the conference, Littleton returned to Wisconsin with Eisch, where they conducted a university summer-school glass course that led to the creation of glass programmes at other schools, most immediately by Robert Fritz (1920–86) at San José State University. At the same time, Marvin Lipofsky (1938–2016), the first Master of Fine Art graduate from the University of Wisconsin glass programme, joined the Design Department at the University of California, Berkeley, and started a glass studio there.

Herman was the first student to receive a Fulbright scholarship to develop his understanding of glass as an artistic form. He left the USA to study at Edinburgh College of Art and went on to introduce the artistic skills and techniques acquired while at the University of Wisconsin to the UK. He also spread the word in Europe with the help of Eisch and Sybren Valkema (1916–96).

One very important point has become obscured over the years in the development of the Studio Glass Movement: the motivating factor for Littleton's initiation of studio glass was the idea, similar to ceramic artists, that artists could utilise glass in their own studios. As was stated in the 1972 programme for the First International Glass Symposium in Zurich by Dr Erica Billeter: 'It was the first manifestation of artists who have chosen glass as a material to express themselves and most of them are intentionally against creating any functional glass. Their works could rather be defined as glass-sculptures than applied arts.'

The Committee of Artists in Glass that was formed in 1972, which included Herman, Littleton, Eisch, Dale Chihuly (b.1941), Valkema, Myers and Lipofsky, resolved to promote and further the material glass as a medium for the artist. These artists heartily encouraged a vital and enthusiastic communication between all artists working in the material. These principles were ones that Littleton had given birth to at Wisconsin during the time that Herman and I were there in that first group of students. Since then thousands of artists around the world have been able to work in glass in a creative way in their small studios rather than only being able to design their artwork and then have it made for them in a glass factory.

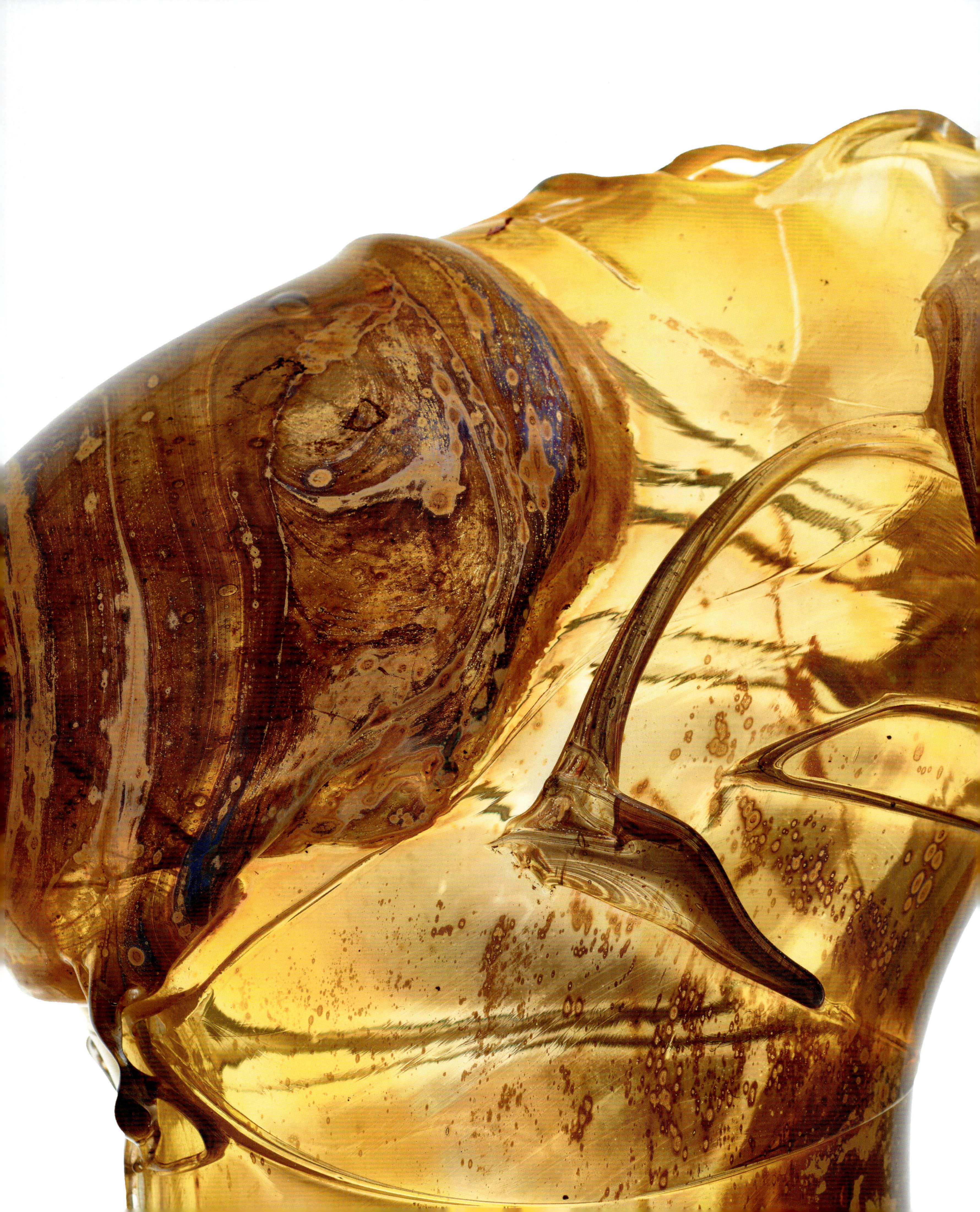

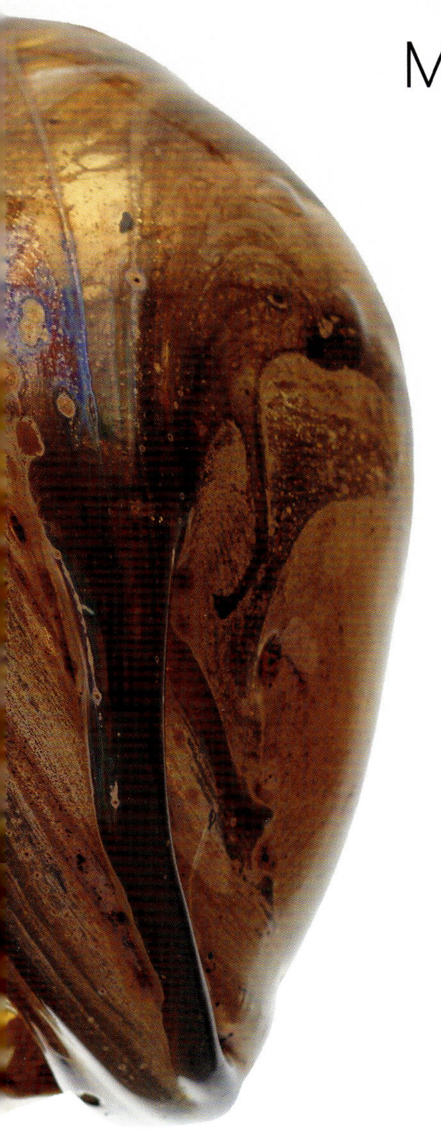

The Studio Glass Pioneer, 1965–84

Mark Hill

Edinburgh, 1965–6

The excitement around the emergence and rapid development of the new Studio Glass Movement was one thing, but Herman soon realised that it was only half the equation. Teaching himself how to handle hot glass effectively was not all he needed in order to understand the medium and all of its possibilities fully. He needed to learn as many techniques as possible and be taught by experienced masters, otherwise, Herman said, it would have been like 'operating with one arm'.[5] For this reason, he began looking for places to learn about cold-working techniques, such as cutting and engraving, which were the mainstays of glass design at the time.

His options in mid-1960s America were limited, however, as there were no educational institutions that taught such courses. Factories were most likely to be closed to him, or would only offer a full-time apprenticeship or starter job that might have eventually lead to learning. Possibilities were more numerous outside the USA but, as he only spoke English, countries renowned for their heritage in cold-working techniques, such as those in Scandinavia, were not options. Following recommendations from colleagues at Wisconsin, he

was attracted to the Royal College of Art (RCA) in London and the Edinburgh College of Art in Scotland, with the latter seeming the 'better option' to Herman. Edinburgh offered a full course led by a highly respected and experienced tutor, Helen Monro Turner (1901–77). She had been classically trained in art, had studied under masters in cutting and engraving, such as Professor Wilhelm von Eiff (1890–1943), and had taught successfully for over 20 years.

Harvey Littleton approved and wrote a letter of recommendation, and Herman prepared a pitch to win a Fulbright scholarship to finance his studies and the proposed year-long trip with his wife, Judith, and their two-year-old son, David. After successfully securing the scholarship, he left Wisconsin and arrived in Edinburgh to be ready for the start of the course in September 1965.

Mere months after arriving, Herman began a task that was to become a constant in his life's work in glass: the promotion of studio glass and its associated techniques across the world. While continuing his studies, he planned to bring over to the UK an exhibition of work produced at Wisconsin, to promote the new ways of making glass and allowing artists to work directly in this exciting medium. He explained to his tutor Monro Turner that hot glass was

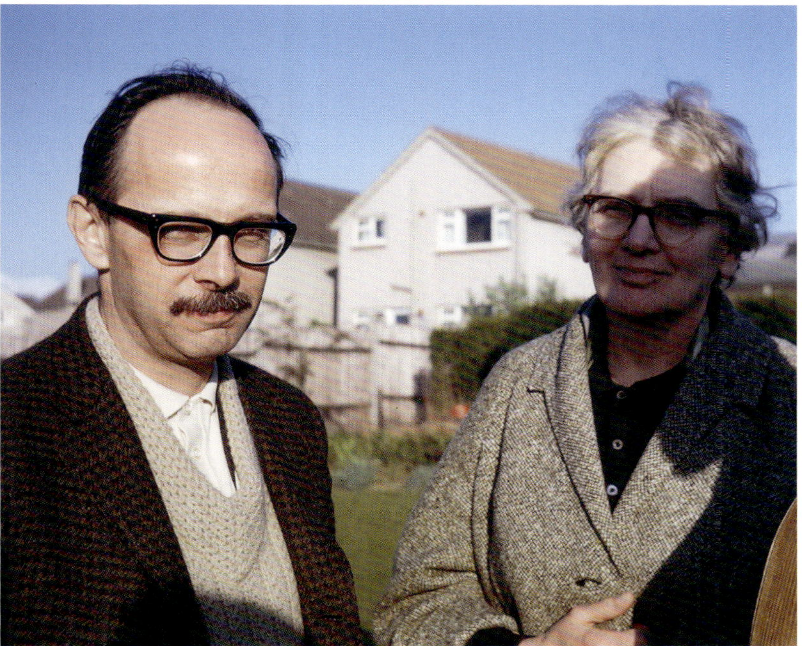

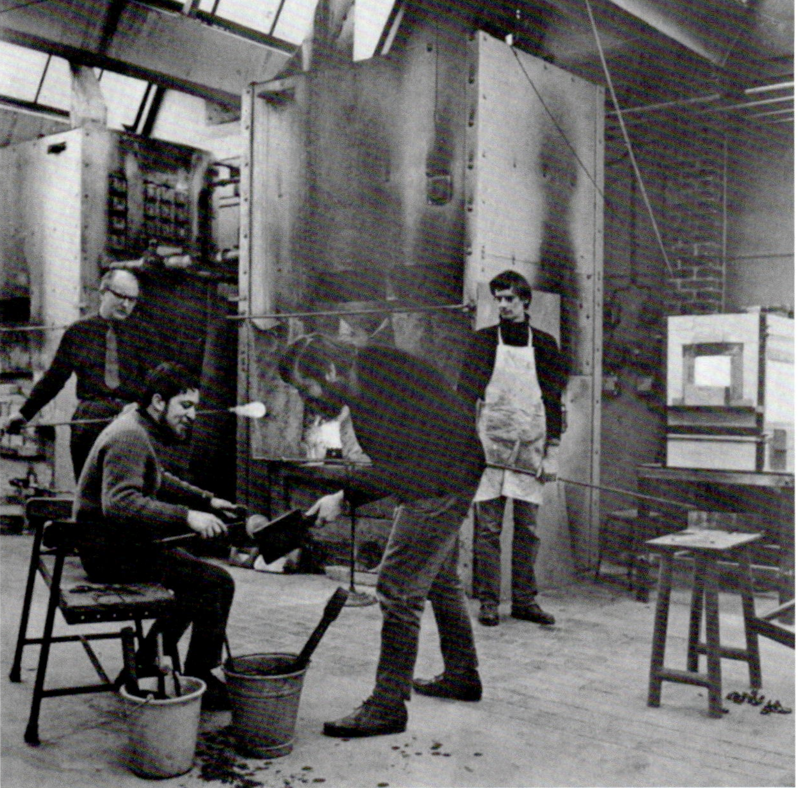

'fantastic, a magical material to work with'[6] and found
her supportive but, reading between the lines, it was
clear that she did not think much of what he was saying.

This may have also been coloured by Herman himself.
There was certainly a clash of cultures between this
stalwart, traditional British lady in her 60s, and an American
less than half her age, whose shaggy bearded appearance
virtually defined the term 'hippie', and who was excitedly
expounding working methods that were completely alien
to her and resulted in what she probably saw as 'lumps
of glass with no control in them',[7] as Herman said.

Even though Monro Turner kept her opinions to
herself, surprisingly her support went further than simply
agreeing to an exhibition. After around 20 pieces had been
selected by Littleton and dispatched to Scotland, the British
customs authorities demanded a financial bond of several
thousand pounds, which neither Herman nor Littleton
could pay. Without being asked, Monro Turner approached
Herman and paid the bond from her own money, thus
enabling the exhibition to proceed.

Despite not liking the look of the results, Monro Turner
almost certainly realised the great potential that the new
techniques offered. About their relationship, Herman said
she was 'an incredible individual with real character and
standards. I really respected her, even though I thought her
work was steeped in classical tradition. She always treated
everyone respectfully and professionally, even if our work
was clumsy by contrast.' Herman learned 'a hell of a lot', but
did not 'find engraving glass enticing. But at least I knew
what it took. I learned those techniques and, although I
personally seldom used them in the future, I could use
them if I felt the piece I was working on warranted them.'[8]

The exhibition opened in Edinburgh in the early
spring of 1966. It was popular, but was largely visited by
students and those interested in the arts as it was not
promoted publicly, or indeed widely. Responses from visitors
were a 'mixed bag', with many comparing what they saw
to fashionable Scandinavian glass of the time. 'You can
imagine what they thought, if they had that mindset. This
glass was flowing, it was alive', explained Herman.[9]

The college's ceramics tutor was, however, fascinated
by what he saw and heard and, with Herman, set up a
crucible furnace, one of the oldest and simplest types of
melting furnace, from which some very rudimentary pieces
were made. Only a few students were interested, as most

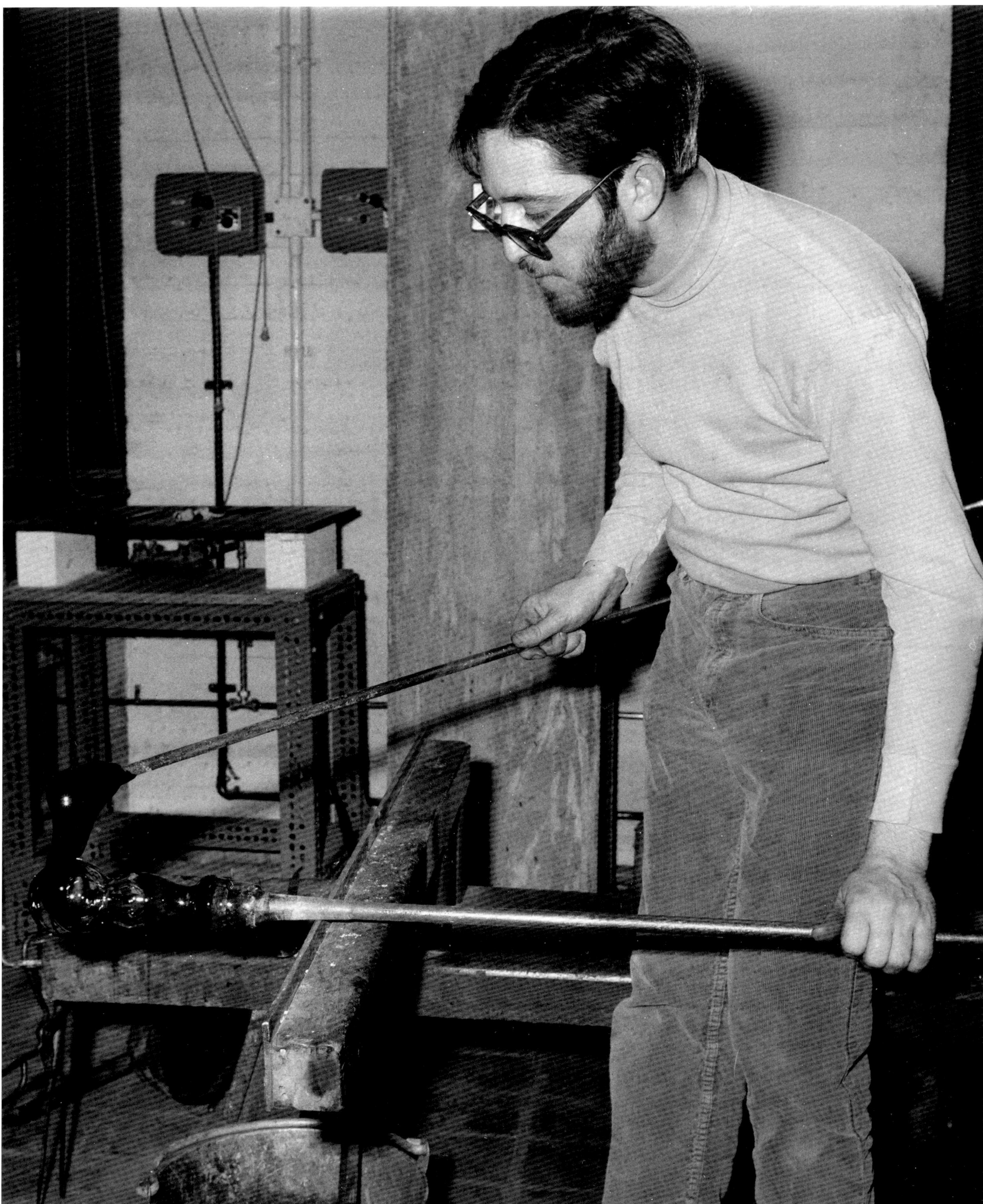

focused on the techniques they were at college to learn. 'They didn't realise that molten glass was within their means', Herman said.[10] Monro Turner, though, was temporarily furious as she was highly protective of her department.

The exhibition travelled from Edinburgh College of Art to Stourbridge College of Art in the West Midlands. Then, in the late spring of 1966, it moved to the RCA in London, and Littleton flew over to attend the opening.

Certainly the most important visitor to the exhibition in London was the Marquess of Queensberry (b.1929). He was Professor of Ceramics at the RCA, and the Industrial Glass Department (as it was then called) fell under his remit. Queensberry immediately saw the vast potential inherent in the new techniques and warmed to Herman personally, and the two went on to build a close relationship over subsequent years. To allow Herman and the techniques he practised to come to the RCA, Queensberry offered him a year-long research fellowship starting in autumn 1966, which Herman gratefully and immediately accepted. Even though it was only for a year, this provided Herman with an income and much-needed stability, particularly as his family had grown with the recent arrival of his daughter, Sarah.

Concurrent with teaching two days a week at the RCA, Herman also accepted the position of Visiting Lecturer for two days a week at Stourbridge College of Art. This role generated additional income as well as the opportunity to promote the Studio Glass Movement in another location, with students who were hungry to learn.

London and the Royal College of Art, 1966–74

In autumn 1966, Herman's first task was to build two small furnaces at the college to the specifications of those built in Wisconsin (he went on to make a third furnace at Stourbridge College of Art). Herman openly demonstrated the construction process of the 1.2m^2 (4ft^2) furnaces to the students, enabling them to repeat this on their own after graduation if necessary. This was the beginning of a radical and unexpected journey for the college's students.

At the time, as the name of the Industrial Glass Department suggests, students at the RCA were only concerned with designing glass, typically for serial commercial or industrial application. Although artistic designs were undoubtedly produced during the course,

the only employment for graduates in glass was in commercial or industrial glass factories, so the course had to cater largely to those targets.

Students produced their designs on paper, which were discussed with the Head of Department, Michael Harris (1933–94). Bill Heaton, the college's glassmaker, then made the designs in glass using the department's industrially constructed furnace. Students were not allowed to handle hot glass and were strongly discouraged from contributing to this part of the creation of their work. As a result, skills actually executed by students only comprised cold-working techniques, such as engraving, cutting, carving, sandblasting and acid etching, on pre-existing blanks or pieces blown by Heaton to their design. A staid traditionalist, Heaton also had his own opinion about work submitted, and was not keen on the use of colour.

The new furnaces were on the other side of the room to Heaton, and Herman recalls 'a widgy bit of resistance'[11] from Heaton. Herman was working directly with students, showing them how to make glass themselves, and Heaton was almost certainly concerned about his position in the future. This caused, as Herman puts it, a 'little unhappiness, but it didn't bother me because it was very exciting'.[12] The situation was very different with Harris, who also saw the potential and grasped the opportunity with both hands, supporting Herman and gaining direct experience from him whenever he could. Similarly, Heaton's assistant Paul Woods, who had joined in 1964, took a positive, open approach to Herman, saying that he realised Herman had 'reawakened the idea of the artist/designer, the craftsman'.[13]

According to Herman, the students took to this new approach 'like ducks to water . . . it was very seductive'.[14] They were able to free their minds and designs by adding myriad colours, while Herman supported them artistically and technically, discussing their work and their aims and the best ways of achieving them. Herman also demonstrated techniques that had not previously been taught because they were not used in industrial or commercial factories, such as fuming or adding glass shards, chips and trails to a body. For the first time, as Woods explained, students could 'make up their ideas rather than design them for others to make . . . and . . . take the approach of making "one-offs" rather than mass-produced ranges.'[15] Whenever possible Herman also produced his own work using the new furnaces (see pp 60–65 for more information about the type of work

Opposite
Sam Herman working at the Royal College of Art, *c.*1966

he created during this time). However, he was so busy teaching techniques and developing his students' artistic abilities that he had precious little time to advance his own work and rekindle his own artistic abilities, meaning that he recalls making fewer than 50 pieces over the course of the academic year.

In the summer of 1967, at the end of his fellowship, Herman travelled across Europe for a month to see first-hand how glass factories in Germany, France and Scandinavia operated. As he had very little money, he was forced to hitch-hike and could only go where he could find a free ride. Nonetheless, for Herman, it was a wonderful opportunity as only Blenko Glass Company in the USA produced this sort of hand-blown glass. 'They might be making a goblet, but the way one factory would make it, such as how to put the foot or stem on, was always slightly different to another. When we started none of us at Wisconsin knew how to blow glass, even Harvey [Littleton]. These guys certainly did.'[16] Standing for hours on public viewing platforms near the factory floors, Herman could 'see all these different techniques, and techniques that I could incorporate into studio glass'.[17]

Herman also visited the pioneering German glass artist Erwin Eisch in Frauenau, Bavaria. The two had first met when Eisch visited Wisconsin on Littleton's invitation in 1964 and they had kept in touch and developed a close relationship built on mutual respect. Some glass was made in Eisch's furnace, and a few examples by Herman were included in the pioneering 'Vrij Glas' (Free Glass) exhibition held in Rotterdam in November 1969.

A few months after Herman returned to London, the situation at the RCA changed dramatically. Over the previous year, Harris had rapidly built his skills and confidence in studio glass, despite the daily demands of his job. He had also devised a business plan and, in July 1967, left his role to found Mdina Glass on the island of Malta. Queensberry asked Herman to take the position as Head of Department, a fortunate turn of events as Herman's next step was unclear and he was expecting to have to return to the USA now that his fellowship and source of income had expired.

Herman's first achievements included changing the name of the department from 'Industrial Glass' to simply 'Glass', and replacing Heaton (already of retirement age) with Fred Daden, who had worked at Whitefriars Glass, the famous British glass factory in Harrow Weald,

Middlesex. At this time, the RCA was a hotbed of creativity, experimentation and excitement that reflected the decade itself. The dramatic changes introduced by Herman fitted in seamlessly. Anything was possible, and change was sought out and accepted. The college was inhabited and run by a roster of now internationally famous pioneers, artists and creators, from Eduardo Paolozzi (1924–2005) to Peter Blake (b.1932), Robert Goodden (1909–2002) to Robin Darwin (1910–74), and Carel Weight (1908–97) to Hans Coper (1920–81). At one point, paintings by Francis Bacon (1909–92), given by the artist himself, hung in the Senior Common Room.

Herman asked his students to think about glass and understand the medium in a free and creative way that had not been taught before, even if a handful of practitioners in the 19th and early 20th centuries had approached this on a personal basis. For Herman, it was about using glass in a natural way:

> Every material has its own attributes. Glass wants to be rounded and amorphic. People far too often make glass do what it can't do – that's unnatural. Use wood for things that wood allows you to do naturally. Use glass to make things that glass allows you to make naturally. Every material has its character and you should utilise that character. That's what the Studio Glass Movement was initially about – using a material in the most natural way possible. But, most importantly, to use it in a creative sense, and in as artistic a sense as possible.[18]

Herman was keen to find again his own innate artistic abilities in glass, but also to balance them against the properties of the material itself. 'You can't control the glass, it controls you. If you start to control it, you lose some of its innate qualities. You're lucky if, at some point, you and the glass work together. It was this synergy I was looking for and teaching. Technique has to submerge, aesthetics have to come to the surface.'[19] Herman looked at each student to identify their individual strengths. He explains, 'You can't teach art, only techniques, but you can bring out the best in that individual by encouraging them to express the theme inside of them. I'd get them to make the best things they could by encouraging the personal – what the hell they're really all about. It had to be an expression of them.'[20] (See pp 127–31 for more information on Herman as an educator.)

Sam Herman in the studio at the Royal College of Art, 1970

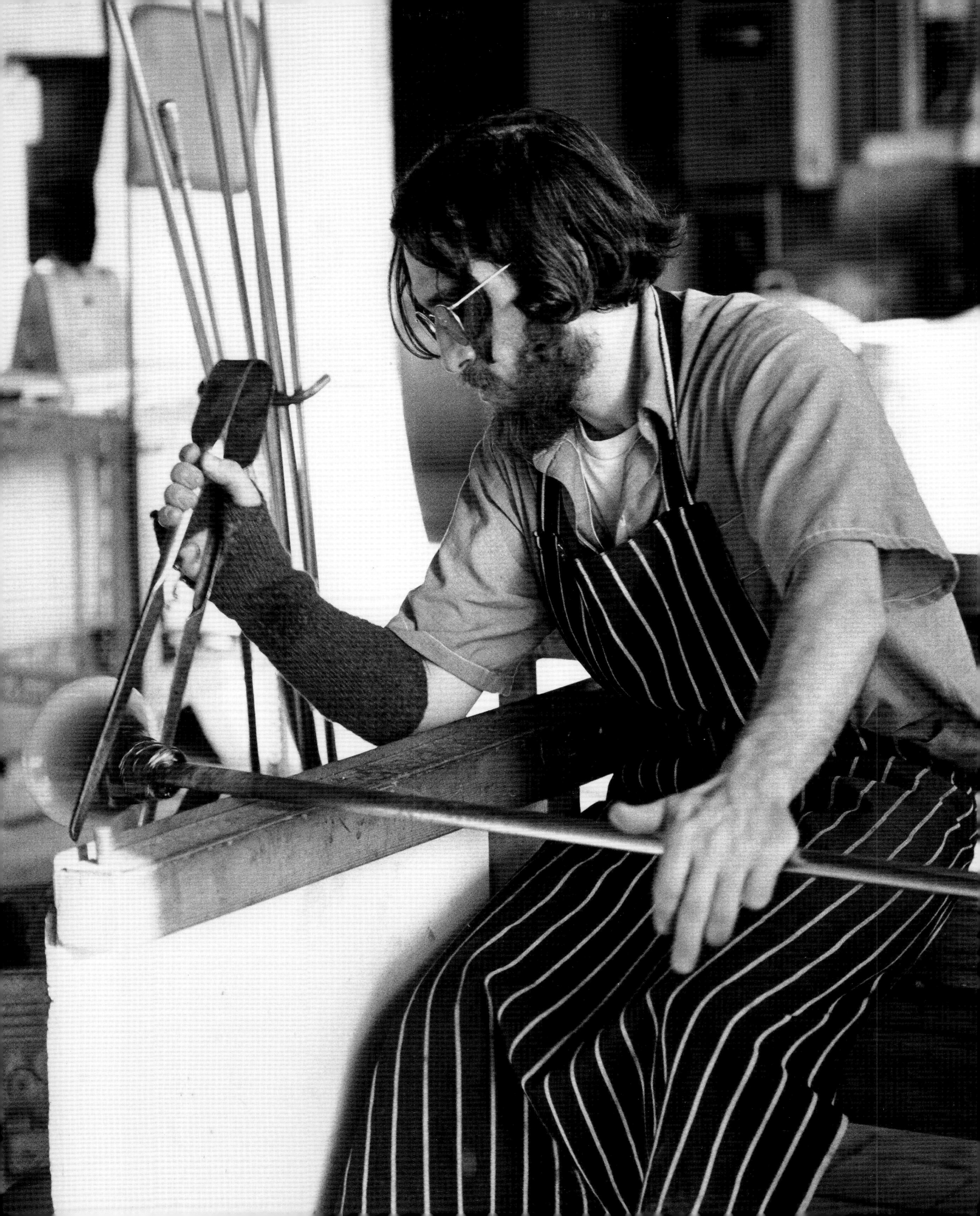

Untitled, 1967, 1969
blown glass, 18cm (7 in) and
36cm (14 in), Mark Hill (left)/
Private Collection (right)

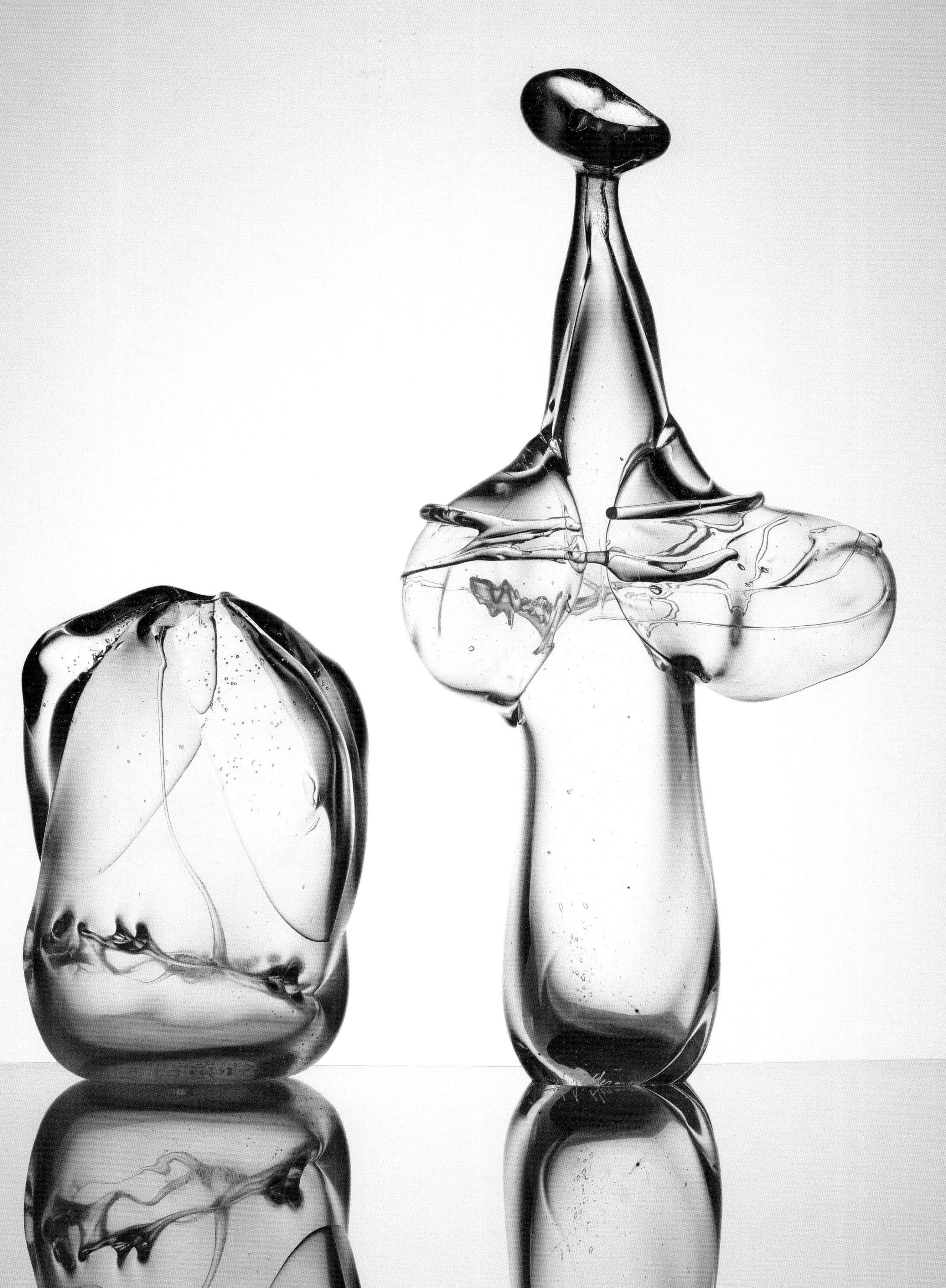

As Head of Department, Herman was free and able to invite visiting lecturers to the department, with many coming from outside the UK to 'give students the greatest range of exposure'.[21] These included Bengt Orup (1916–96) from Sweden, Sybren Valkema from the Netherlands and Erwin Eisch from Germany, but he was most excited about those he invited from communist Czechoslovakia. The Czechs were, as Herman put it, 'a million miles ahead of anything anyone else was doing'[22] and had esteemed and respected artists working in glass. Jiří Harcuba (1928–2013) had been invited for a year as a visiting professor, demonstrating cutting techniques, so the precedent had been set. Pavel Hlava (1924–2003) visited more than once, the longest period being from 1966 to 1967, and built a close personal and working relationship with Herman that resulted in Herman being invited to Czechoslovakia in 1968 as a guest of the Czech Government. A card-carrying member of the Communist Party and a progressive glass artist, Hlava ensured that Herman was exposed to as much as possible, including meeting now internationally renowned pioneers such as Stanislav Libenský. 'Stanislav was a real artist – he understood scale, he was creative. He understood form, art and aesthetics, as well as technique', Herman explained. Although Herman did not make anything during his visit, had the political situation following the Prague Spring not made a return impossible, he felt sure that he would have been invited back to work. From 1968 to 1971, the well-known Czech glassmaker and designer Jiří Šuhájek (b.1943) studied at the RCA under Herman, and the effects of this experience can be seen clearly in Šuhájek's work across subsequent decades.

Early exhibitions

Based on his desire to spread the word of the Studio Glass Movement and its possibilities, Herman organised exhibitions of his students' and his own work wherever possible, but these were usually small in scale and not widely publicised. Herman's first major exhibition was held in 1967 at London's prestigious Primavera Gallery, founded on Sloane Street in 1945 by Henry Rothschild, a scion of the influential banking family. The gallery contacted him at the RCA to offer him his first one-man show in the UK, which comprised new and existing work produced at the College.

The pressure was immense as, within two years of arriving in the UK, he had been asked to exhibit at one of the most highly respected galleries for craft and art. 'I was scrambling – promoting the Studio Glass Movement, giving lectures, building furnaces, teaching.'[23] The show was a total success and every piece was sold, with the highest price being £18. The gallery continued to stock Herman's glass, where it was displayed and sold alongside work by his peers, including ceramics by Hans Coper. This success and Primavera's formidable influence opened many doors for Herman. Not only was he quickly offered other exhibitions at galleries around the world, but also his work had begun to attract a high calibre of collector.

On the back of the Primavera show and his growing network of contacts, Herman had his work included in exhibitions in Stockholm, Jablonec (Czechoslovakia) and Bremen (Germany) in 1968. In 1969, he contributed to exhibitions in three Dutch museums, in the Crafts Centre of Great Britain and in two department stores: Heal's in London and Seibu in Tokyo. Herman considered department stores important as he wished to promote glass as art and to advocate the idea of unique works as opposed to the serial consistency of production ranges made in factories and sold in most shops. He wanted to persuade more shops to open themselves up to individual artists, which in turn would provide more places for his students to sell their work and, thus, to survive and develop when they had left the secure world of academia. The Seibu exhibition was additionally important because it was organised by the Crafts Council, and included many top British designers and craftspeople of the period: Gerald Benney (1930–2008, silver) Robert Welch (1929–2000, metalware), Gerda Flöckinger (jewellery), and Bernard Leach (1887–1979), Lucie Rie (1902–95), Hans Coper and Gordon Baldwin (b.1932) (ceramics). As well as Herman's work, glass by John Cook (1942–2012) and Pauline Solven (b.1943) was also shown, putting studio glass firmly in the same league as work in more traditional media by these recognised masters.

Nevertheless, there was no master plan as regards exhibitions. Herman was aware that he had to keep his name known and earn money, and he wanted to continue to promote studio glass generally. But this was countered by a desire to appear in the right galleries, and not to seem too 'easy' by accepting every opportunity offered. He was also affected by the incredible level of stress caused by

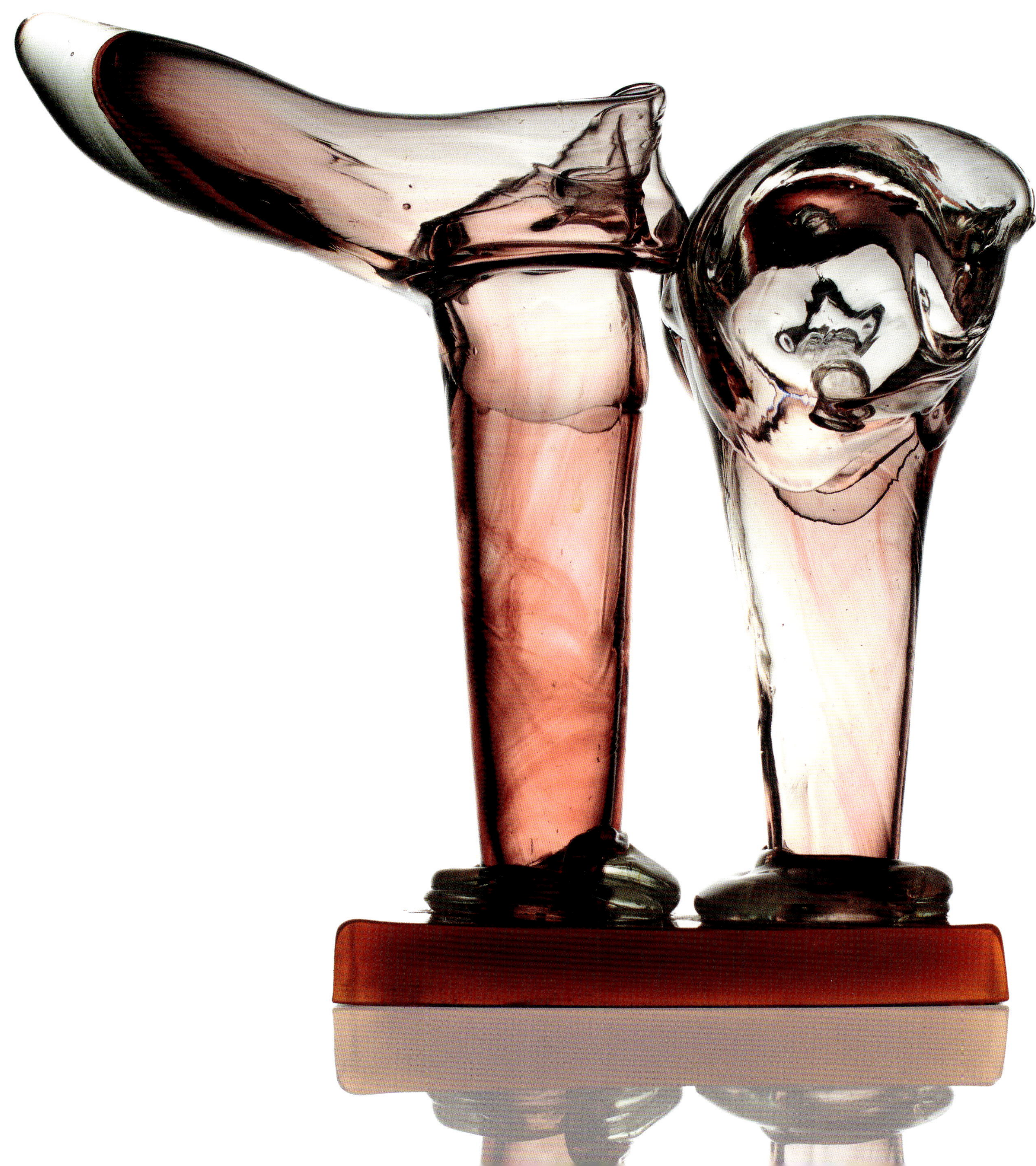

the preparation for an exhibition: 'My greatest enjoyment is being able to work, and being able to make anything that I feel like making, and not having to concern myself with whether it will fit into the next exhibition or not. I'd always worry if the work was going to be anywhere near good enough to exhibit.'[24] As a result, he tended not to accept an exhibition unless he had already produced all the work necessary. This also limited the amount of his work available in the marketplace at any time, creating a feeling of scarcity that usually served to boost desirability – and price.

The next major exhibition came as unexpectedly as Primavera. In late 1970, Belgian gallerist Gilbert Weynans, who had founded Galerie L'Ecuyer in Brussels in 1952 with his partner Hubert Meurrens, contacted Herman. The gallery had a strong reputation for selling fine European decorative arts, from glass by Emile Gallé (1846–1904) to furniture and decorative effects in the Beaux Arts and art nouveau styles, but typically combined with contemporary art. Weynans and Meurrens had become excited by Herman's work after seeing the Primavera exhibition, and finally tracked him down at the RCA. The resulting exhibition ran from December 1970 until January 1971, and introduced his work to a new high-end audience of European collectors. Weynans and Meurrens were extremely well-connected and also presented Herman's work to a number of European museum curators, thus ensuring that it entered a number of public and private collections, including the Royal Family of Belgium, the Palais Stoclet in Belgium, the Badisches Landesmuseum in Germany, the Gulbenkian Museum in Portugal and the Kunstindustrimuseet in Sweden.

Val St Lambert, Seraing, Belgium

The exhibition at Galerie L'Ecuyer also had another important effect. Weynans and Meurrens knew the owners of the prestigious Belgian glass company Val St Lambert, founded in 1826. Well-known for their high-quality sparkling cut glass, they were keen to experiment in new areas as sales for their largely traditional designs were slowing. They had also recently closed their in-house design department in order to cut costs, and had begun to invite consultant designers in to modernise production. Weynans and Meurrens suggested that Herman became one of them. In 1971, Herman was asked to visit Val St Lambert to produce a small collection of unique pieces to be sold in Galerie L'Ecuyer. The collection sold out, and Val St Lambert asked

Herman to devise a range that could be produced by a team of its glassmakers for commercial sale.

Herman designed and produced ten special pieces himself at the factory to use as model examples. He showed these to the glassmakers and then directed every step of the initial production process to replicate them. The result was the 'El Dorado' range, produced from 1972 onwards, and based on Herman's work. The pieces were deemed a perfect fusion of commercial concerns (as Herman said, 'they were in business!') and a desire to react to the growing popularity of the 'new' studio glass.

The path to the final range was unusual on both sides. Firstly, unlike any other place he had been employed so far, Herman was working only with a team of highly trained glassmakers. Secondly, they had been trained (and expected) to produce technically and formally perfect colourless or cased glass on a consistent basis. This total control of the material was diametrically opposed to Herman's aesthetic and his desire to let the glass have an input on the final design of the piece. Furthermore, commercial considerations needed to be factored in. The designs had to be repeatable and also immediately appealing to the public when retailed. During the time that Herman was at Val St Lambert he worked with a number of the gaffers there, one of whom was Louis Leloup (b.1929). Leloup eventually went on to set up his own studio where his work was heavily inspired by Herman's designs and his experiences with him.

Herman visited Val St Lambert a number of times during the 1970s to monitor and feed back on the production of his 'El Dorado' designs, and also to create unique works (see pp 66–70 for further information on work made at Val St Lambert).

The Victoria and Albert Museum, London

At around the same time as Herman had been contacted by Weynans and Meurrens, he had also been approached by representatives of the Victoria and Albert Museum (V&A) in London. In 1969, the V&A had begun a sadly short-lived series of exhibitions about contemporary craftspeople and artists that had launched with a joint exhibition of ceramics by Hans Coper and textiles by Peter Collingwood (1922–2008). The museum's noble stated aim was to give 'the work of outstanding craftsmen . . . the emphasis more frequently accorded to the work of painters and sculptors.'[25]

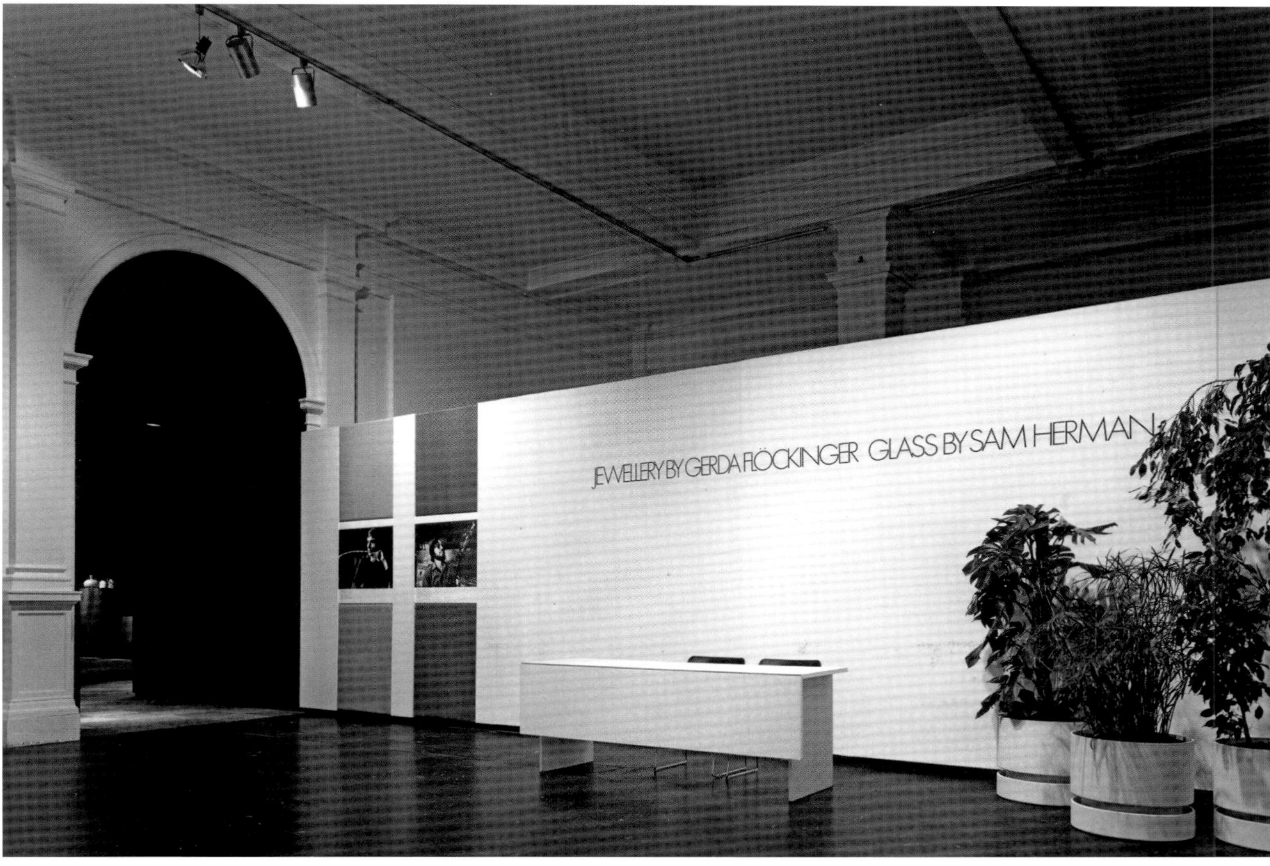

In 1971, Herman's glass was exhibited alongside the innovative and rich jewellery of the British designer and maker Gerda Flöckinger (see p.19). The organisers visited Herman in his studio and asked him to make new pieces as the exhibition was intended to show the subjects' mature and current work, rather than their development. Sixty-nine pieces of Herman's glass were included, and 25 were photographed and presented in the accompanying catalogue. These were both single pieces and sculptures comprising multiple components mounted on a base. Forms varied from the sculptural and torso-like to the more vessel-like. The pieces represented Hermar's increasingly mature work at the RCA, and offered a detai ed snapshot of his style and artistic direction at the time.

Despite the obvious stresses of contributing to an exhibition in an internationally renowned museum, Herman took it all in his stride. It was not until he visited the exhibition just before it opened that its immense significance hit him: 'As I wandered in to give my two penn'orth, I passed through the galleries and realised that there was 2,000 years' worth of amazing art here and people were passing it on the way to see my glass. That was quite a jolt'.[26]

The exhibition ran from February to March 1971. It was an incredible achievement for Herman for so many reasons, not least because he had only been practising studio glass since the mid-1960s and had only arrived in the UK six years earlier. It also gave Herman the double accolade of being the first contemporary glass artist and the first living glass artist to have an exhibition at the Victoria and Albert Museum. The show rightly put Herman at the centre of the Studio Glass Movement in the UK and Europe, placing his work firmly on the same level as Hans Coper's renowned ceramics: as pioneering artworks in media other than the more traditional ones of paint, pencil, bronze and stone. It also led to a dramatically increased level of interest from collectors, museums and galleries, resulting in around 30 important exhibitions across the globe over the next eight years.

Not everything ran smoothly with exhibitions, primarily because of the preconceptions that glass making was a craft rather than an art (as was even stated by the V&A in the catalogue), and that glass could not be a medium for art. In the early 1970s, Herman carefully approached Heinrich (Harry) Fischer (1903–77), one of the founders of London's prestigious gallery Marlborough Fine Art, who dealt in names ranging from Claude Monet to Edgar Degas, and Francis Bacon to John Piper. Fischer had founded his own gallery, Fischer Fine Art, in 1971, and Herman was keen to break down the barrier between craft and art and thought that such a gallery and personality could help him achieve this. Despite showing initial interest in his sculptural forms, Fischer stated that his company only dealt in fine art and that Herman's glass was craft in his mind. As a result, contact was severed.

Other gallerists at the same level saw things differently. At the time of the Victoria and Albert Museum exhibition, Herman was approached by Andrew McIntosh Patrick and Simon Edsor of London's esteemed Fine Art Society, based on Bond Street in the heart of London's gallery district. He was given an exhibition there, and his work was also shown in their galleries in Glasgow and Edinburgh. Moreover, the Fine Art Society continued to stock Herman's work, and the resulting slow but steady sales provided extremely helpful income to Herman, as well as serving to maintain his profile. Other early exhibitions took place at the Pace Gallery in London, the Gemeentemuseum and the Museum Boijmans von Beuningen in the Netherlands, the Archer Gallery in London, the Oxford Gallery in Oxford and the Röhsska Konstslöjdmuseet in Sweden.

The Glasshouse, London

Herman had built himself a strong profile across the UK and Europe, and was regularly selling work through galleries to a growing base of collectors. He also had a full-time job as Tutor at the RCA. As far as any artist and creator can be, he was secure, well known and able to develop his work, despite the daily responsibilities of his job. However, the question of what would happen to the students who passed through his department after they graduated played heavily on his mind. The glass industry was comparatively small and only a very limited number of jobs existed. Although it was now practically possible for a graduate to build their own furnace and continue to develop and make their own

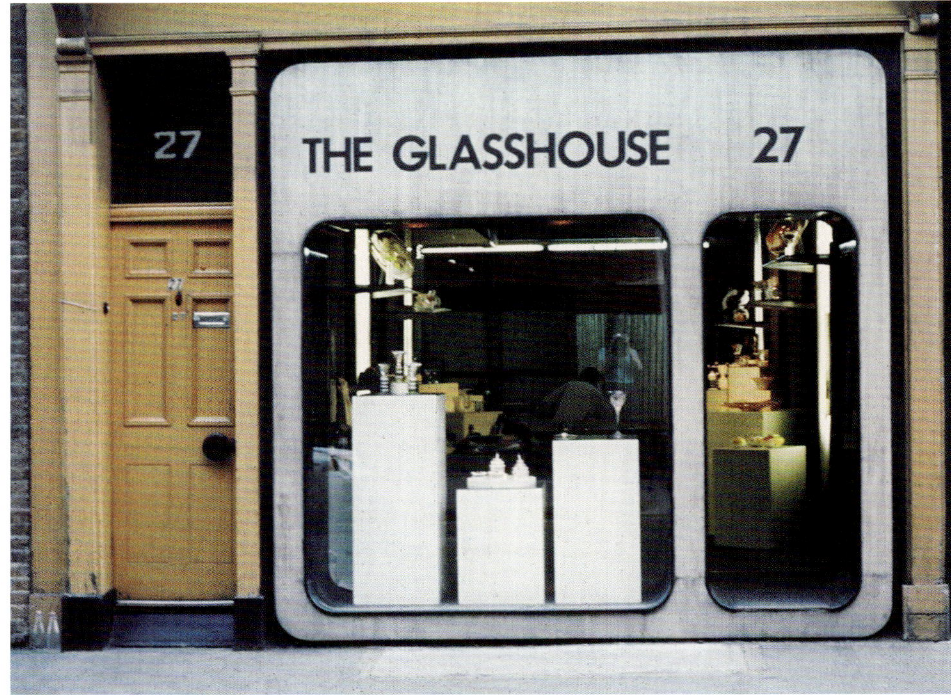

The frontage of The Glasshouse, 27 Neal Street, Covent Garden, London

glass, the costs of fuelling a furnace, together with renting a location and constructing it, were prohibitive. Even if a graduate had the money to do all this, how would their work be sold, and where? Who would promote it, and how? All these issues were compounded by the shock of coming out of the 'protection' of the RCA, where students were cosseted and encouraged, and sheltered from the harsh realities of life. Consequently, Herman said that after graduation 'most students fell into oblivion. They realised that galleries weren't interested and they just couldn't deal with it. It's terrible, as you helped these people develop and then they disappeared. Their work disappeared too.'[27] Herman explained, 'I feel a moral obligation to my students. Where can they go when they leave college? Sometimes you feel as though you're pushing them over a cliff.'[28]

In early 1969, Herman was discussing these serious issues over lunch in the Senior Common Room at the RCA with his friend Graham Hughes (1926–2010), a director of The Worshipful Company of Goldsmiths. Herman pointed out, 'It'd be great if there was a halfway house for them to get on their feet' and a way 'of creating a life in glass away from the industry'.[29] Hughes asked for more information and a rough idea of the cost of setting up and running such an organisation. Herman provided some rough estimates, and a week later Hughes responded, 'OK, let's do it.'

Later that year, The Glasshouse opened in a retail shop at 27 Neal Street in Covent Garden, London. Hughes secured funding from the Crafts Council and also put some of his own money into the risky and pioneering venture – without his support, the project would have never got further than estimates on a piece of paper. Herman built the furnaces himself, Susannah Robins, a director of the Crafts Centre of Great Britain, was taken on to act as administrator and Pauline Solven, who had graduated under Herman in 1968, ran the operations. For nearly three decades, hundreds of graduate glassmakers and glass artists passed through its doors, first in Neal Street, then at Long Acre in Covent Garden from 1975 and finally at St Alban's Place in Islington from 1992 until its closure in 1998.

Working as a collective, students were able to lease a furnace for periods of time, produce their work and then sell it in the shop on the ground floor. The business took a commission from sales to cover its operating costs and the costs of marketing and promoting the business. Sales were never easy, due partly to the British public's lack of understanding of contemporary craft at the time, and the business met regular funding challenges. Without Herman's and Hughes' determination to keep the venture afloat, it is almost certain that the Studio Glass Movement would not have flourished as vibrantly as it has. Now-renowned names who benefitted from kick-starting their careers there include Pauline Solven, Annette Meech (b.1948), Fleur Tookey (b.1950) (all of whom also helped to manage the business), Jane Bruce (b.1947), Catherine Hough (b.1948), Helen Millard, Steven Newell (b.1948), Bob Crooks (b.1965) and Simon Moore (b.1948).

The Glasshouse was intended as a stepping stone, but many students chose to spend as much time as they could there, enjoying the benefits of low and flexible costs, ease of production and a prestigious sales venue in the centre of London where their work and names were actively promoted. The business was also unique and had no direct precedent – there was no other option. The Glasshouse may have been Herman's first major foray into commercialising studio glass beyond his own work being sold in galleries, but it was not his last.

The Jam Factory, Adelaide, 1974–9

In 1971, Dick Richards (b.1938), the progressive Curator of Asian Art at the Art Gallery of South Australia in Adelaide, was asked by the Australian government to travel to Scandinavia, the UK and Ireland to report on commercial craft-based industries. The Australian government was aware that overseas competition, mainly from Japan, in the automotive and white-goods industries was affecting Australia's economy and causing growing unemployment. One option was to develop the country's vast natural resources – gemstones, clay, sand and leather – on a craft basis.

During his visit to London, Richards was introduced to Herman via the Crafts Council and the British Council of Industrial Design. Richards had heard not only about Herman's achievements at the RCA and in the promotion of studio glass across Europe and the UK, but also about The Glasshouse, which he saw as a potential model to be duplicated. Furthermore, another of the directors of the Australian project, the notable pathologist Dr Earle Hackett (1921–2010), had seen Herman's exhibition at the V&A Museum in 1971 and was keen for Herman to be involved somehow.

Herman responded positively to Richards' suggestions. He was extremely excited about replicating and expanding the model behind The Glasshouse, and creating a business that allowed people to learn a craft and also potentially develop their artistic abilities in glass. Moreover, as well as apprenticeships, their ongoing professional development would be supported, and their work sold in a central gallery space to generate income for them and the business. Herman had also watched with interest the growing success of Michael Harris's business at Mdina Glass in Malta.

Over subsequent discussions, Herman was offered total control of the department, a salary and the freedom to work on his own glass. As Herman and his glass had an international reputation, this was seen as a major boost to the venture. In 1974, Herman took the brave and bold step to resign from his position as Head of the Glass Department at the RCA and move to Adelaide to found and run the glass division of what would be called The Jam Factory. There were also personal reasons behind the decision. Herman had fond memories of his early childhood in Mexico, and he wanted to give his children a taste of life in another country, under the warmth of a blazing sun and away from grey city life in the centre of London.

For safety reasons related to the furnace, the glass department was located in a large corrugated-iron structure outside the main building, a large disused factory that had once produced jam. As well as glass, other departments produced textiles and leather, jewellery, metalwork and ceramics. When Herman arrived, the daunting scale of the project dawned on him immediately. He was unable to find suitable materials to build the furnaces, and he had to order them from Japan, the USA and the UK. Glass to melt was similarly hard to source, so Herman resorted to using empty wine bottles that had been collected from the greater Adelaide area as rubbish. Although this glass was inexpensive, readily available and plentiful, the working time of the material was extremely short, so soda ash was added to the batch to try and extend it. This affected the shapes and designs that could be made (see pp 81–2 for more information on this). Initially, they worked with colourless glass, but they soon ordered colour glass rods from Kugler in Germany.

Herman acted as both the director and the tutor. Apprenticeships in the glass making team were advertised widely and paid a salary. Herman would show potential recruits how to gather the right amount of glass for the piece, and then blow simple forms like a small drinking glass. He could tell who had a natural aptitude, making it easy to decide whom to offer a job to. Once the recruits had mastered producing drinking glasses, the mainstay of production as 'they felt right in the hand and they really worked',[30] they moved on to larger forms such as vases, which were ostensibly larger glasses. Then they would learn how to handle colour. 'It was all skill-driven. The design had to be based on the skill. As the skills developed you could develop the designs. It was baby steps. In the end, it all got quite sophisticated.'[31]

Herman set his team daily targets for each product, as he said, 'It was a proper factory, there was no fooling around.'[32] Even though the gallery and shop handled sales and marketing, freeing Herman to focus on design and production, commercial concerns constantly dominated any potential artistic avenues: 'They weren't trying to create artists, they were trying to create jobs.'[33] As such, they produced easy-to-sell practical tableware, ranging from drinking glasses to jugs, and simple vases and bowls.

Sales drove production, with unsuccessful or uneconomical designs rapidly discontinued. Herman learned a lot about bureaucracy and dealing with government committees, as he also sat on the board, making the whole 'a wonderful experience'. Despite employing people to do production work, Herman was delighted when some individuals who had trained at The Jam Factory went on to set up their own studios and became artists in their own right.

Due to the responsibilities of his job, Herman was typically only able to produce his own work at night, when the commercial glass-making team had gone home. The work he created took on elements unconsciously inspired by the Australian landscape. Occasionally, he was able to make use of one or two more experienced members of the glass-making team, especially if he was preparing for an exhibition at The Jam Factory and larger pieces were required (see pp 81–93 for more information about this, and the general style of his work at the time). These unique artworks in glass were sold in The Jam Factory's gallery, generating revenue and promotion for the venture, and were also collected for exhibitions in Australia and around the world.

Herman remained in contact with his existing network of galleries when he was in Australia, making long and expensive trips to the UK and Europe, or exporting crates of his work at his own cost. Due to the limited amount of work he could produce at The Jam Factory, and the smaller demand for his work in Australia, he restricted his exposure there to around three exhibitions in major cities per year. Back in his core markets of the UK and Europe, this limited supply created a feeling of scarcity, tipping the balance of supply and demand in the right way for Herman. Although he was keen to hold regular exhibitions and maintain his status and earn extra money, he found that if he was unable to supply the quantity of pieces a gallery initially required, demand and prices for his work would rise. Similarly, he felt it better to have a greater number of small exhibitions than one or two large ones. During his time in South Australia, he took part in just over a dozen exhibitions across Europe and the UK, and just over a dozen exhibitions in Australia, including at The Jam Factory.

By the late 1970s, The Jam Factory project was deemed successful, but the government's approach to the venture had begun to change. A new director was brought in to streamline production and control costs as it was still not making a profit and continued to drain government

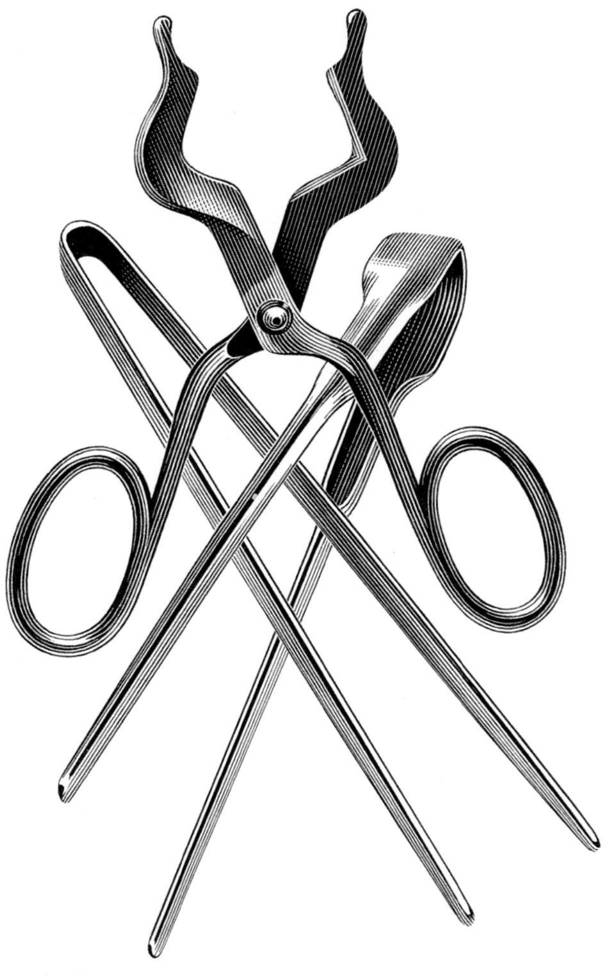

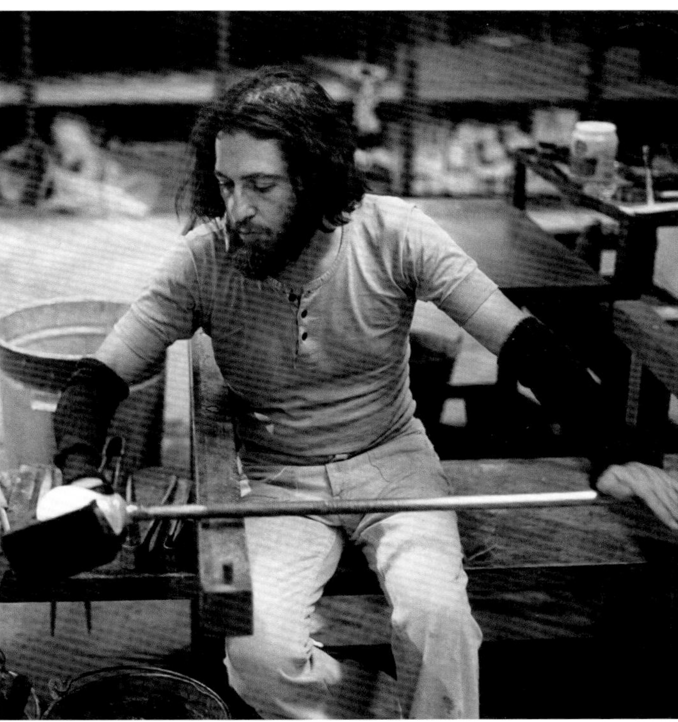

funds. The open positivity and feeling that anything could be achieved were suppressed by the cold, hard bottom line. Herman's colleagues also began to perceive and treat him differently, as he had been in Adelaide for a few years and was considering making it his permanent home: 'In Australia at the time, if you were from somewhere else they were in awe of you. I was precious. But if you said you wanted to stay living there, the awe vanished.'[34]

The tide had also changed in Herman's marriage, which, after 14 years, had begun to break up. His wife Judith had been a wonderful mother to their two children and had also fully supported Herman through every difficulty and success as he developed his groundbreaking career and travelled from Bellingham to Wisconsin, Edinburgh, London and Adelaide. 'It was all a big adventure!', Herman said.[35] In 1977, she became involved with a feminist group in Adelaide. Deeply influenced by their way of living, she left Herman and their two children to become further involved with the movement. She no longer wished to care for the children, and so Herman took on full responsibility for them, adding to the pressure already generated by his considerable responsibilities and concerns about his career.

In 1979, the board of The Jam Factory agreed to buy Herman out of his contract, providing him with a cushion of money and the freedom to make his next step. The most obvious choice was to continue with what was a very good life, if you did not want to be 'cosmopolitan and fancy',[36] and remain in Australia. Sydney College of the Arts opened discussions with Herman about him joining as Head of the Glass Department, but they could not find the funding immediately. With a dwindling sum of money and two teenagers reliant on him, he could not wait, especially as there was no guarantee that the funding would ever be found. Furthermore, the market for his work in Australia was comparatively small and the country's long distance from his main markets in the UK and Europe made it expensive and impractical for him to act as an independent glass artist based there.

Return to Europe, 1979

On one of Herman's previous trips to the UK, he had met Jonathan Stone, a wealthy barrister friend who was an ardent collector of Herman's work. A supporter of the

Polish artist Feliks Topolski (1907–89), among others, Stone was, as Herman described him, 'a real patron of the arts'.[37] Herman had discussed the difficulties he was facing at The Jam Factory, so when he further elaborated on the situation to Stone by letter, Stone offered to help him return to the UK. Stone organised enough funding to allow Herman to return and set up his own studio in central London, where he would be free to create what he wished. 'It wouldn't have been possible for me to come back if Jonathan hadn't come forward', Herman stated.[38] A location for the studio was found in Lots Road, Chelsea, and Joanna Shellard, a relative of one of Stone's business contacts, was asked to help Herman found his studio when he and his children arrived. A new chapter was about to begin.

The Lots Road studio flourished until 1984 with the added support and encouragement of John Campbell, another true collector and supporter of the arts. However, in 1984, it became clear that to continue in the Chelsea studio it would be necessary to either share the space with another artist or start a production line. Neither option was in keeping with Herman's philosophy of producing only unique pieces. More importantly he wanted to have the opportunity to explore his first love of sculpture and to develop his creativeness in painting. He was already establishing a painting and sculpture studio in Camberwell, and was also in the process of buying a property in Mallorca, where he was keen to spend more time. The Lots Road studio closed in 1984 and his glass-making tools were packed away until he returned to make blown glass in 2007.

Reminiscences with Erwin Eisch, 2017

To summarise the aims of those early pioneers of the Studio Glass Movement, Erwin Eisch's daughter, Katharina Eisch-Angus, reminisced with her father and the following words, written by her, bring together the feelings and ambitions of those artists:

A Sunday afternoon in late April in Frauenau, Germany, sitting around the big table in Erwin and Gretel Eisch's kitchen, an occasion for sharing memories. Gathered on the table are old photographs, yellowed newspaper cuttings, handwritten notes and machine-typed letters,

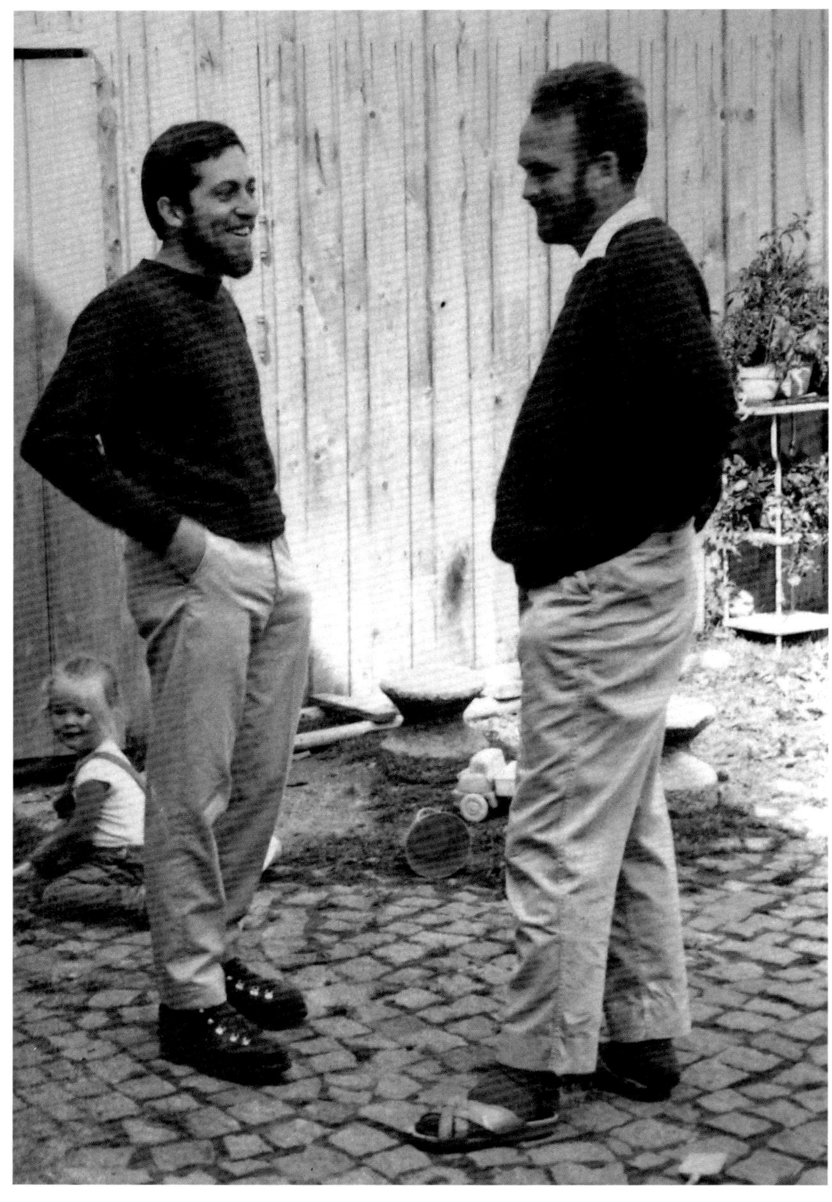

Sam Herman and Erwin Eisch at the Eisch home, Frauenau, 1967

to help trace the memories of Sam Herman and the early days of the glass movement.

All of us recognise the black and white photographs in the family album, taken in August 1967 in the enclosed cobbled courtyard that screened off our home from the bustle of the Eisch glass factory outside. There are Erwin and Sam standing in animated discussion, both smiling. For me, as the then five-year-old, Sam was different to the many American glass people who visited our house in those years. Over the years, he somehow held a gentle presence in our house and I would always have recognised the white vase that carried his name in our sitting room (and later in the Frauenau Glass Museum).

Erwin is very clear about their first meeting in 1965, which for him is linked to the overwhelming experience of his first US visits at the commencement of the Studio Glass Movement: 'I was also in London, visiting Sam up there where he then had his furnace'. 'Up there', means the Royal College of Art, high up, maybe on the sixth or seventh floor. With Erwin and Sam, and with Sybren Valkema, studio glass was now developing across Europe. Another slip of paper is an invitation for a private view for the exhibition 'Vrij Glas' – Free Glass – in Rotterdam, on 1 November 1969, organised by Sybren Valkema and featuring Erwin Eisch, Sam Herman, Harvey Littleton and Marvin Lipovsky. Photos show Sam, bearded and with long hair, in discussion with his contemporaries. We can sense an atmosphere, where the idea of 'free glass' resonates with the sentiments and movements of the time, but is brought to life in an ongoing border-crossing exchange of ideas and knowledge between like-minded friends, and in their working together at the studio furnaces in London, Frauenau and elsewhere.

When Sam wrote his perceptive foreword for Erwin's book entitled *Erwin Eisch – Clouds Have Been My Foothold All Along*, published in 2012, he talked about their early meetings in the 1960s, about the intensity of learning together in Wisconsin and of repeated family visits in Frauenau. Yet at the same time he observed in Erwin's work a feeling of being 'very alone', and an expression of 'the conflicts that lie not only within Erwin but are probably also hidden in most of us'. I believe that this loneliness and the awareness of the dark side of life might be a secret foundation of the deep bond and of the speaking silence between these two renowned artists. Erwin was also aware of murderous brutality and oppression that marked his growing up in a predominantly communist-minded glass workers' community in Bavaria. With their pasts on adverse sides of the inhumane history of the Second World War, they both, and the early founders of studio glass, knew about the value of friendship, and when they talked about free glass, they could appreciate what freedom really means.

Erwin's focus on art and his self-understanding as a painter and sculptor is another shared direction that they have pursued. Having accomplished their mission of free glass, they both needed to liberate themselves from glass, towards art and the expression of content. Two artists and friends who were founders of the Studio Glass Movement in Europe and who both continued to successfully expand their artistic expression into painting and sculpture.

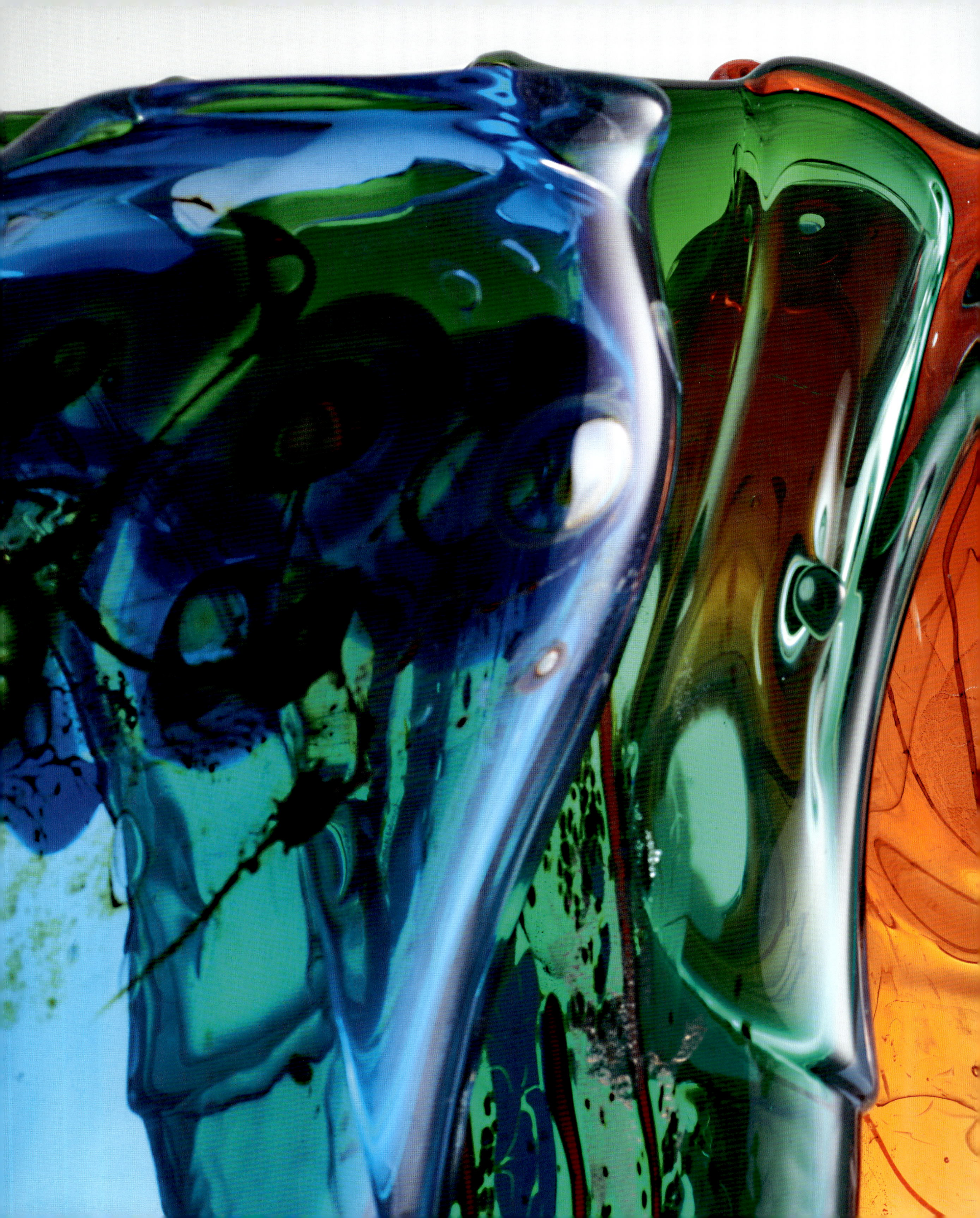

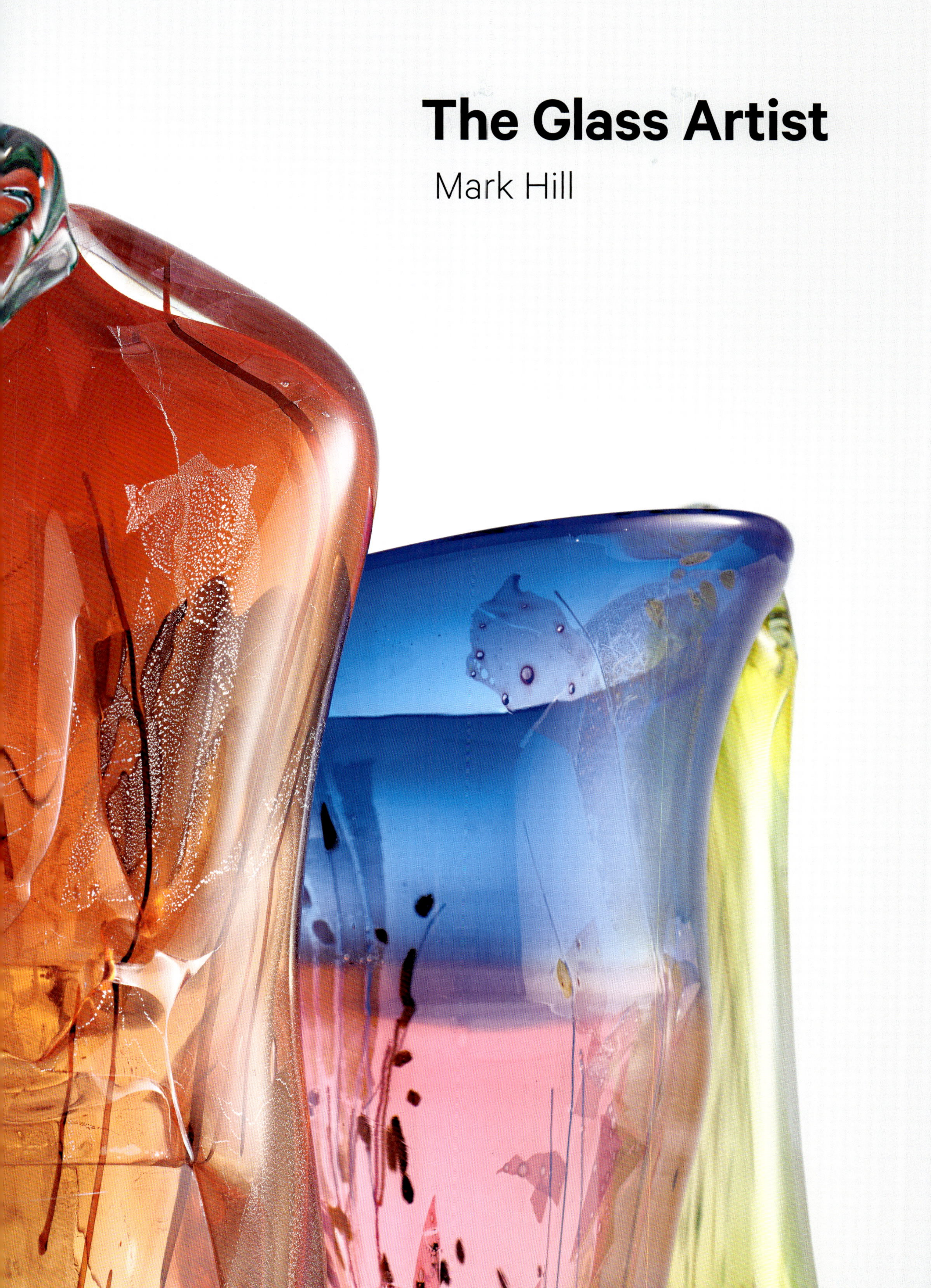

The Glass Artist

Mark Hill

Across his career, Herman's designs in glass comprise many different sculptural forms. There are no defined signature styles, such as a spindle or cylinder. Size varies widely, as it was dictated by whether Herman was working alone or with the assistance needed to produce large-scale pieces.

Each piece is unique because it was handmade at the furnace, even though certain forms or themes recur. Producing a functional vessel was not the reason behind the creation of a piece, but some pieces lend themselves to a practical use. Herman explains,

Regardless of what they are, they are an expression of myself, my consciousness or my subconscious. I don't make the distinction between fine art and crafts. In spirit, I am in line with the Japanese – it's a work of art whether it's a doorknob or a sculpture. I didn't make things to be functional or non-functional, if they happened to be functional, so be it. I don't feel damaged or hurt if someone puts flowers in a piece, or drinks out of it.[39]

Two core themes underlie Herman's career in glass: the nature of the material of glass and a sculptural approach to the form of the human torso. Herman has generally followed Harvey Littleton's initial principles and the original ethos of the Studio Glass Movement, working the glass alone, without any assistance, and staying true to the material by not forcing it to do something that it would not do on its own. As such, any cold-working techniques – cutting, engraving, sandblasting, applying transfers or painting on enamels or gilding – were not used. The molten glass was allowed to act naturally, permitting the properties of the material to come through as part of the final piece. Thus, techniques used regularly were hot-worked, and included blowing, shaping with hand moulds and paddles, and the application of further quantities of glass in the form of wings, trails, straps, prunts and powdered or chipped enamels.[40] Metal oxides, silver chloride and gold or silver leaf were also added. All were applied freely and in a sculptural or painterly manner when the glass was molten and ductile, just as a painter mixes and manipulates pigments and wet paint. Form, colour and pattern often gave a sense of dynamism or movement to a piece, either individually or in combination.

Periodically, the glass was cut with shears or impressed with a pattern, with the hard cut edge or firmly

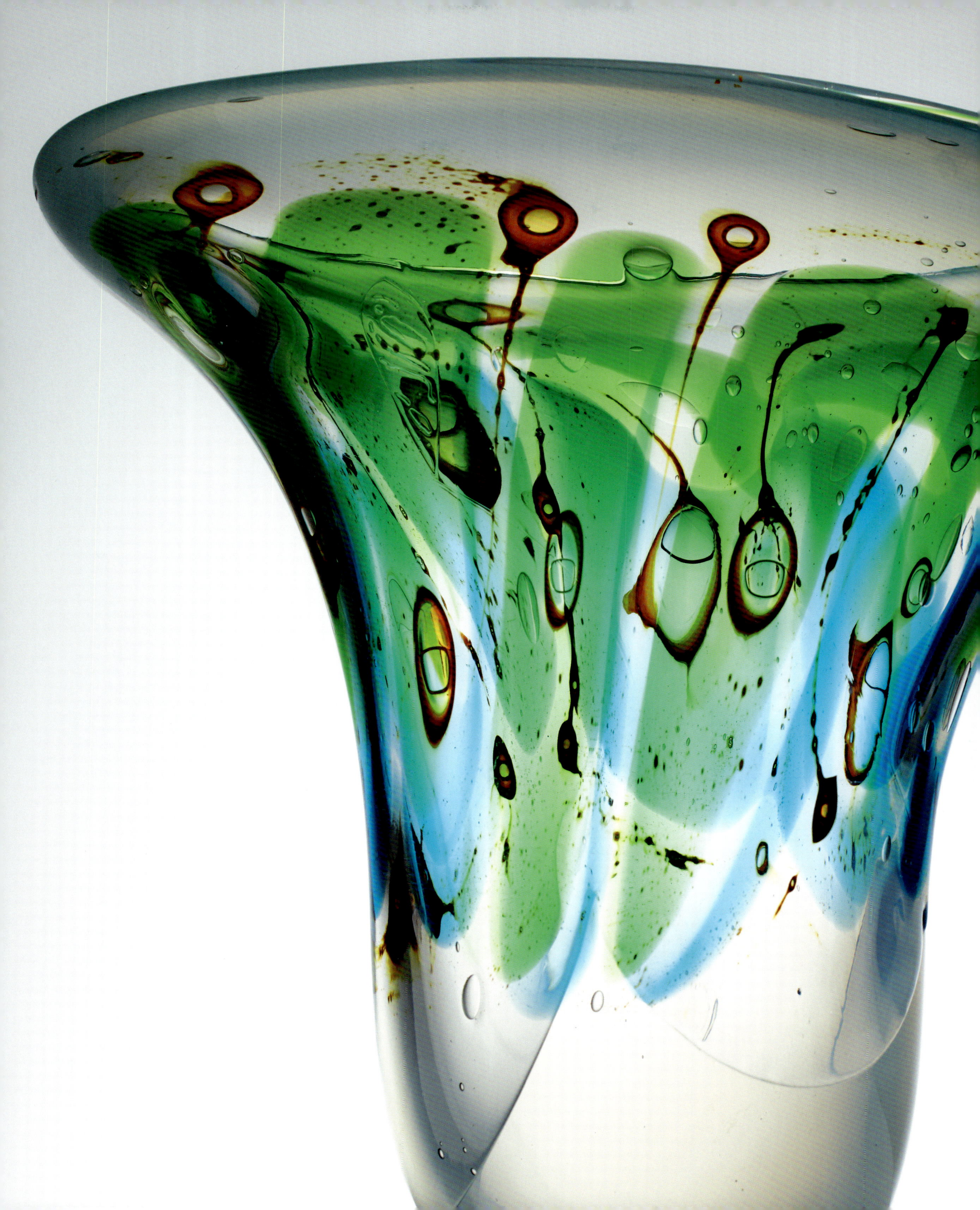

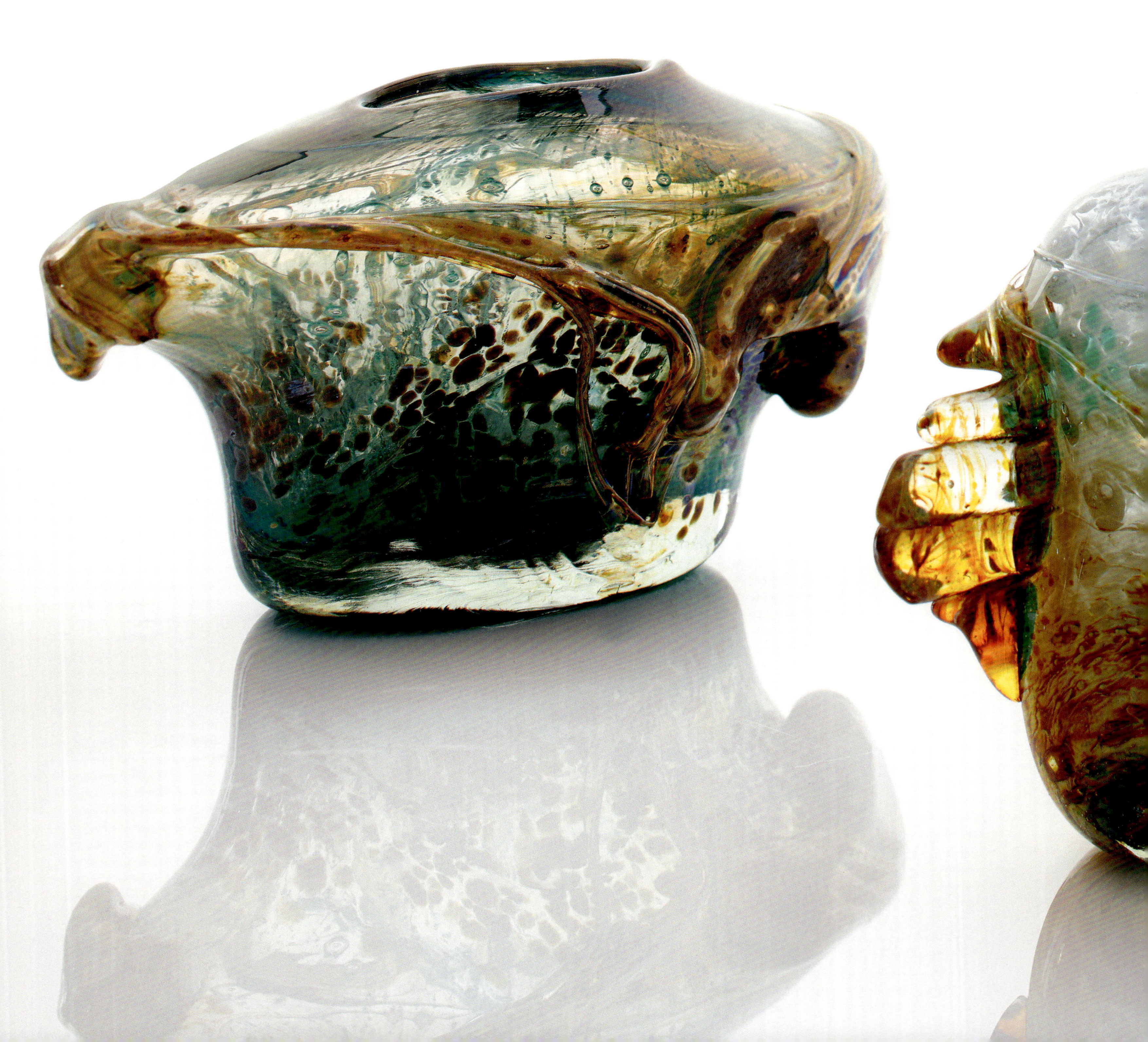

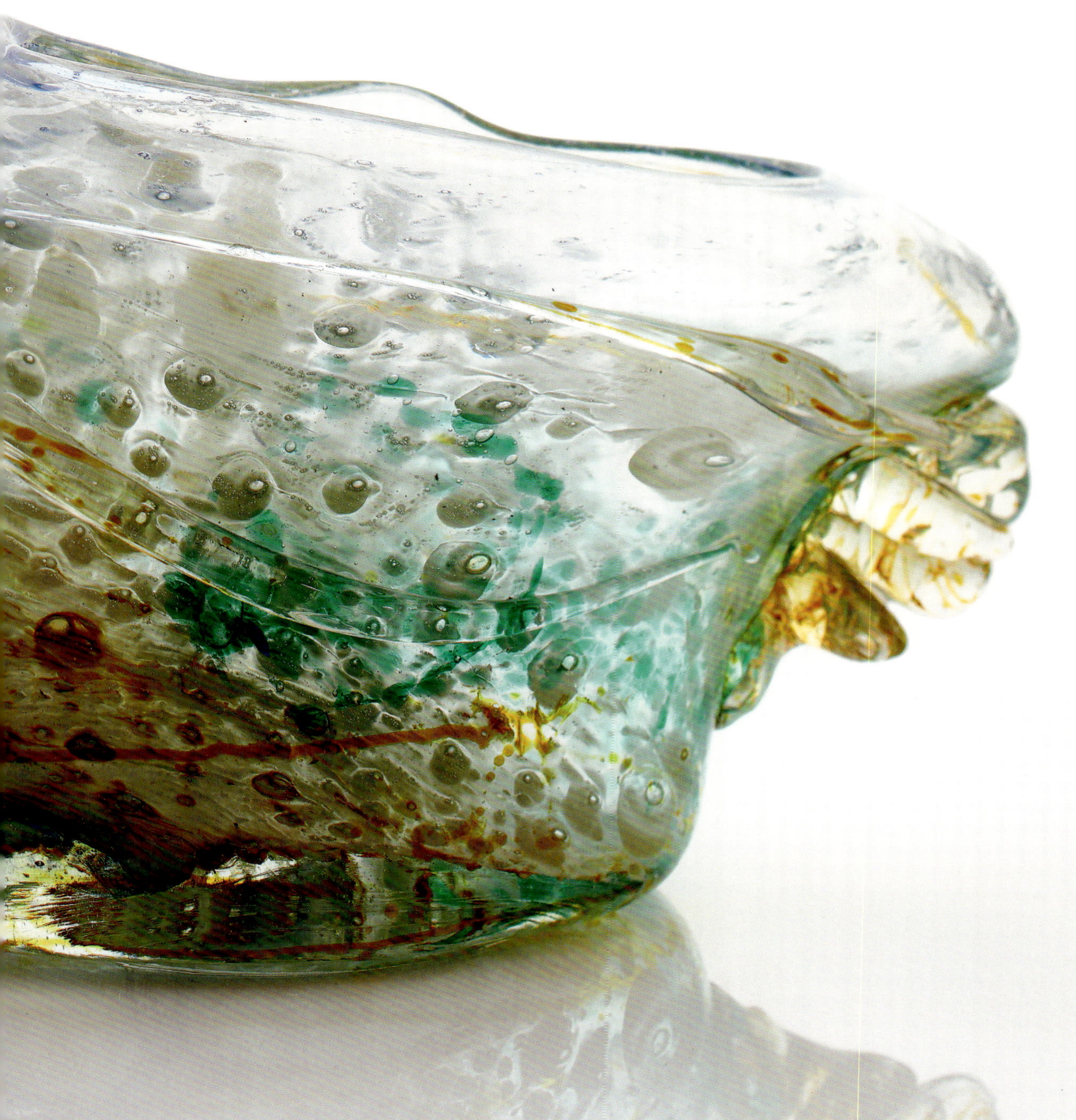

Opposite
Untitled, 1970
blown glass, 14cm (5½in),
Private Collection

Left
Untitled, 1970
blown glass, 13.5cm (5⅜in)
Private Collection

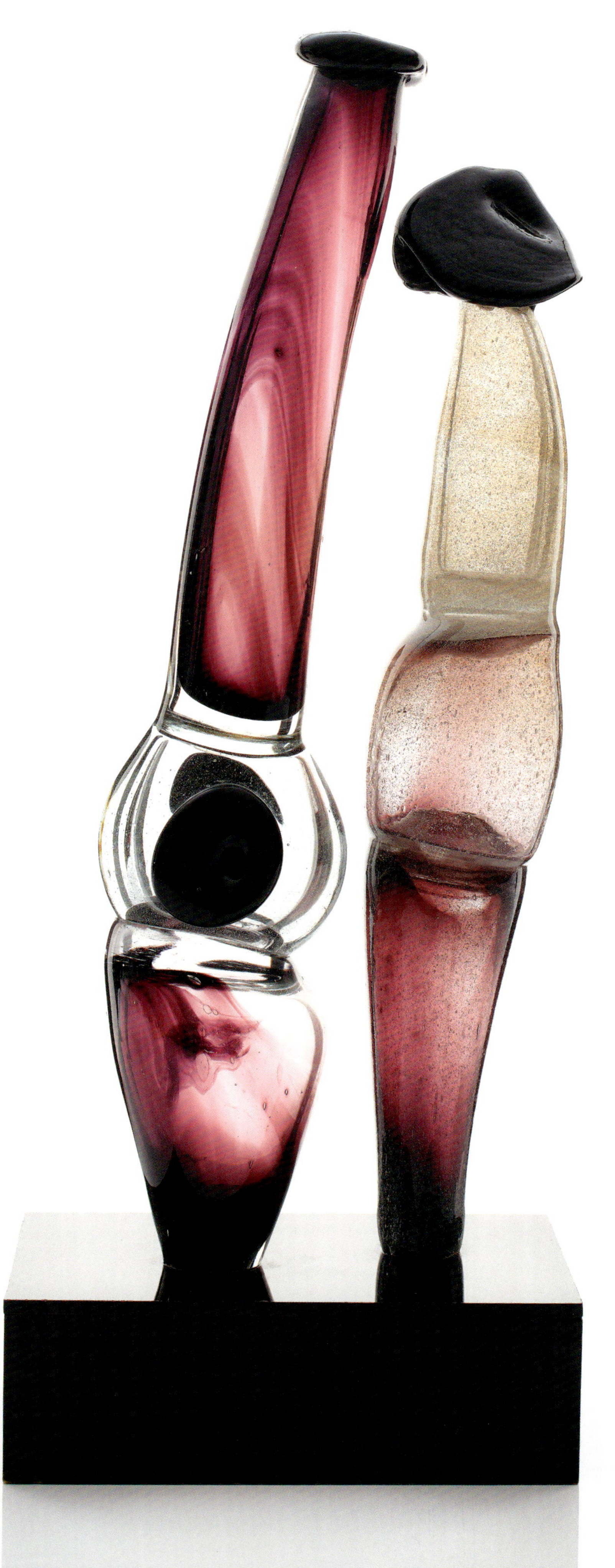

Untitled, 1970
blown glass, 47cm (18½in),
Private Collection

demarcated form being melted into a more undulating, rounded and watery final shape in the furnace to make it more fluid and 'glassy'. 'Why make glass look like something that it isn't?', Herman asked.[41] On rare occasions, such as in the early 1970s, separately blown pieces were assembled and mounted on a base or frame made from another material such as wood or metal. Glue, metal screws and flanges or pins were sometimes used to join these components together.

Herman often approached a piece with a preconceived idea, sometimes sketching or using his paintings to explore a theme before turning to glass. However, this idea was often modified during the creative process by the glass itself – spontaneity and reacting to the mass of glass, and any patterns or forms applied to it, were all equally important. Herman elaborates,

> Sometimes I may start out with an idea, I know exactly where I'm going and the end result is like the idea I started with. Other times, I start out with an idea and I discover a better idea in the process. By some fluke, I heat the glass too much or the colour changes, and I think, 'Hey, that would be better like this'. So I follow it.[42]

Alternatively, there was no preconceived idea, and Herman chose how much glass to gather himself and then worked the gather, applying further masses of glass, colour and pattern as necessary, letting instinct and experience guide him. Again, the actions of the mass of glass itself had a part to play in this creative process, with the final piece also guided and developed 'through the plastic changes that occur during creation. In effect, it is to be hoped that the glass itself will initiate its own final form.' As Herman noted, 'Glass is a dance of immediacy.'[43]

Although there are hallmarks that combine to give Herman's work a strong, instantly recognisable identity, and often enable it to be dated to a specific period, these hallmarks do not govern him. He explains, 'I just instinctively know when something works, and when something doesn't work. There is something recognisable, but not definable. I'm not influenced by style or fashion, I just think "Yeah, that works for me right now".'[44]

As stated above, a sculptural and abstract approach to the human torso lies at the core of many of Herman's glass designs. He comments, 'The human torso is a very beautiful thing. Hasn't it been utilised for centuries?'[45] However, although frozen in a moment in time, this torso is not static but is dynamic and indicative of the posture and personality of the person who inspired him. 'I'm a people watcher; I look at the way they posture themselves. Next time you go to a bank, watch the person who goes to the counter. Then watch the next person. They will stand in different postures. The way a person postures themselves reveals their personality.'[46] The fluid nature of molten glass as it moves with gravity and with the glassmaker's actions also fits with this, linking idea and narrative with the material. 'The form defines a person's character and posture. Once you start playing around with that, it becomes interesting.'[47]

It is estimated that in the 20 years up to 1984, Herman made just over 2500 successful pieces in hot glass. Herman did not consider every piece a success, and those he deemed unsuccessful were smashed, with the decision process typically happening quickly after the finished piece was cool. He often saved the shards from broken pieces to use later to create sculptures or lighting sculptures. As such, there are no 'seconds' in Herman's glass oeuvre. All pieces that met with Herman's approval were signed, and sometimes other information was included such as a number or date, or both (see p.170). Unsigned pieces were either stolen from a lehr,[48] or were (extremely rarely) pieces that Herman deemed unsuccessful but kept because they contained an idea that he liked and wanted to explore and develop later.

Taking into account the above, Herman's work in glass can be divided stylistically into five key periods, each relating to his geographic location and working activities: the Royal College of Art and The Glasshouse, Val St Lambert and Rosenthal, The Jam Factory, Lots Road studio and 21st-century work. Each period has its own recognisable features and elements of style. However, they cannot be employed to accurately date a piece to a period as they could also have been used earlier or later: 'Do you want the same thing for dinner or lunch every day?'[49] The pieces that Herman produced at symposia or similar events, or as a guest glassmaker, may or may not differ from these general guidelines. Work created before his arrival in the UK was highly experimental, cannot be characterised and is extremely rare.

Royal College of Art and The Glasshouse

London, 1966–74

During this time, Herman started to work directly with hot glass more frequently and used glass as a medium for art. This resulted in highly experimental pieces that were spontaneous, fluid and wildly diverse in terms of form, colour and pattern. He was beginning to connect properly with the material, attempting to re-engage with his artistic abilities developed in his background in sculpture and anthropology, and marry these themes successfully. His work was, however, tempered and limited by the availability of materials and his evolving glass-making skills. There were no set standards to reach, and every piece represented a successful learning experience, even if the piece was not a success in itself. Herman was finding himself.

Colour was applied either by rolling the body in powdered oxides, as at Wisconsin, or through the use of industrially manufactured coloured glass rods made from oxides combined with powdered glass. These were applied to the body in powder or chip form, or heated until molten and then applied. Rolling a body in oxides creates a series of uncontrolled, random tiny bubbles, while the use of coloured rods gives a more consistent and uniform effect. From the late 1960s onwards, patterns were often cloudy and mottled with largely colourless areas, but could also be so heavily decorated with oxides, coloured enamels and/or silver chloride that they were barely translucent or opaque. During the early 1970s, similar patterns and trails melted into the body were often set against a single opaque coloured background, which ranged from green to cream.

Right
Untitled, 1973
blown glass, 15.5cm (6in),
Mark Hill

Opposite
Untitled, 1970
blown glass, 30cm (11¾in),
Private Collection

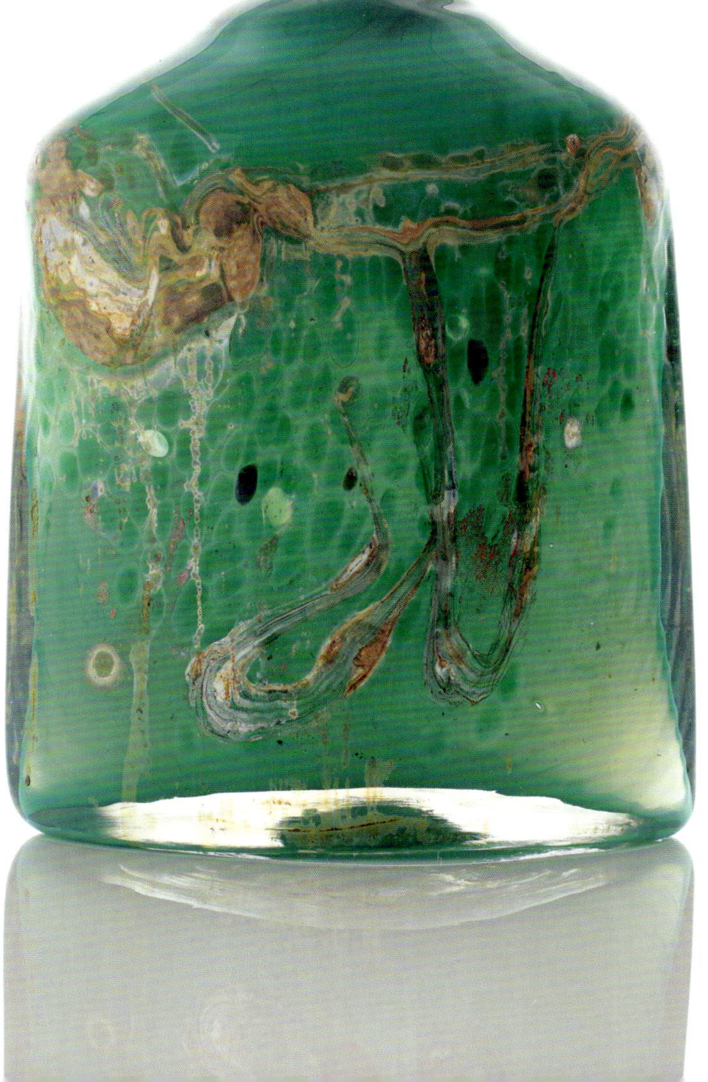

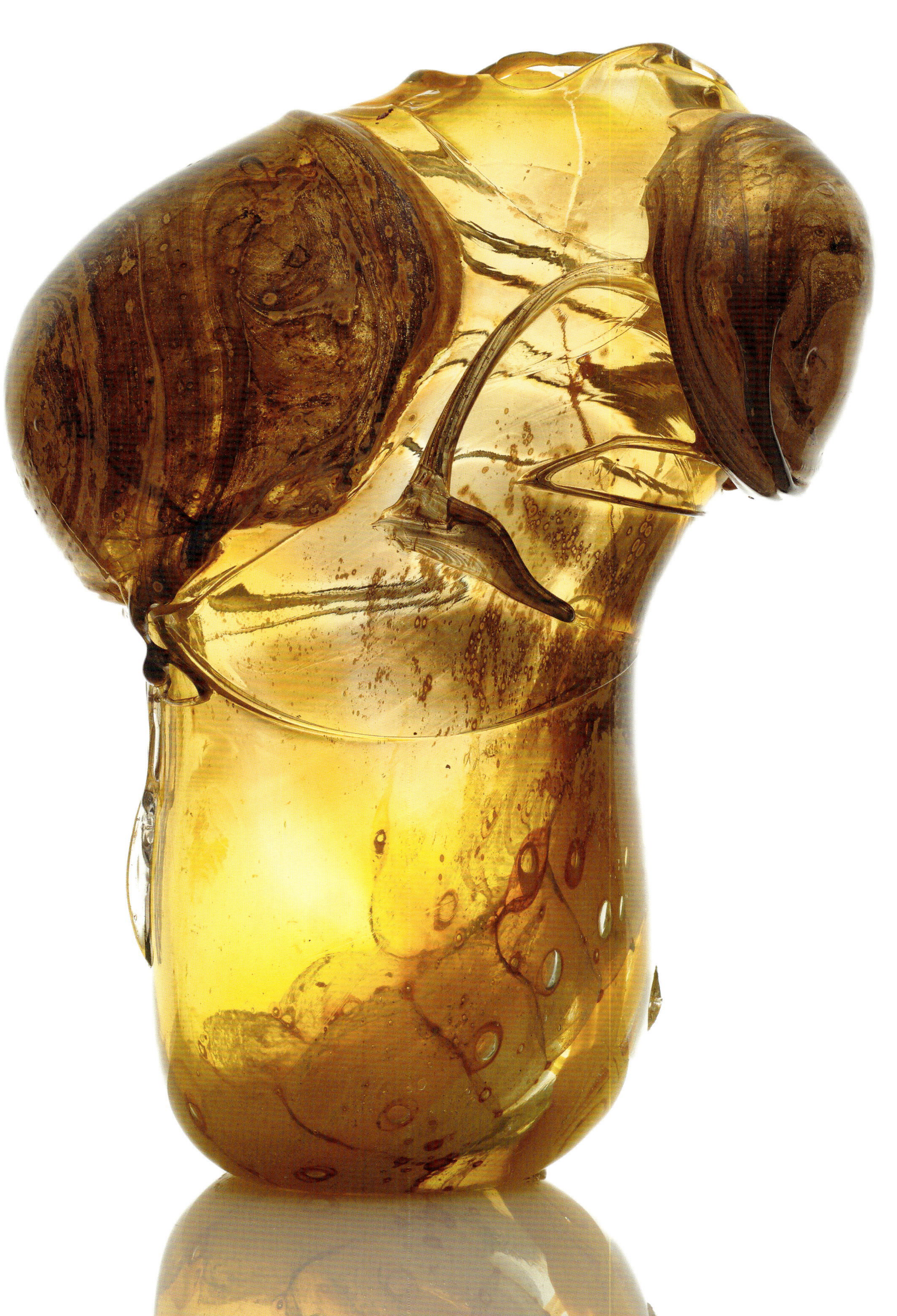

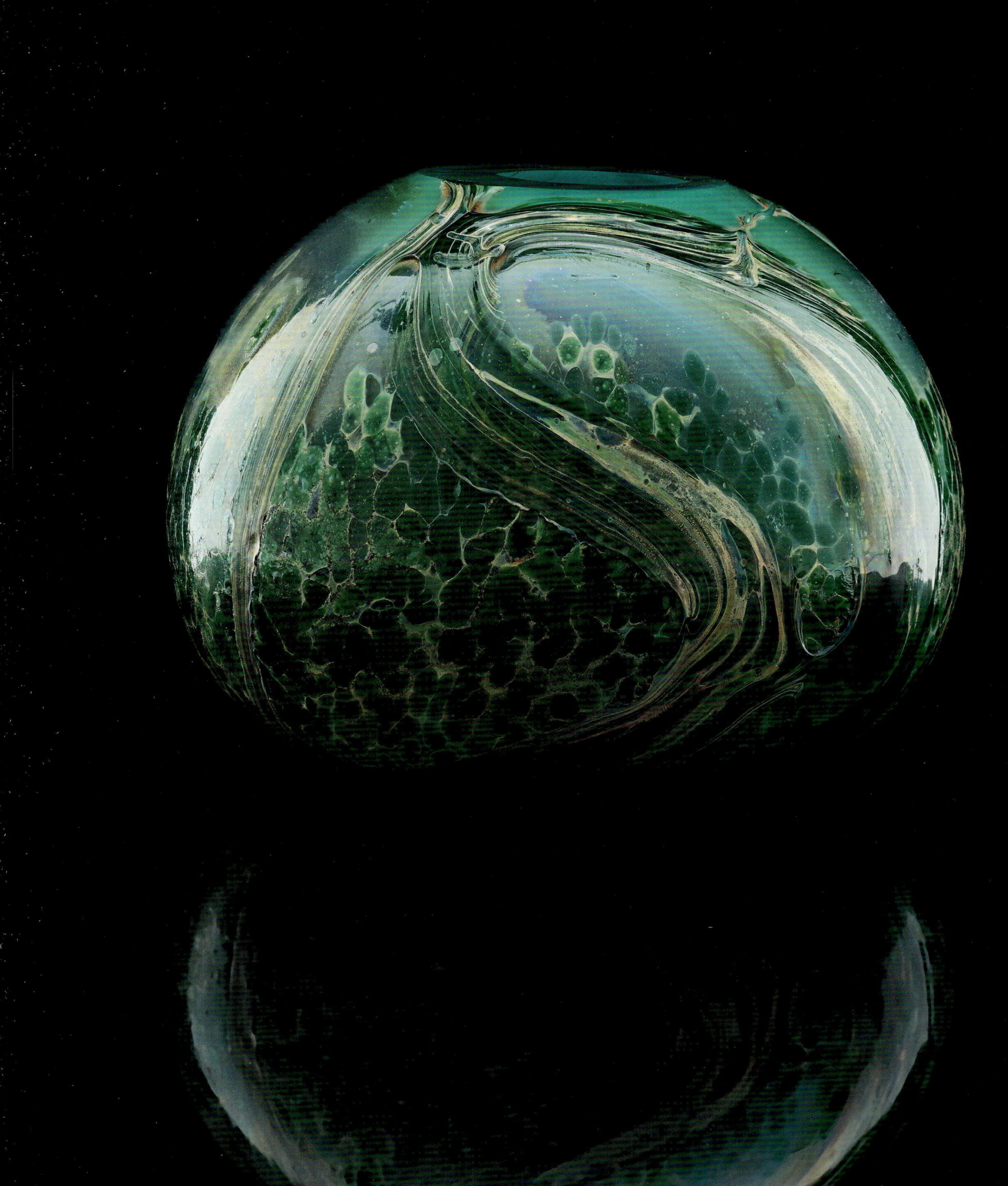

Herman brought the use of silver chloride in powdered form to the RCA from Wisconsin, developing and popularising its use in studio glass. Employed frequently at the time and into the late 1970s, silver chloride gave effects ranging from sandy- or brown-coloured mottles, streaks and cloudy patterns within the glass to an iridescent, metallic finish on the surface. It could also modify colours, for example, changing green to blue. The surface finish of a piece could also be altered: a reduction flame (more gas than oxygen) gave a shinier finish while an oxidising flame (more oxygen than gas) offered a more matt finish.

The glass Herman had used at Wisconsin had a short working life and was very brittle, meaning glassmakers needed to work quickly to achieve the desired result. At the RCA, cullet[50] from Dartington was used, which had a comparatively long working life before it became too cold to manipulate and gave Herman great freedom. He compared the two glasses by saying, 'It was like night and day'.[51] The inclusion of 45 per cent lead oxide in Dartington's cullet also gave it a certain brilliance. Three-dimensional wings, trails and prunts were often applied by Herman, as the molten glass acts naturally when used in such a manner, and the shapes of these additions lent themselves to Herman's concern with the human torso. However, many of the 300 or so successful pieces produced by Herman at the RCA and The Glasshouse were (often rudimentary) bottle or bulbous vessel-like forms, sometimes with slightly flared small button rims with thin necks. Some examples from the early 1970s have an elliptical cross section and opaque and trailed decoration giving them a cowled or caped torso feel. Herman also created sculptures made up from assembled components during the early 1970s, including for the exhibition at the V&A Museum in 1971, and he also began using silvery 'mirrored' glass at this time.

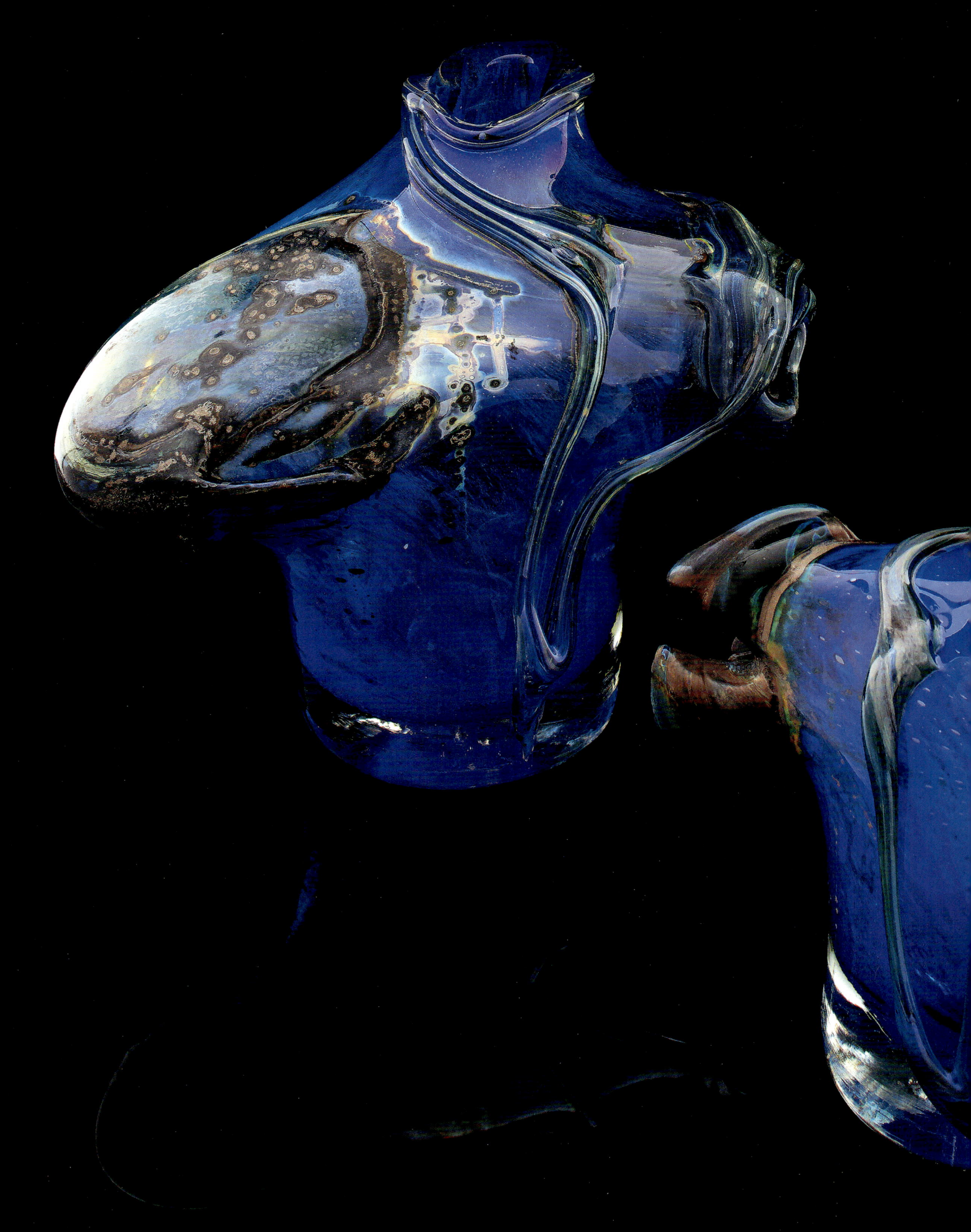

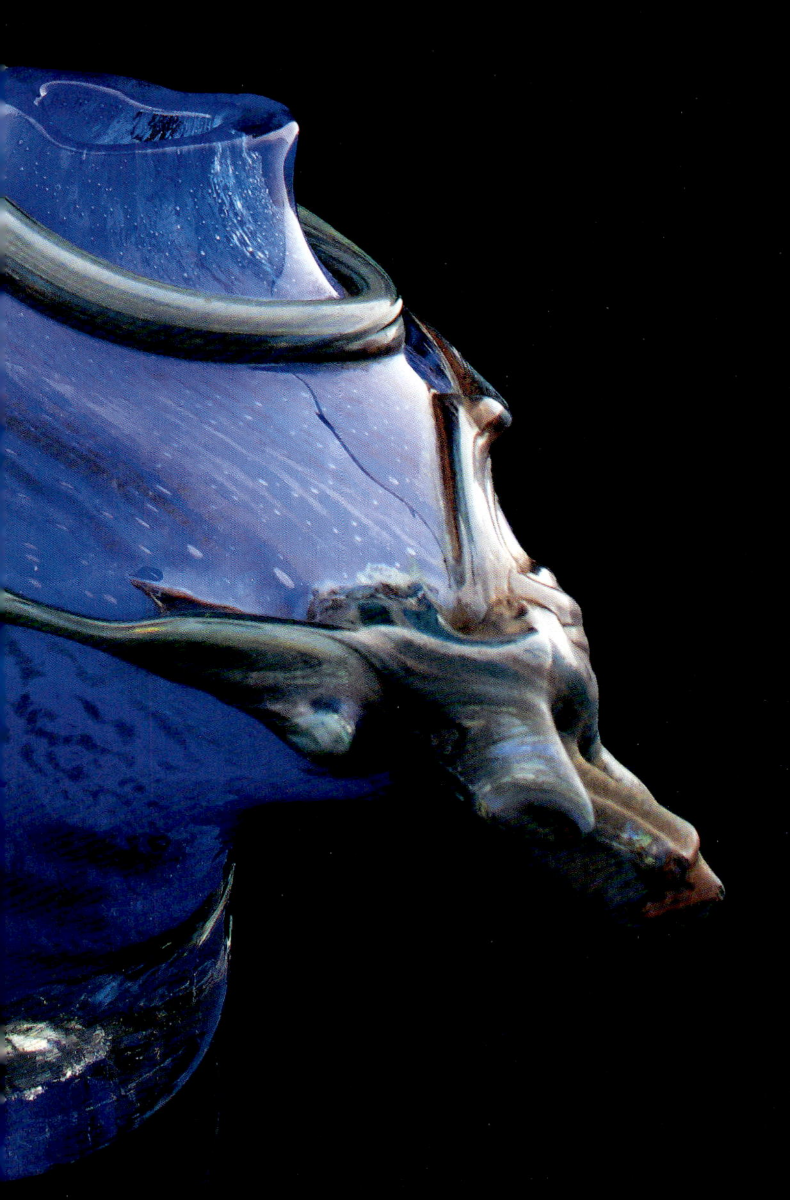

Untitled, 1971
blown glass, 20cm (8in) and
18cm (7in), Private Collection

Val St Lambert and Rosenthal
Belgium, and Germany, 1970s

Herman's work over various short periods across the 1970s at esteemed Belgian company Val St Lambert can be divided into two types: the work he designed and trained the in-house glassmakers to produce, sometimes under his direct supervision; and the pieces that he made with assistance from the team. Herman's signature on the base of the piece indicates those made by Herman himself and the team under his direct guidance (see p.170 for more information on how to recognise these pieces). Pieces produced by Herman at Val St Lambert are considerably scarcer than those made to his designs by the team, regardless of the level of Herman's intervention in the creative process.

For the individual pieces, Herman carefully gathered and executed the amount of colour needed to start each item. Once he had started the line, he ran from position to position to ensure that his works were being actioned correctly at every step – a mentally and physically exhausting exercise. Despite their initial concerns, the gaffer and his team quickly adapted to the new ways of working and were soon able to produce Herman's unique work under his close supervision. For the first time in his career, Herman was working with a team of ten to 12 highly trained glassmakers. Working under their gaffer they were used to repeatedly producing consistently perfect forms that would then be cut with a pattern. This training and the preconceptions it had created had a direct effect on the forms. Whilst Herman was able to draw the glassmakers away from strict regularity and train them to let the glass itself contribute to the final piece to a certain extent, forms were more recognisably traditional, functional and regular. Most were based on ovoid or bulbous vases, near-cylindrical vases with flared rims, rounded bowls or bottle shapes. The resulting pieces were also deemed a perfect fusion of commercial concerns (as Herman said, 'They were in business!'[52]) and a desire to react to the growing popularity of the 'new' studio glass.

Right
Untitled, 1979
blown glass, 31cm (12in),
Private Collection

Opposite
Untitled, 1979
blown glass, 20cm (8in),
Private Collection

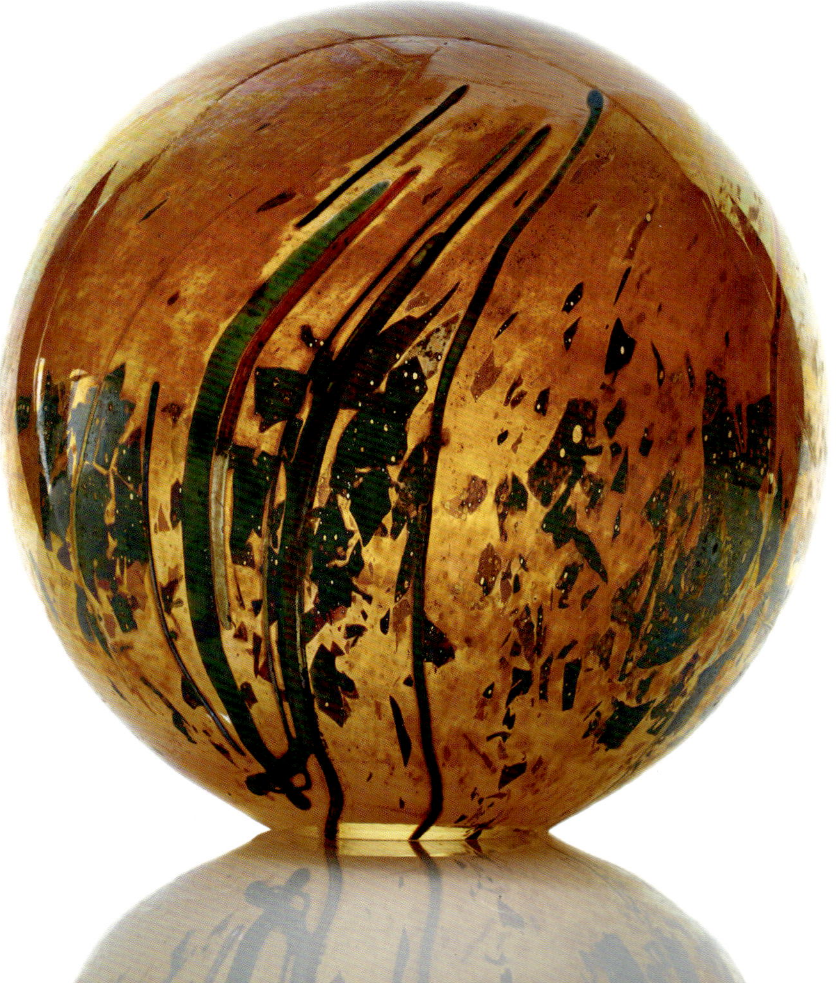

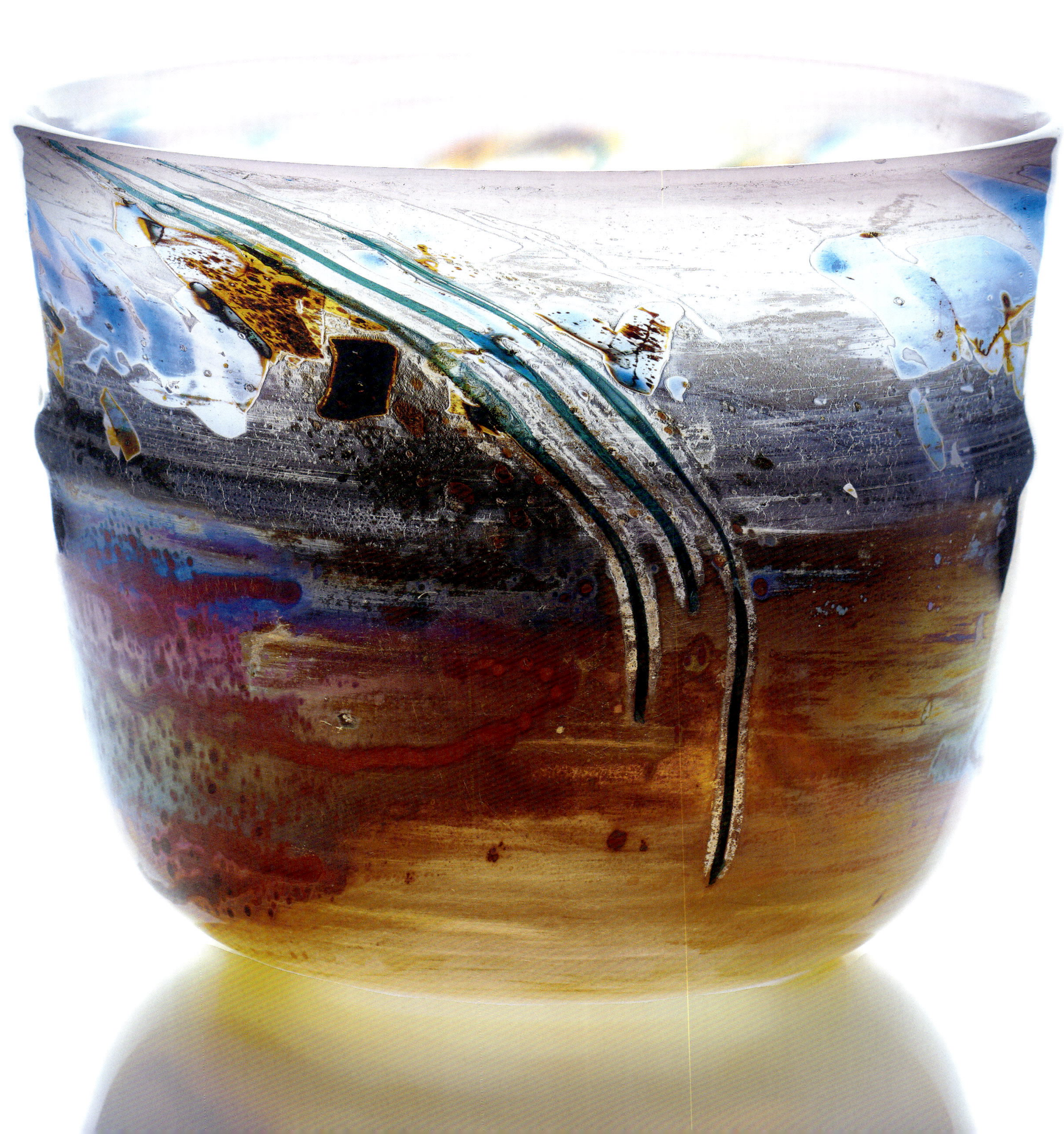

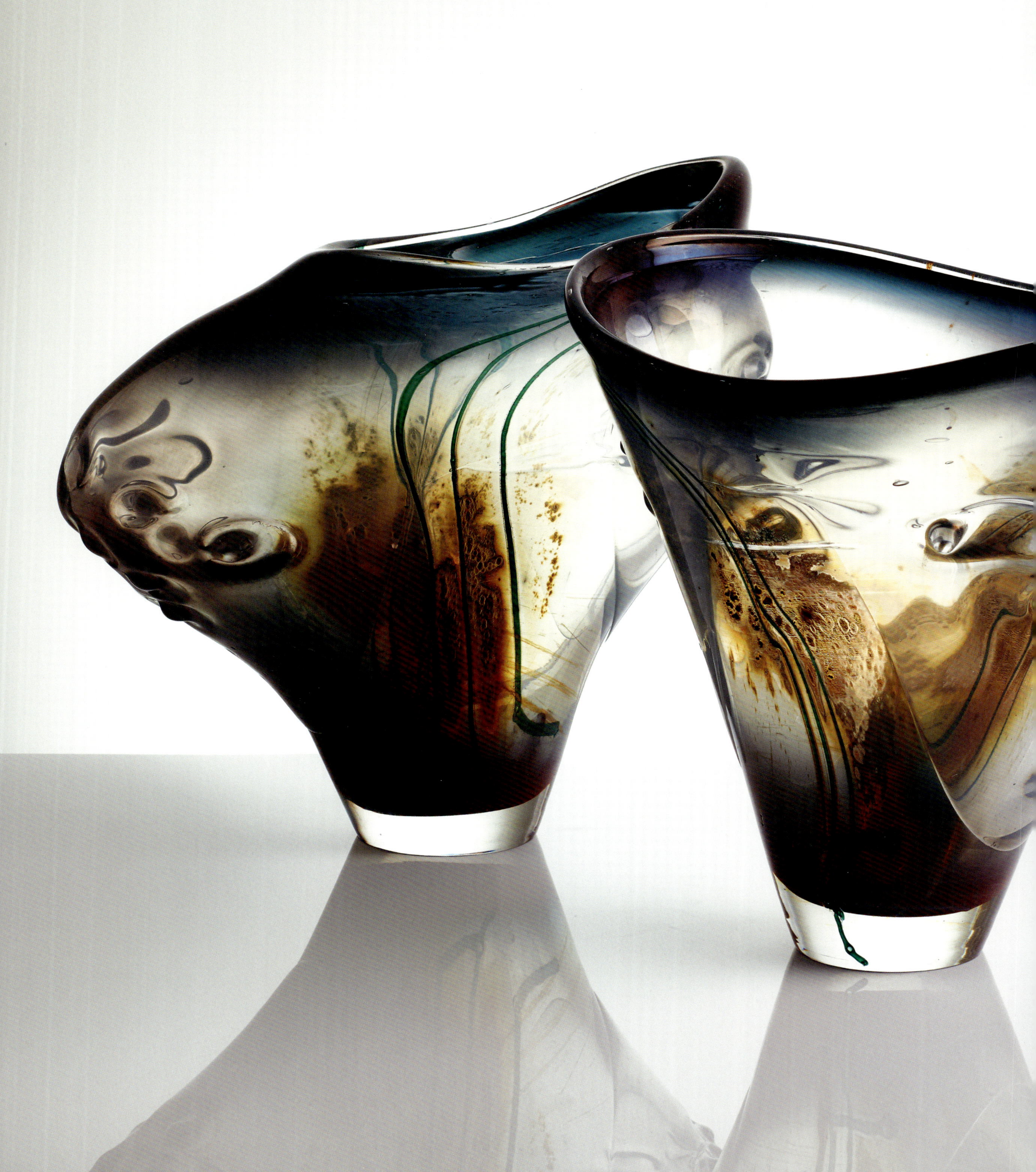

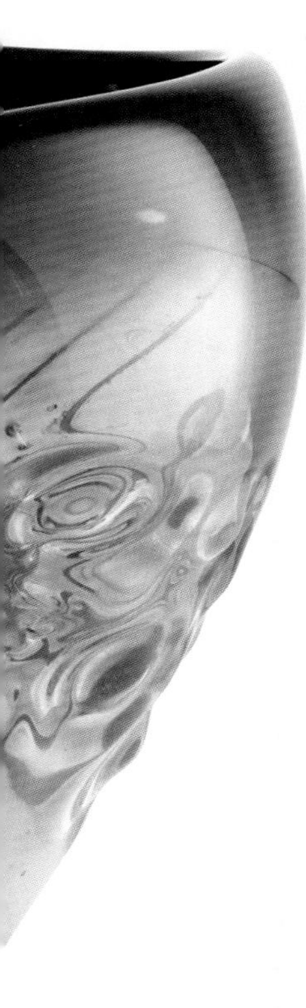

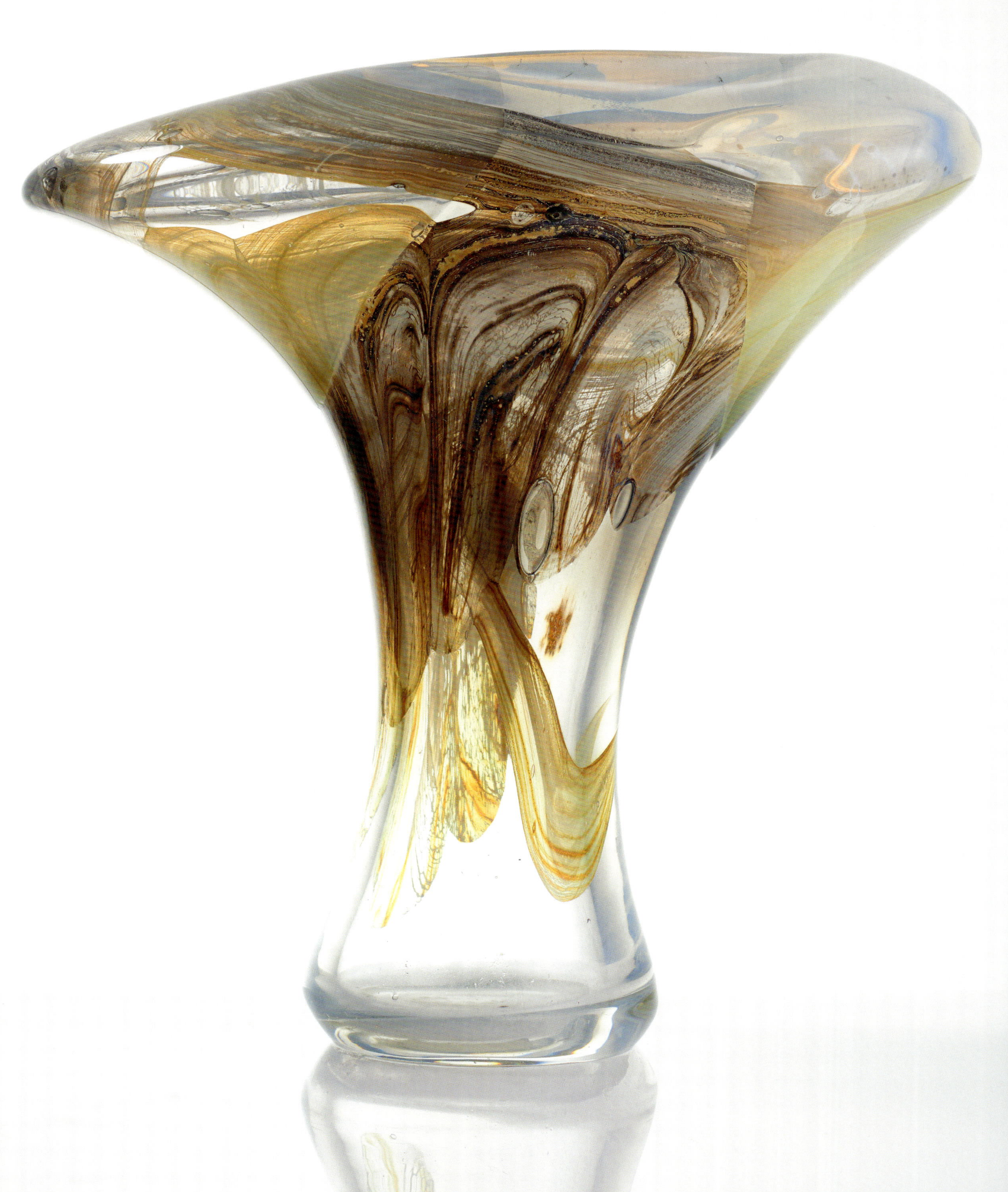

Trails or spots, typically melted into the body of a piece, were as bold and broad as on pieces produced later at The Jam Factory, but were instead often strongly demarcated and contrasted in terms of colour against the body. They ranged from roughly horizontal bands to dramatic loops. Iridescent and opaque or strongly coloured and dark, they nearly always had a complex swirling or mottled internal pattern and trails were typically contrasted against a lighter and barely translucent or opaque body such as a creamy white, which was sometimes tinted with another colour such as violet or blue. Some appeared almost metallic, with mottled and swirling bronzy tones. Detailed mottles and swirls in the body were also commonplace.

At Val St Lambert, Herman was also able to make larger pieces as he had experienced glassmakers to help him. They were not only able to physically handle larger pieces, but were also able to gather the right level of glass and apply the right level of colour through the development of a piece. Furthermore, Herman thought that the quality of glass used was fantastic, allowing him and the glassmakers greater freedom.

Iridescent effects were commonplace, created by heavy use of silver chloride. A silvery-golden all-over fragmented external finish, almost resembling a Tiffany product, was only created at Val St Lambert during the late 1970s. Platters and dishes, often large in scale, were made with decoration on both sides. The silvery-golden finish was an unusual and difficult effect to create, and this work was inspired by ancient Roman glass that Herman had seen in the V&A, and he was able to find a process that gave a similar effect.

Herman's designs for a limited-edition range produced at Rosenthal in Germany in the 1970s were similar, but even more strict and regular in form. Forms largely comprised clean simple cylinders, sometimes with necks, and bowls. Patterns were simplified and typically made up of a swirling or gently zigzagging coloured band that tended to be regular and bright in colour tone, and set against a contrasting creamy background. Herman did not produce any of his own work at Rosenthal. At both factories, the external colourless casing was usually more visually evident than on pieces produced elsewhere by Herman. Bases tended to be ground and polished, as each company took the time to finish them highly for sale. In other locations, Herman did not feel it necessary to finish his unique pieces in such a manner.

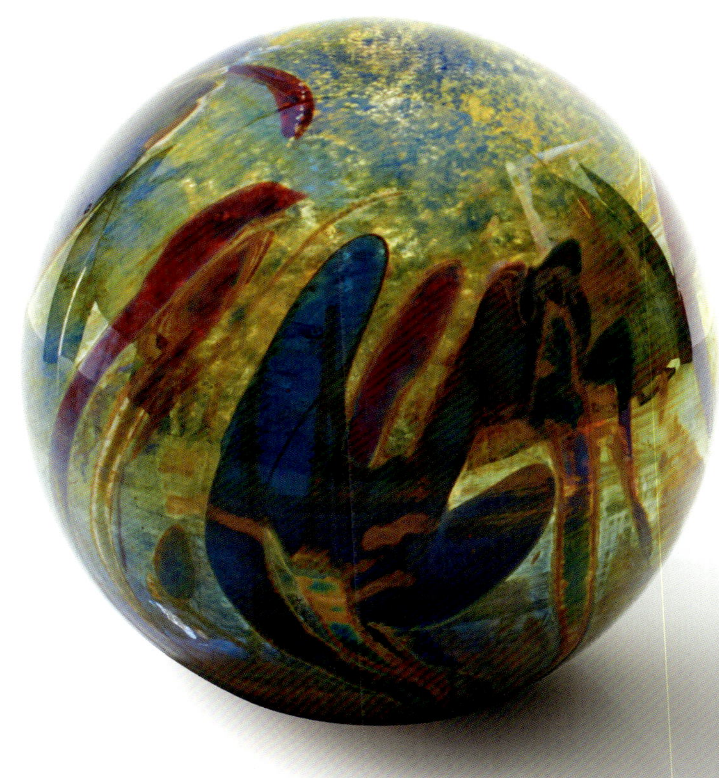

Untitled, 1971
blown glass, 23cm (9in) and
22cm (8¾in), Private Collection

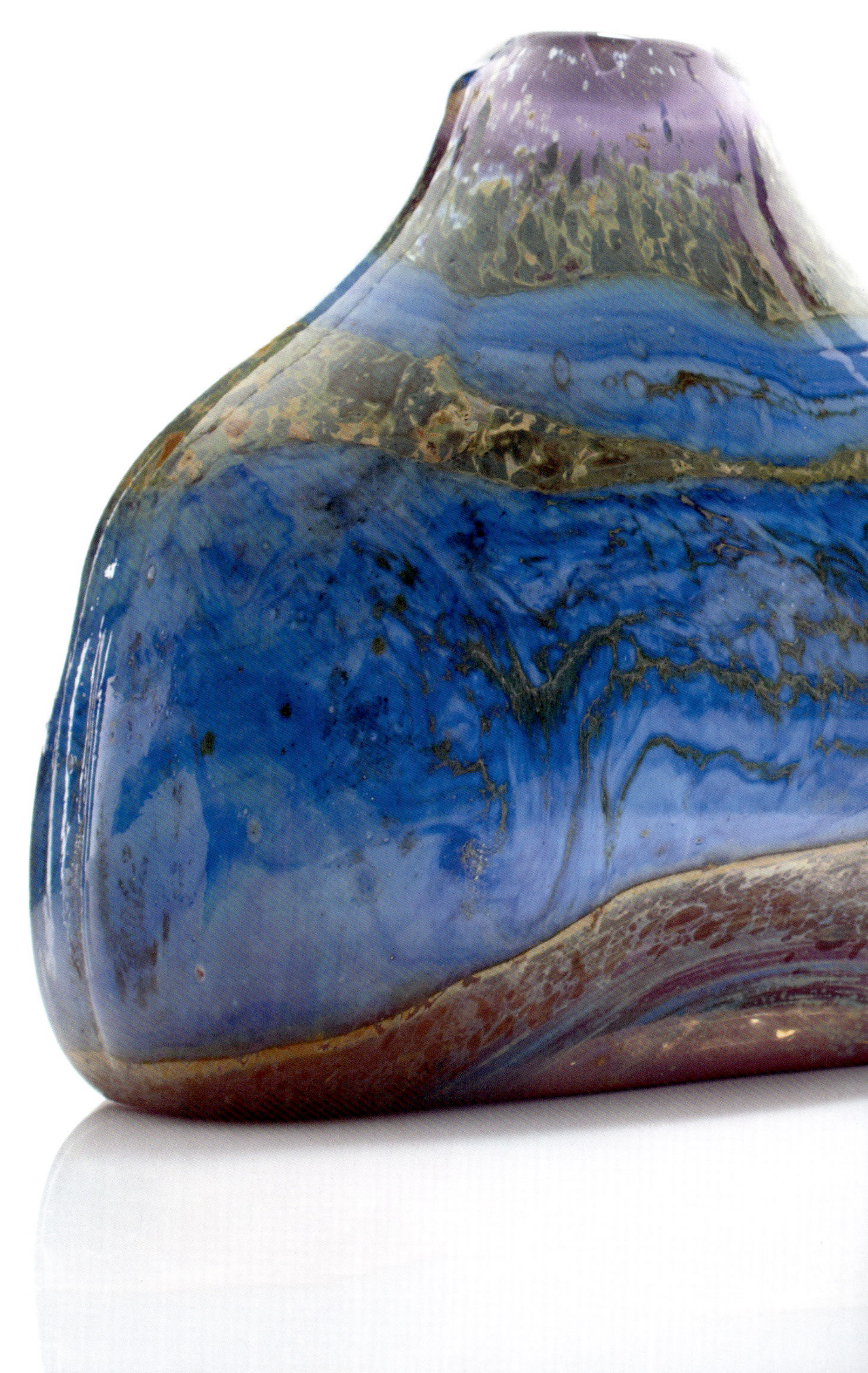

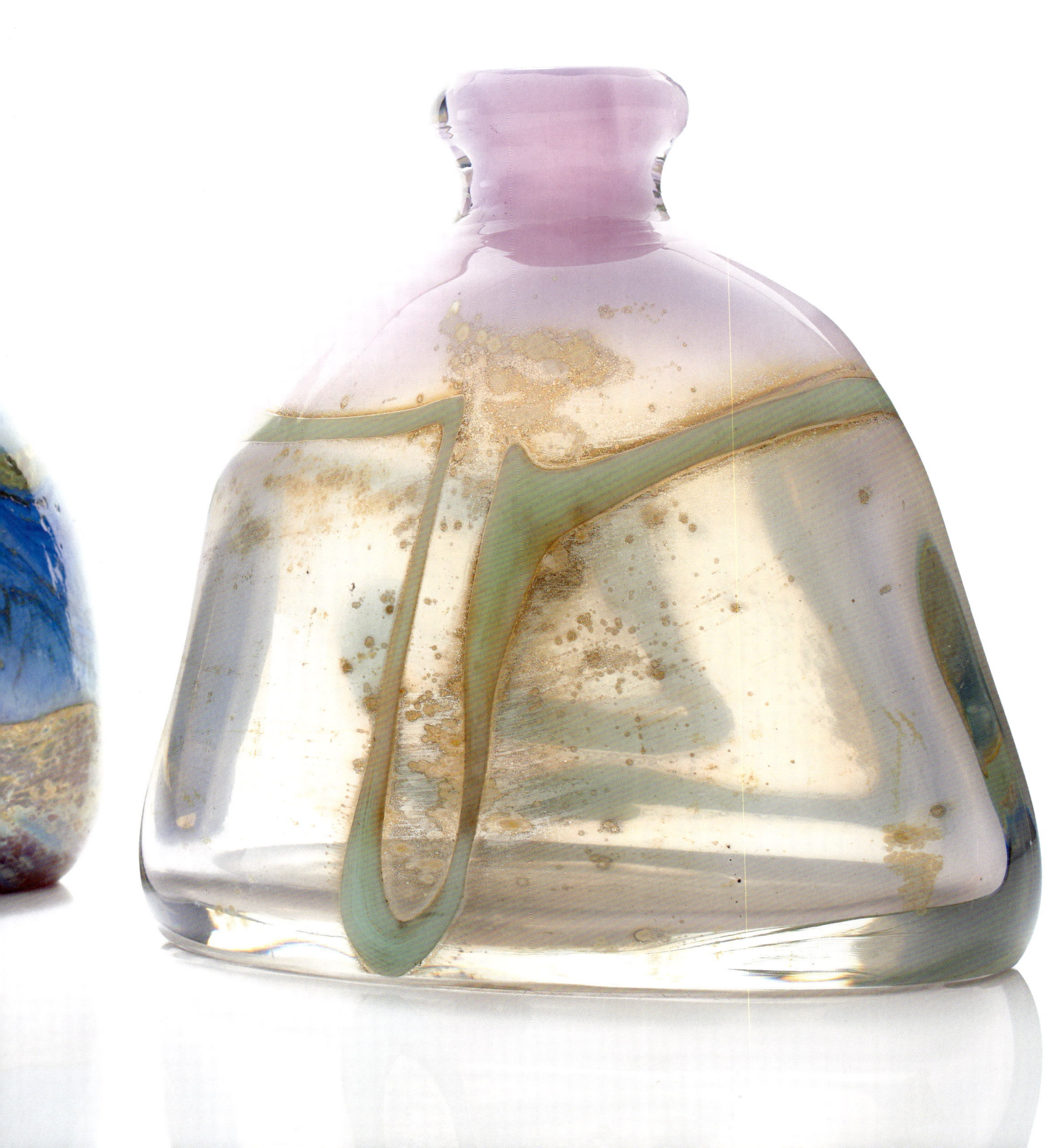

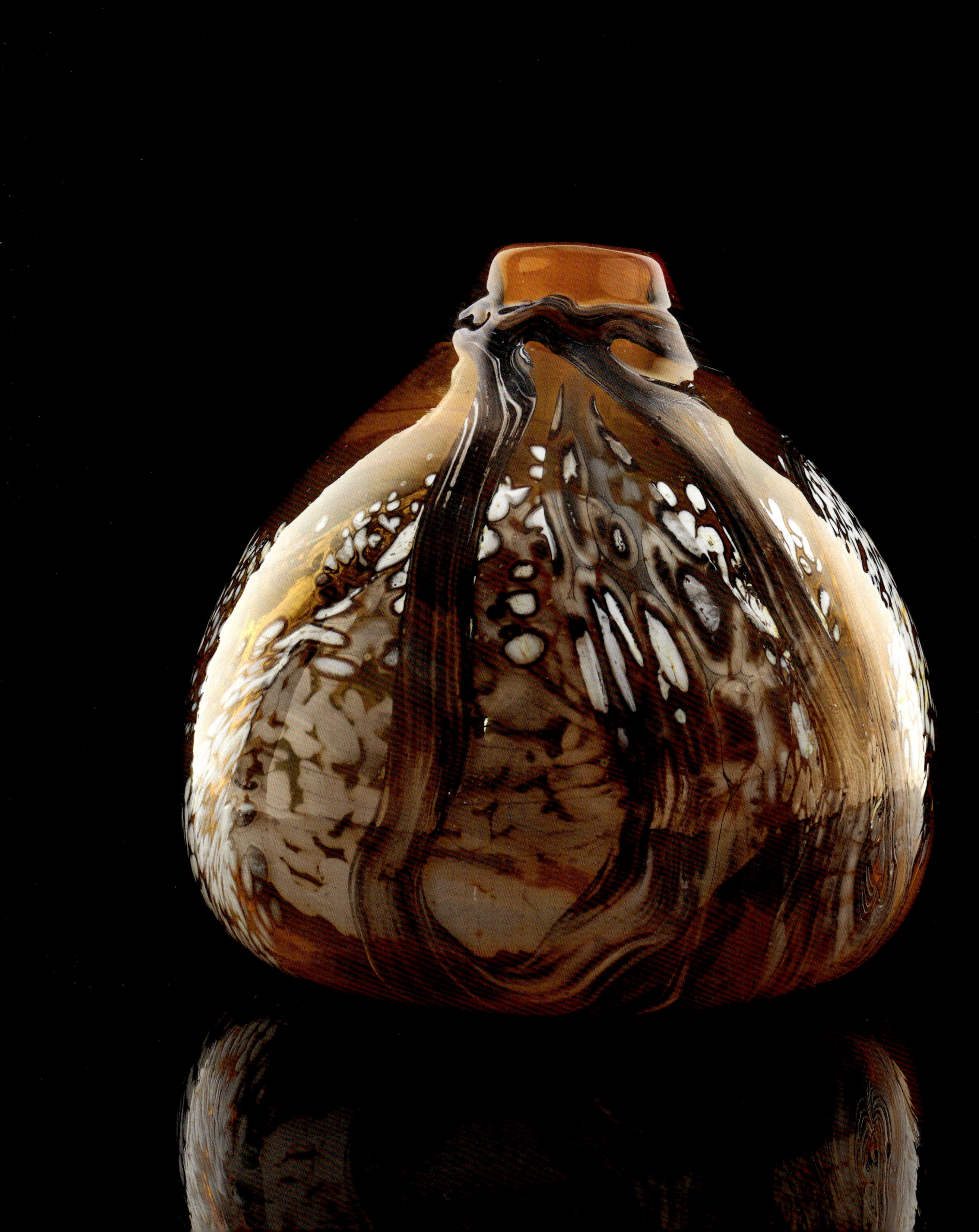

Opposite
Untitled, 1977
blown glass, 15cm (6in),
Private Collection

Below
Untitled, 1977
blown glass, 15cm (6in),
Private Collection

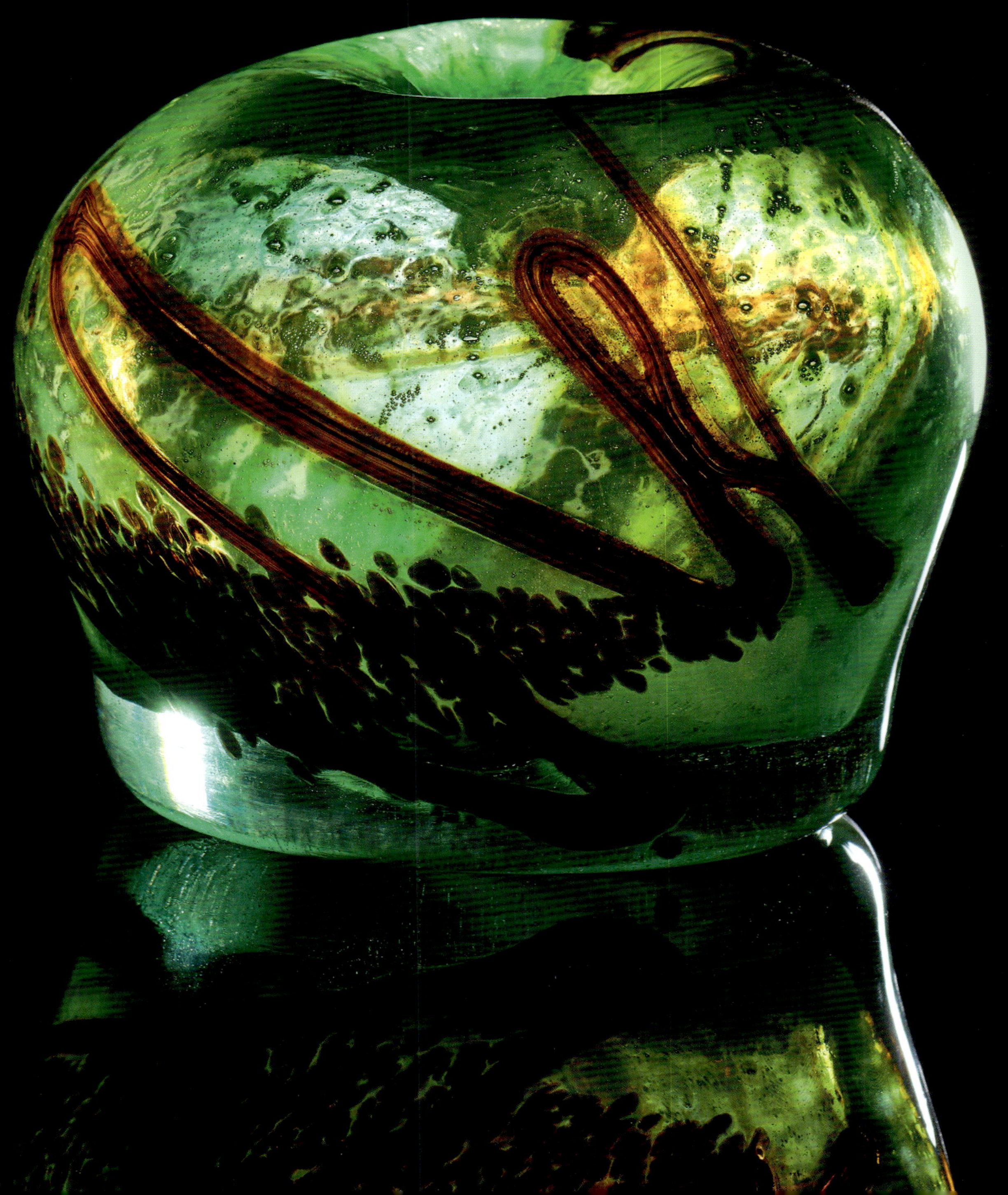

Below
Untitled, 1979
blown glass, 30cm (11¾in)
and 34cm (13½in),
Private Collection

Opposite
Untitled, 1971
blown glass, 32cm (12½in),
Private Collection

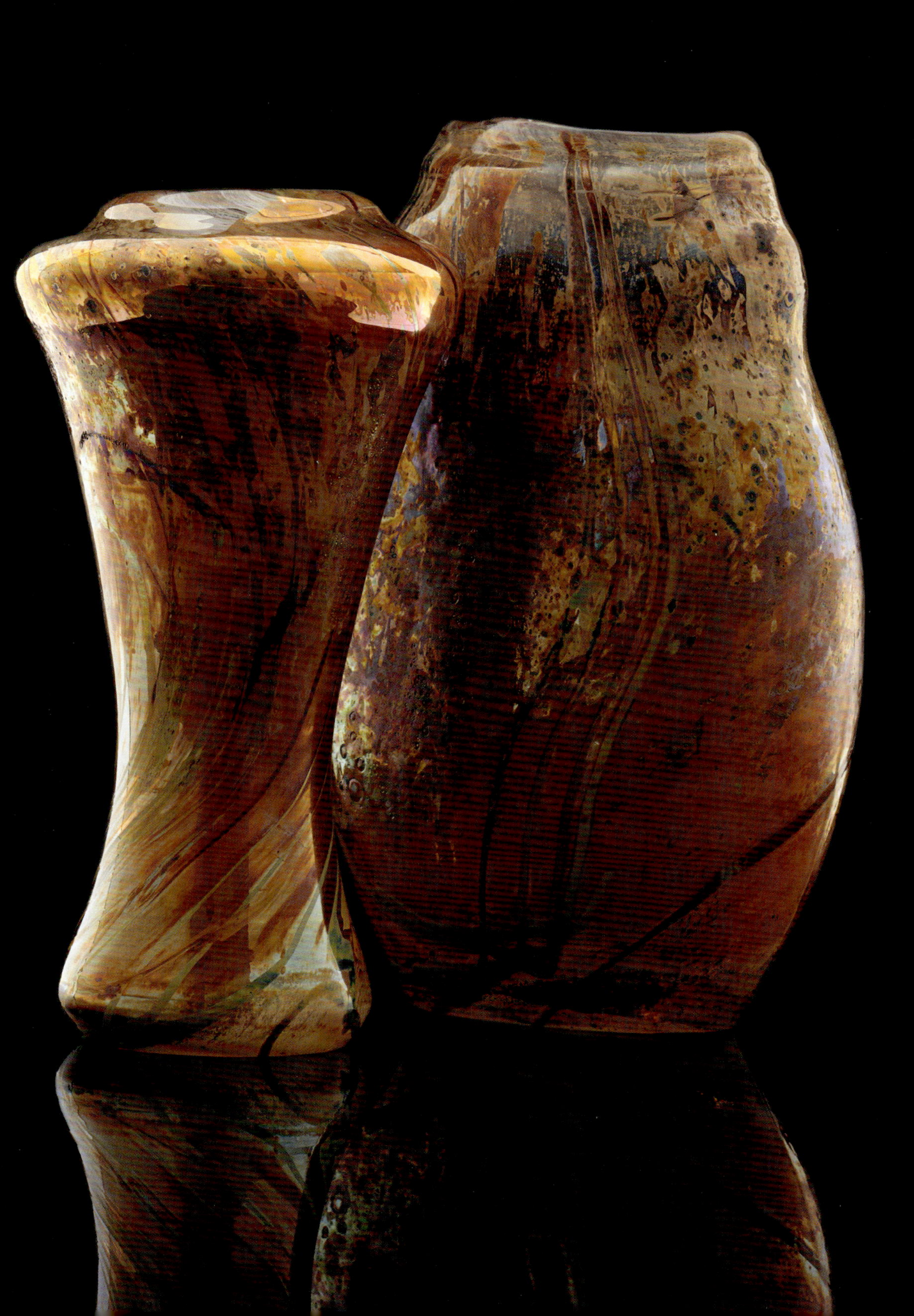

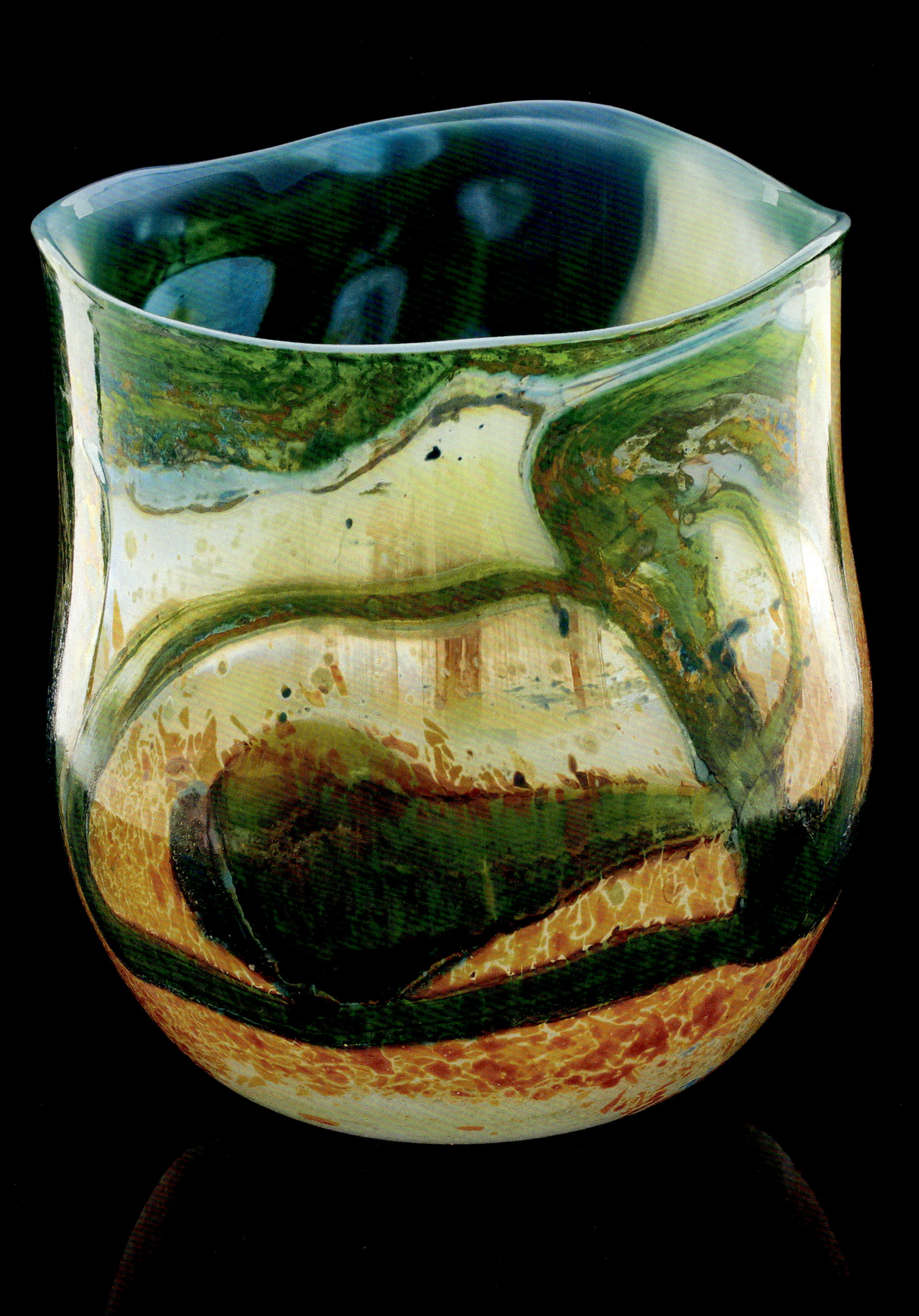

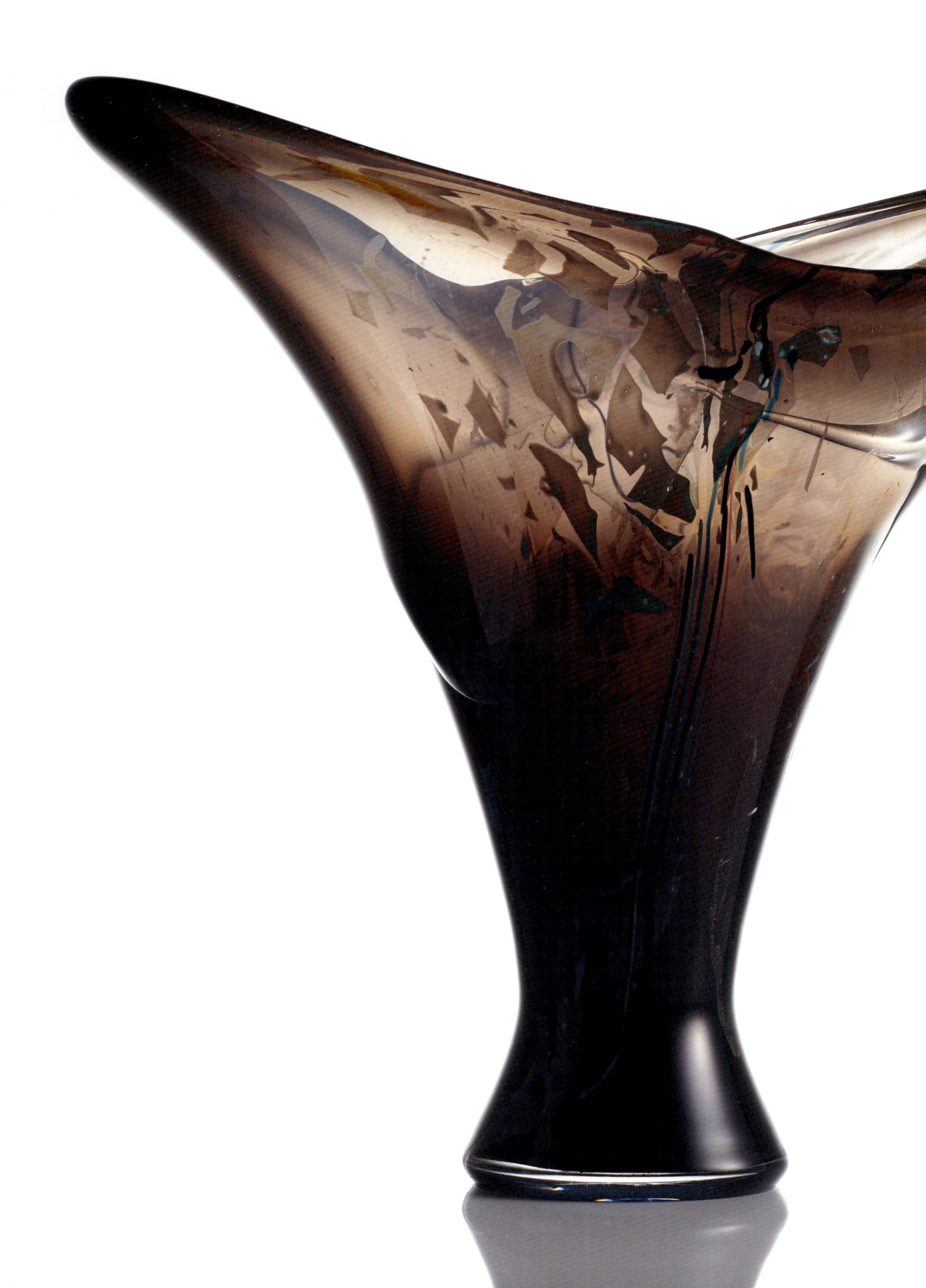

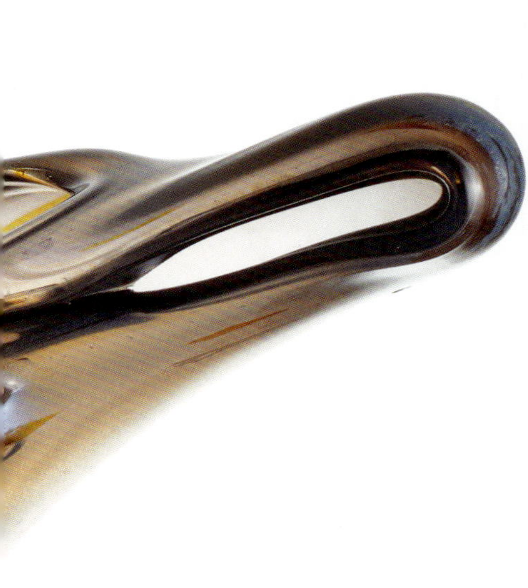

Untitled, 1979
blown glass, 42cm (16½in),
Private Collection

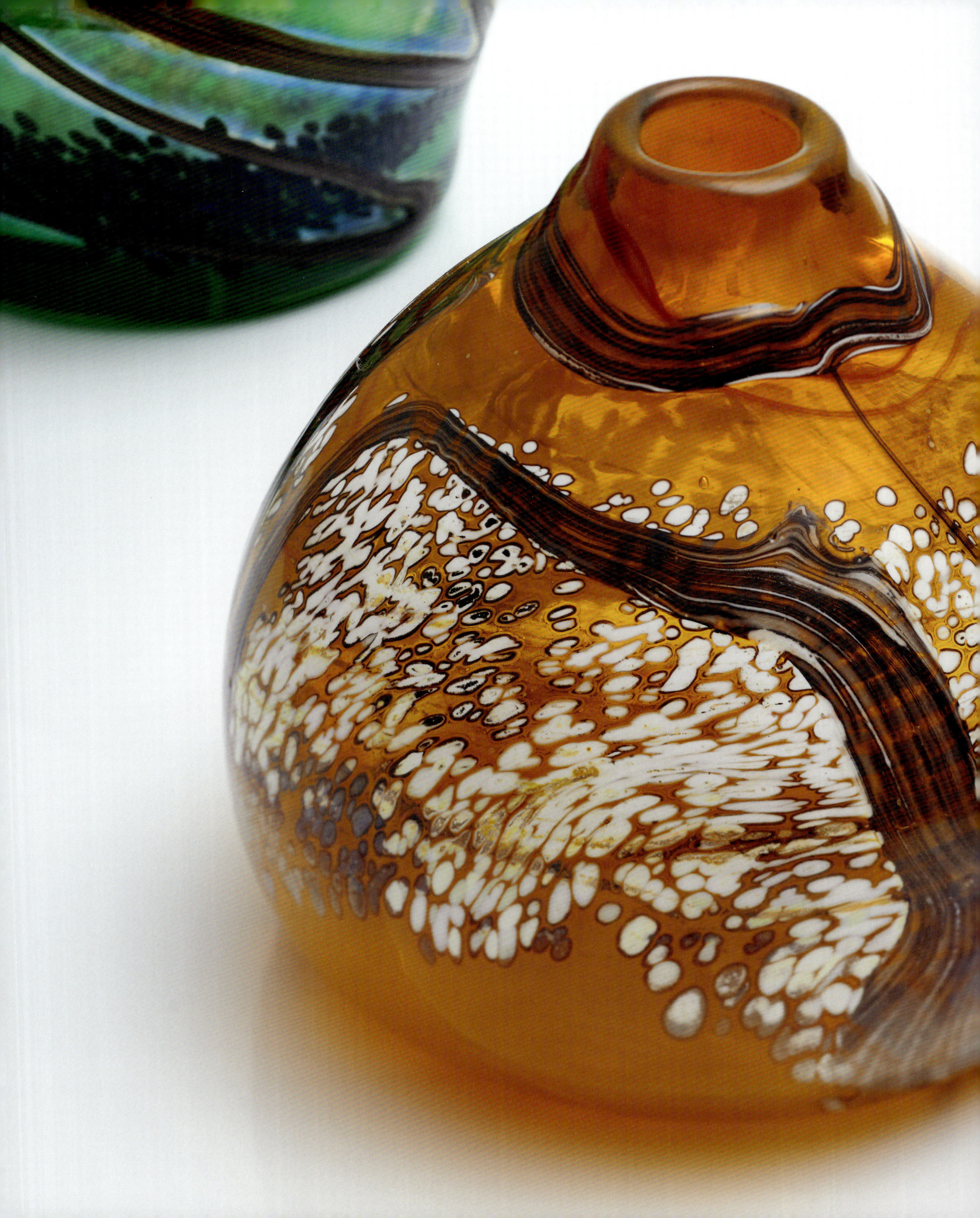

The Jam Factory
Adelaide, South Australia, 1974–9

Herman was not usually concerned by external factors such as location or period styles or fashions, but at The Jam Factory he was unconsciously affected by the Australian landscape around him. As such, he used earthy and sandy tones, iron reds and muddy greens more frequently here than at any other point in time, or in any other location.

The expansive, panoramic nature of the Australian landscape also seems to have influenced forms, patterns and sizes, which were dramatic and often monumental. Forms were bulbous or pillow-like, wide and puffed out, with great surface area. Platters tended to be asymmetric and almost lobed, showing off patterns well. Trails were bold and broad, consistent with the background in colour and were usually melted into the body, thus echoing strata in rock or even Aboriginal art. To a certain extent, large sizes were only possible because Herman enjoyed the use of assistants. Furthermore, as it was a commercial venture, Herman produced large sizes (despite smaller pieces often being aesthetically as good or better) because they commanded a higher price when sold in the enterprise's gallery, generating much-needed income.

With all of this in mind, Herman introduced the use of the 'wet stick' technique, first shown to him by Roya College of Art glassmaker Fred Daden, and used to great acclaim by Finnish glass designer Timo Sarpaneva (1926–2006) in 1952 for his 'Orkidea' (Orchid) design produced by Iittala. This technique allowed Herman to create large

Opposite
Untitled, 1977
blown glass, 15cm (6in),
Private Collection

Right
Untitled, 1978
blown glass, 24cm (9½in),
Private Collection

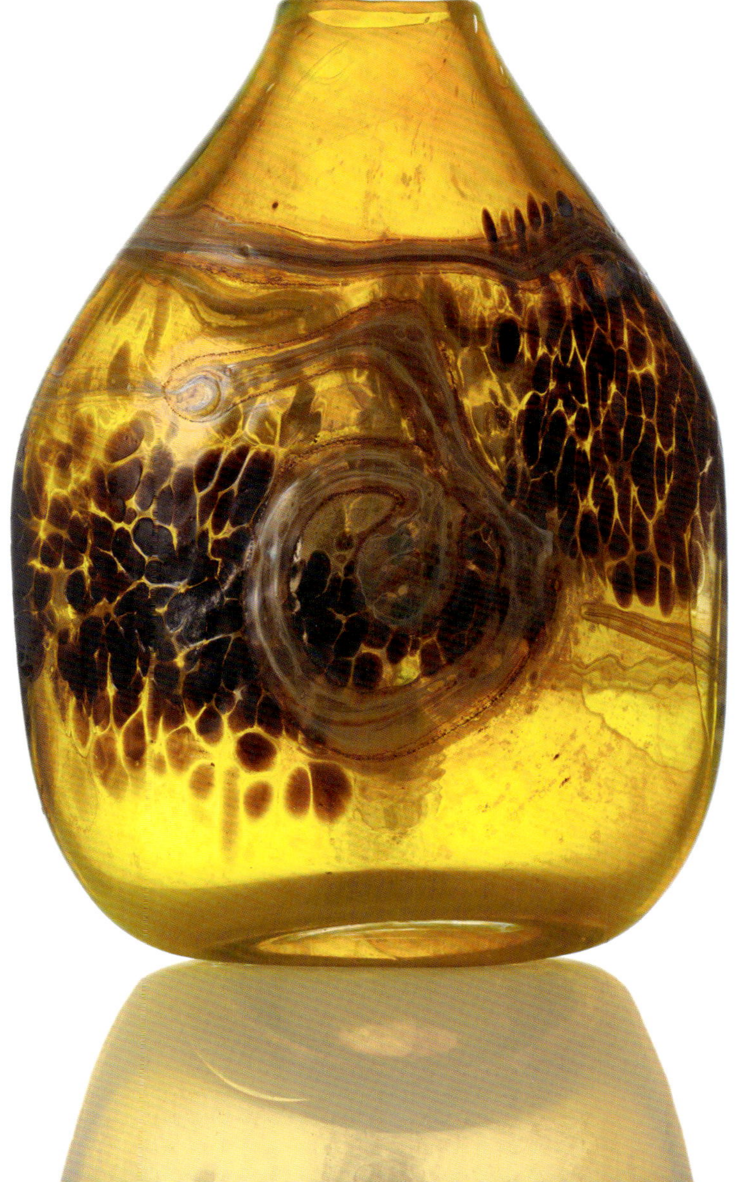

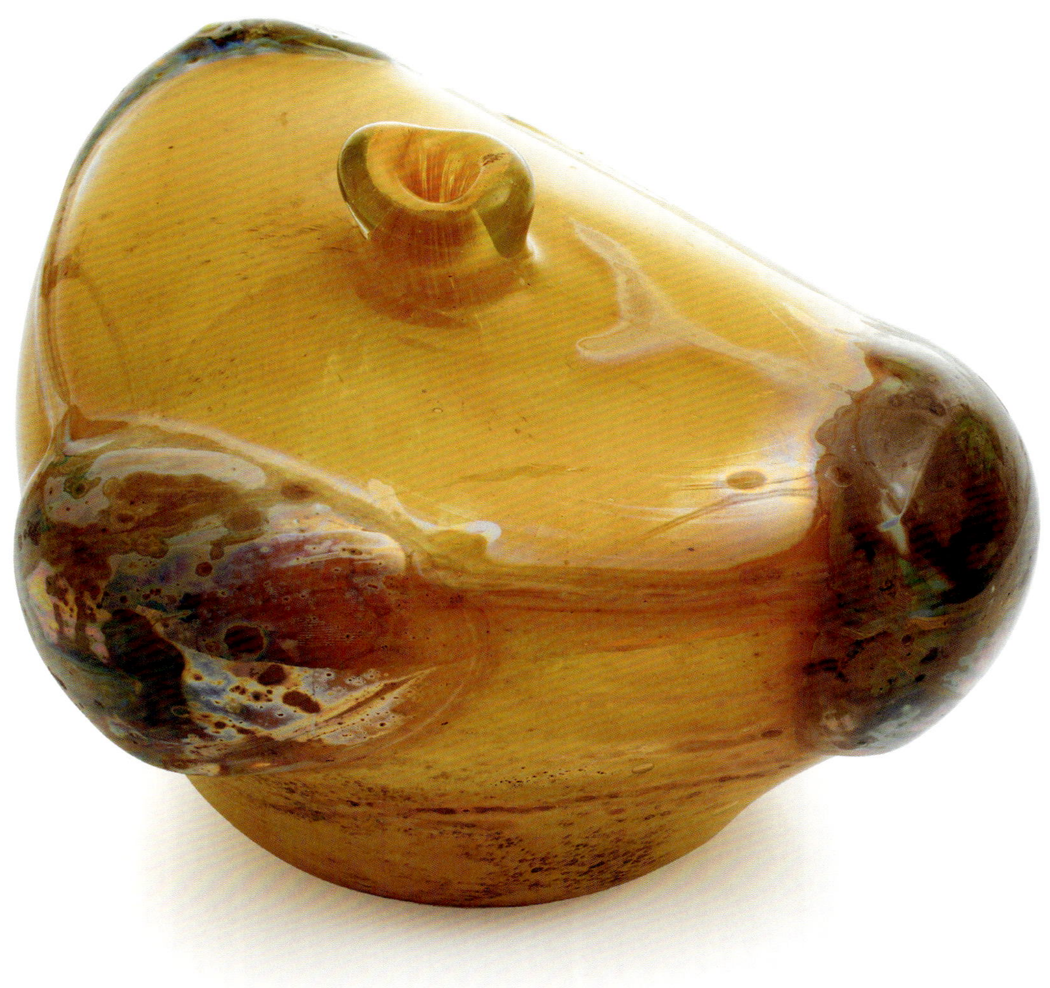

pieces on his own, without the need for support from assistants. A wet stick was forced into a partially blown gather of hot glass, with the steam released from the stick causing the body to expand and swell, creating a random and large bulbous form.

This technique also worked well as the end result was achieved very quickly. The glass used at The Jam Factory was made from melted-down wine bottles that had been collected as rubbish. The glass used to make these bottles was intended to cool very quickly so that it only needed to stay in the mould in the bottle factory for as little time as possible. As such, when re-melted at The Jam Factory, it had a very short working life, even shorter than the glass used at Wisconsin, before it became too hard to manipulate. Attempts were made to soften and extend the working life of the glass by adding soda ash, with limited success. This factor affected the forms that were made, and narrowed the use of three-dimensional applied features.

Untitled, 1975
blown glass, 16cm (6¼in),
Private Collection

Opposite
Untitled, 1975
blown glass, 18cm (7in),
Private Collection

Opposite
Untitled, 1983
blown glass, 36cm (14in),
Private Collection

Below
Untitled, 1980
blown glass, 29cm (11½in),
Private Collection

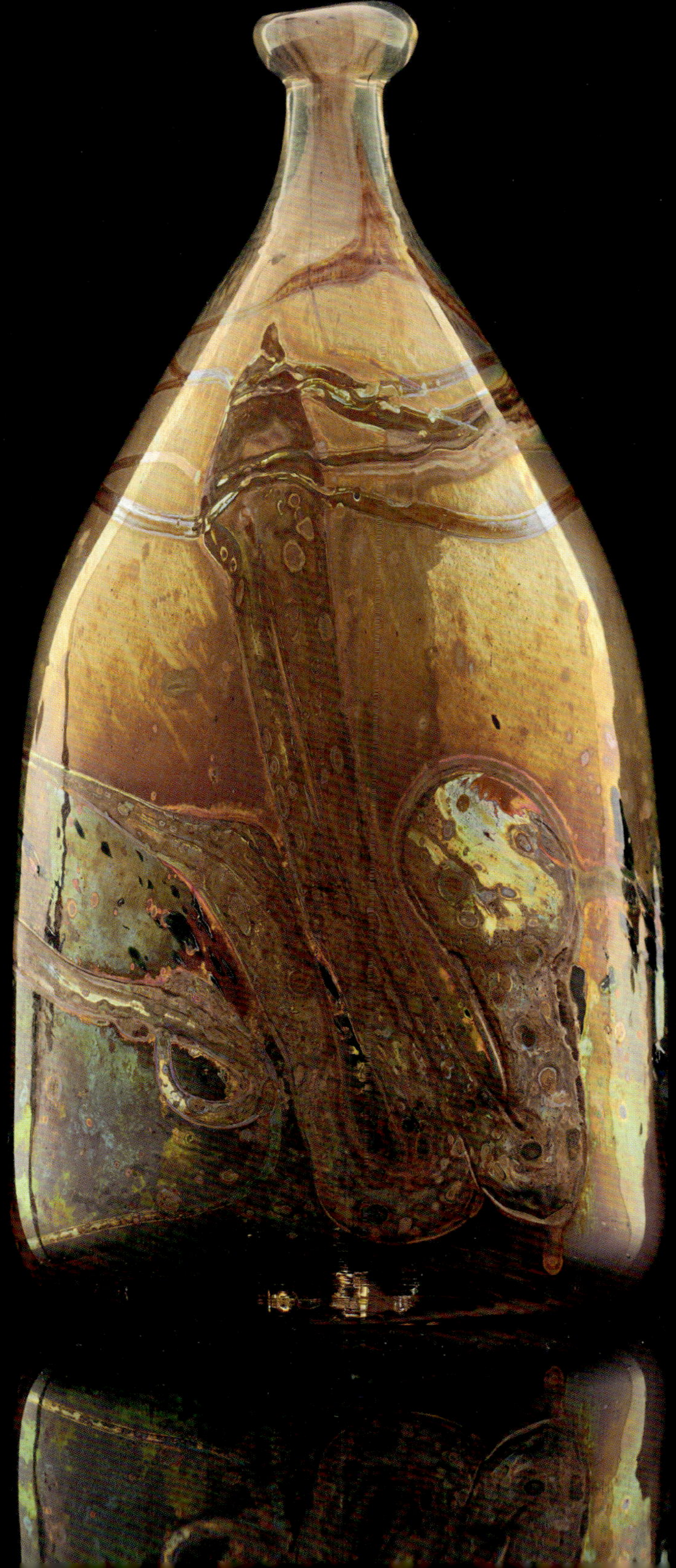

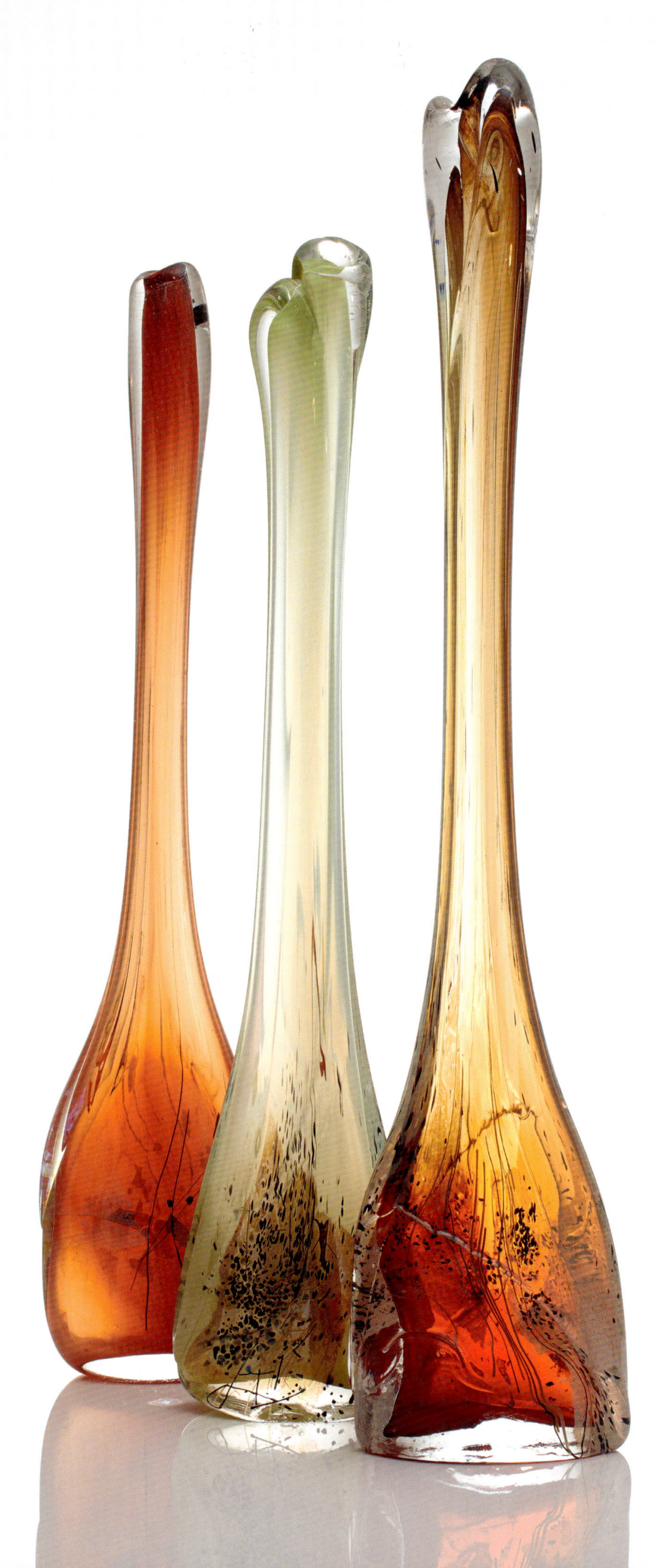

Below
Untitled, 1982
blown glass, 15cm (6in) and
12cm (4¾), Private Collection

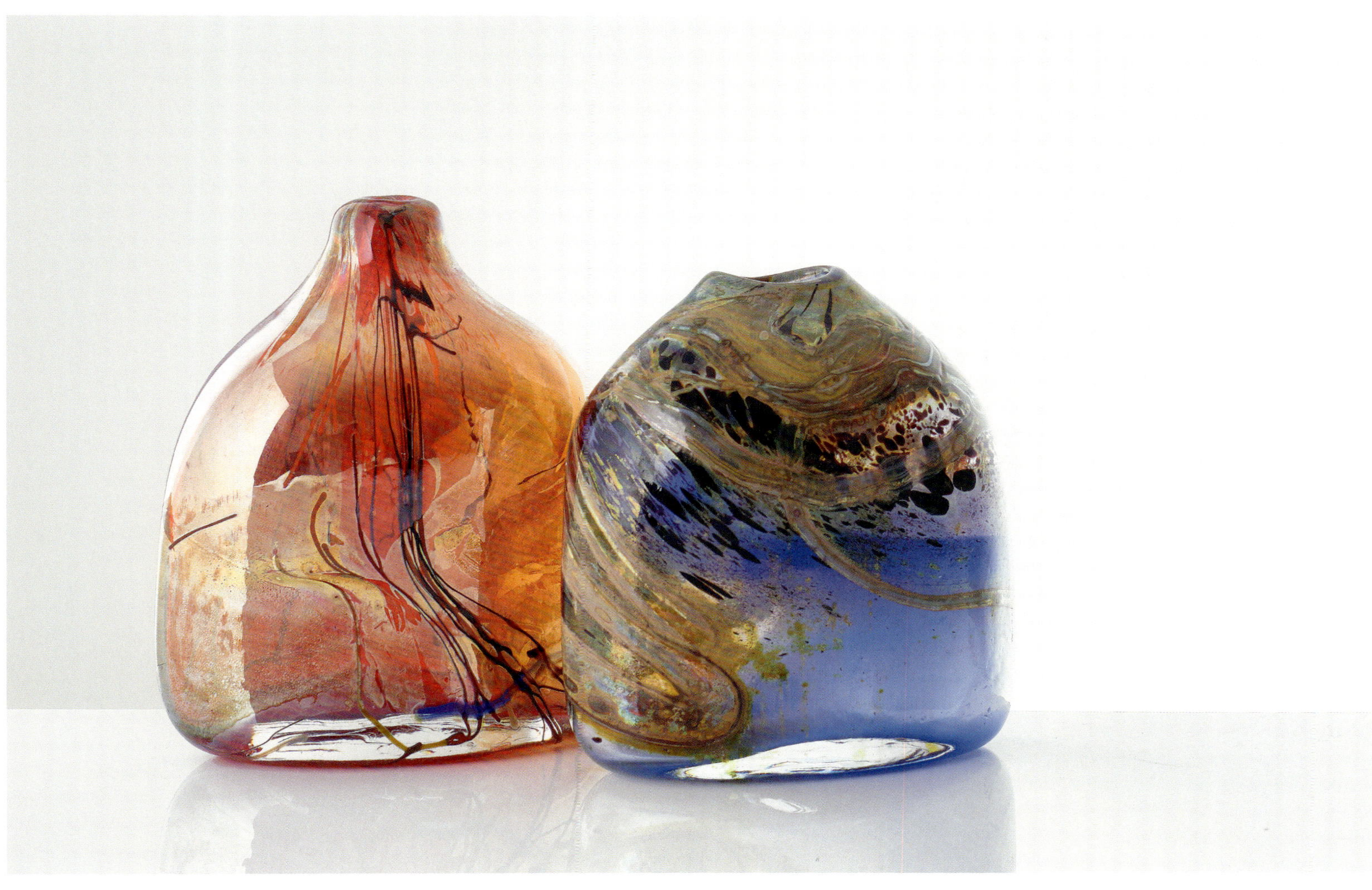

Opposite
Untitled, 1980
blown glass, 60cm (23½in),
59cm (23¼in) and 65cm
(25½in), Private Collection

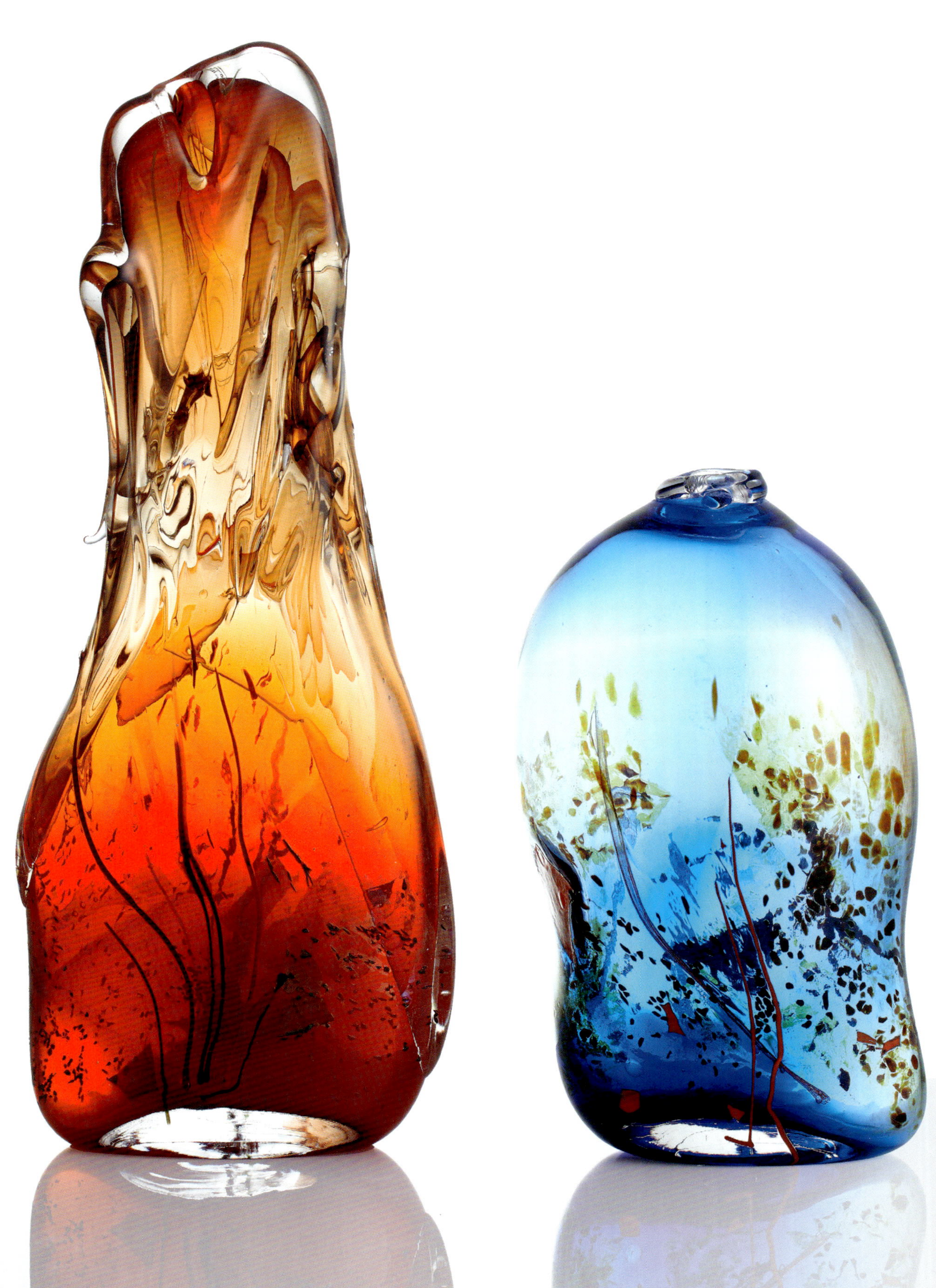

Opposite
Untitled, 1981
blown glass, 34cm (13½in) and
20cm (8in), Private Collection

Right
Untitled, 1983
blown glass, 24cm (9½in) and
28cm (11in), Private Collection

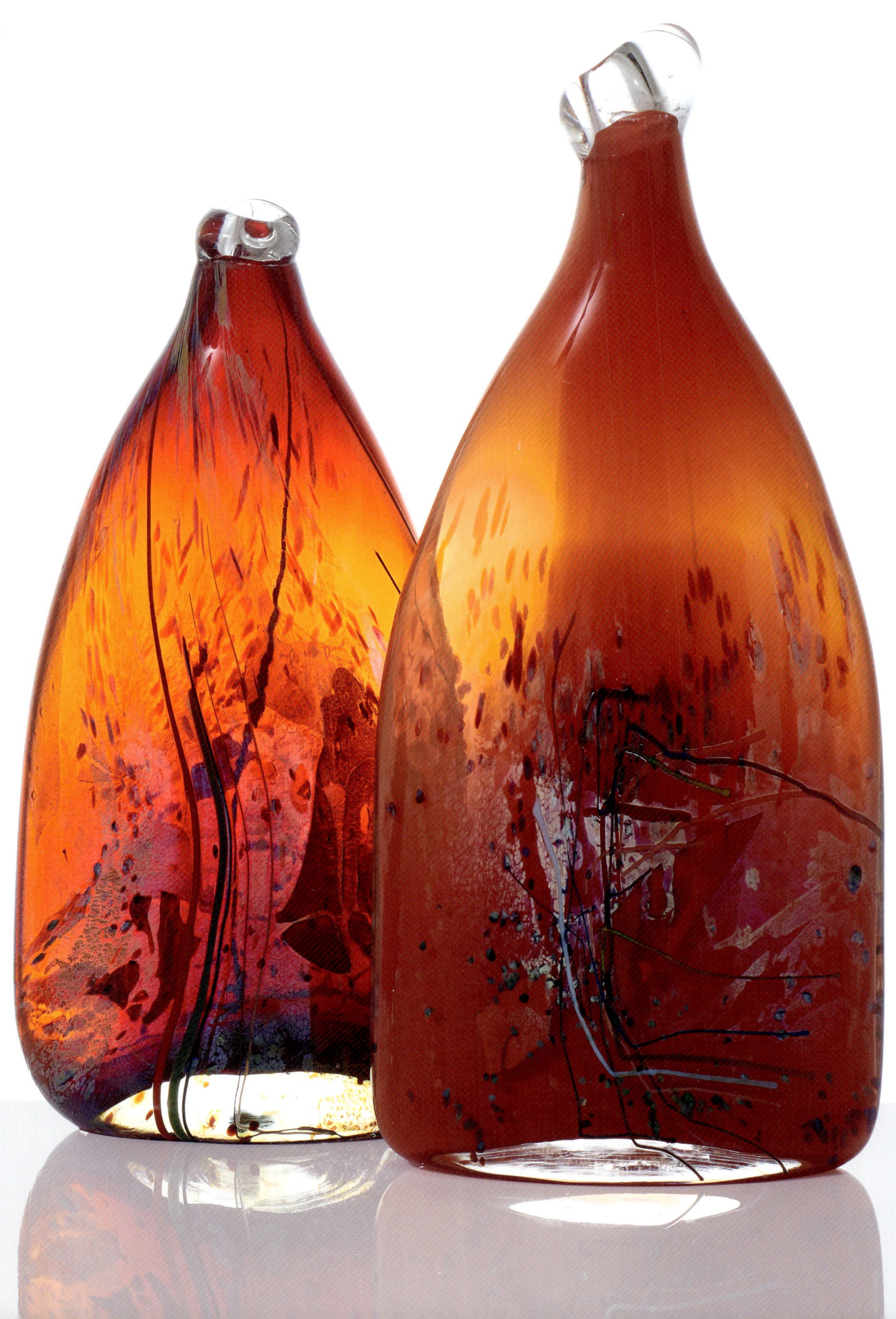

Below
Untitled, 1982
blown glass, detail,
Private Collection

Opposite
Untitled, 1982
blown glass, 30cm (11¾in) and
38cm (15in), Private Collection

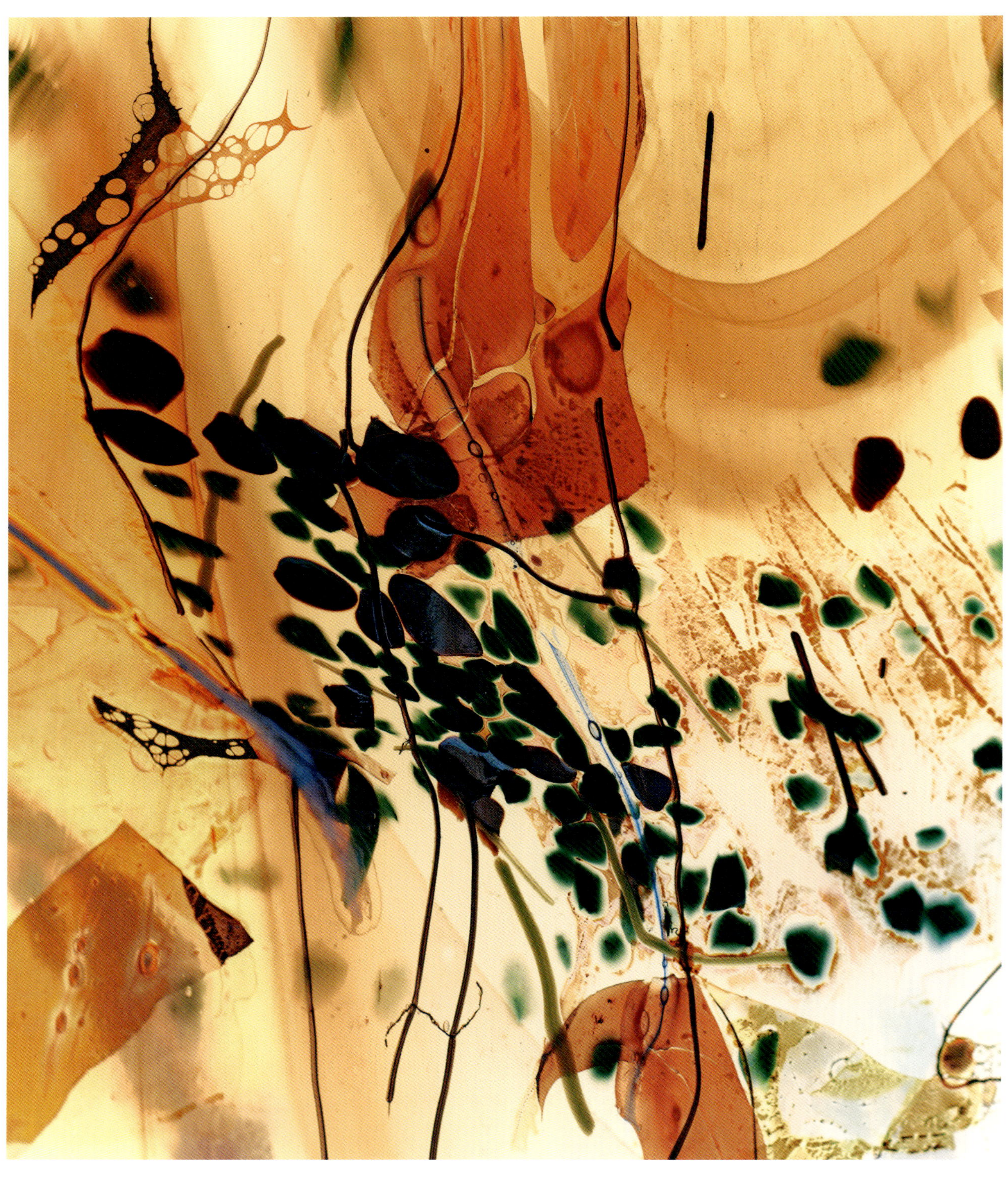

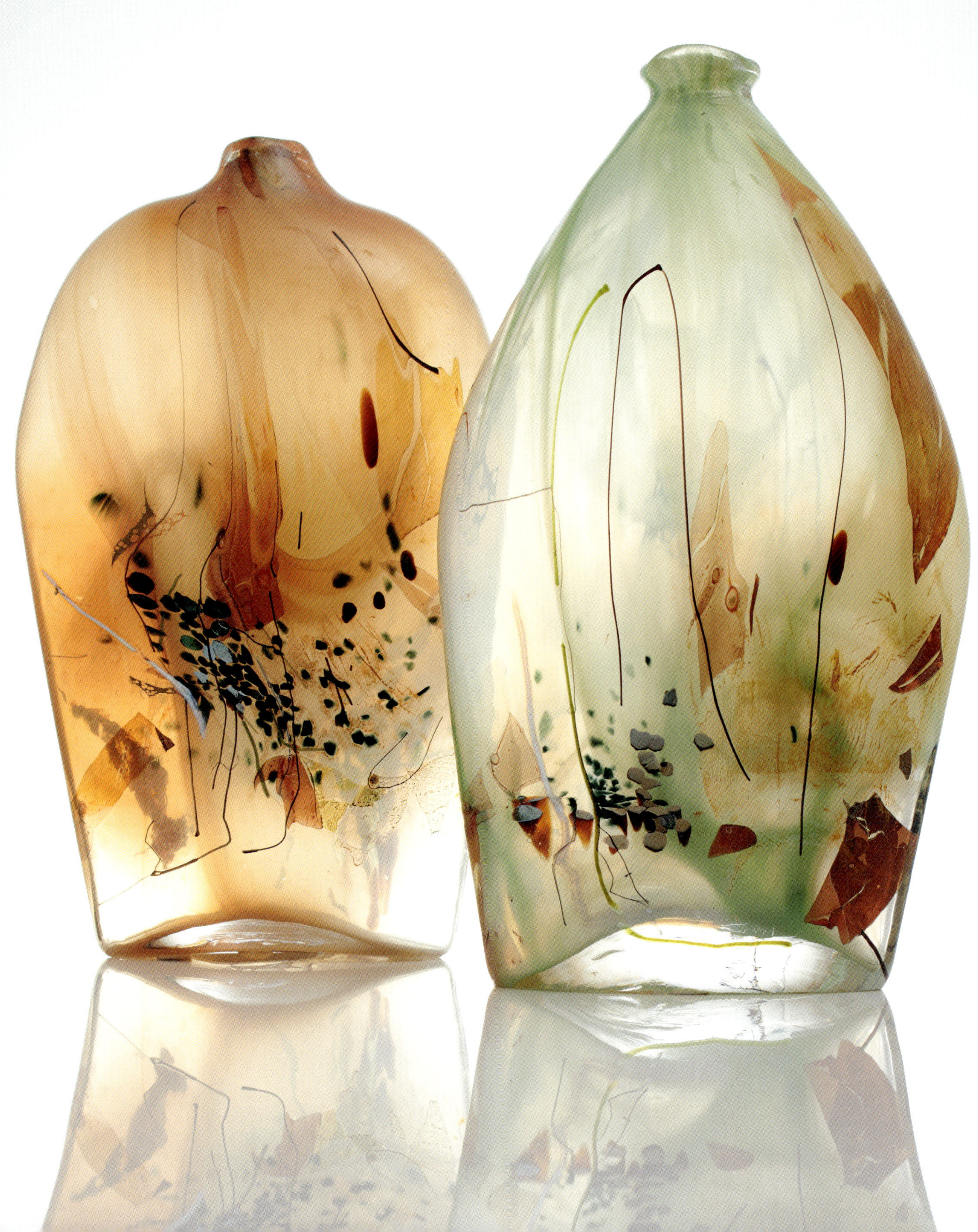

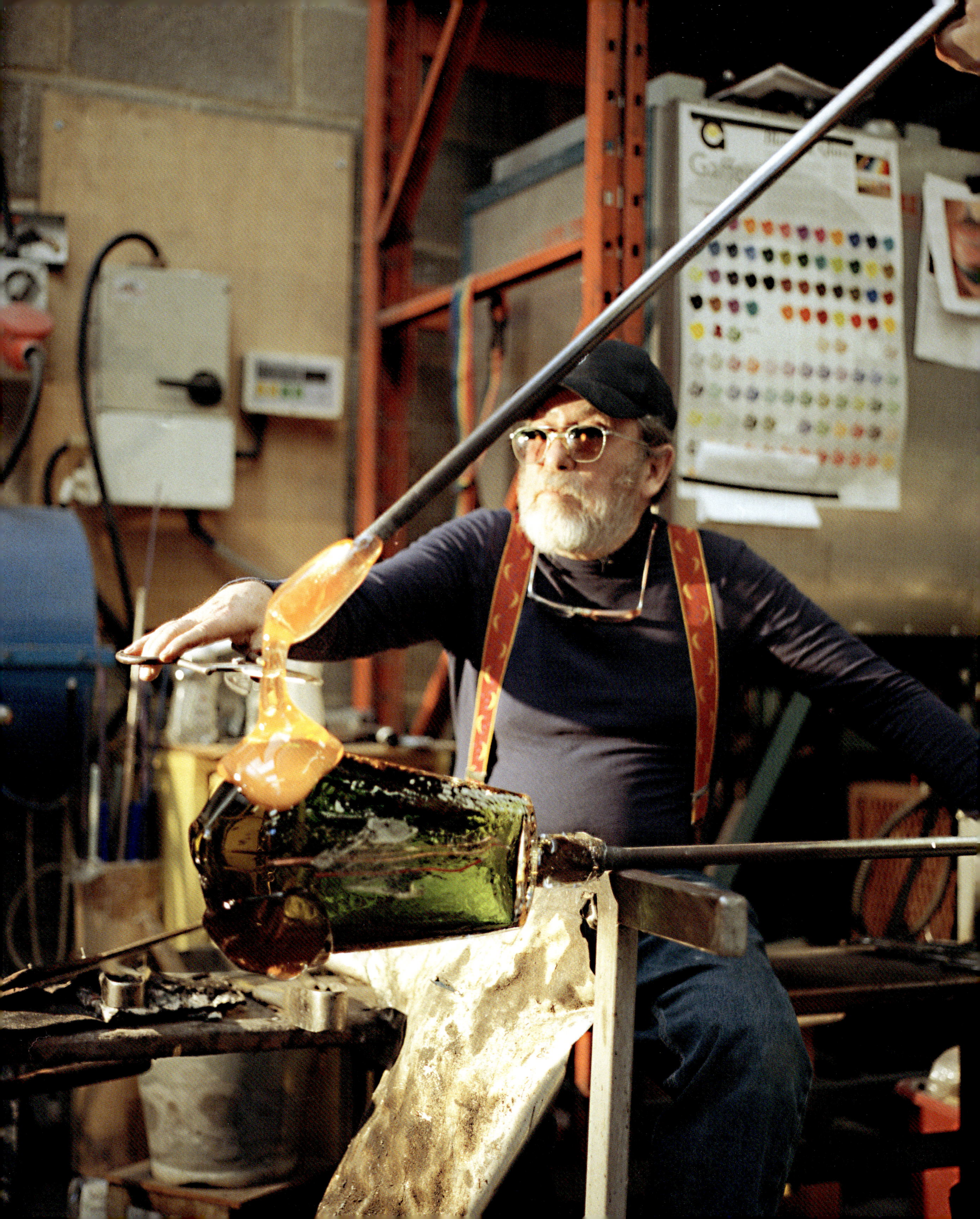

Twenty-first-century work
Various glass studios, UK, 2007–17

After Herman closed his Lots Road studio in 1984, he took a 23-year break from glass making to focus on his painting, lighting and sculptural work in other media. However, in 2007 he was persuaded to return to the furnace by Adam Aaronson of Aaronson Noon Studio and Gallery in London. Since then, he has made glass for short periods of a day or a few days only, each time at Peter Layton's London Glassblowing studio (2012) and at Colin Hawkins' Loco Glass in Gloucestershire (2015–17). Over a total of no more than a few weeks across this decade, it is estimated that around 80 to 90 successful pieces were produced.

In all instances, Herman worked with the support of experienced glassmakers and glass artists. This was partly due to the fact they were available and partly because, in his 70s, he was physically less able to handle the glass he wished to make. On a positive note, this support allowed him to make large-scale as well as small pieces, and some pieces measure over 40cm (16in) in height (see p.115 and p.120).

In his work across the three studios, Herman returned to the dynamism of form seen at the RCA and Lots Road, but the 'glassiness' was further accentuated. The large size of many pieces added drama and, combined with their forms, reinforced their nature as sculpture in glass. Many had applied and melted-in wings or extravagant lobes giving a torso-like form, while others were near-cylindrical or conical, sometimes with open, flaring and asymmetric rims that gave them a strong functional vase-like appearance. As throughout his career, functionality was not the intention, and Herman said that he would have also made less

Opposite
Sam Herman working at London Glassblowing, 2012

Right
Untitled, 2008
blown glass, 52cm (20½in), Private Collection

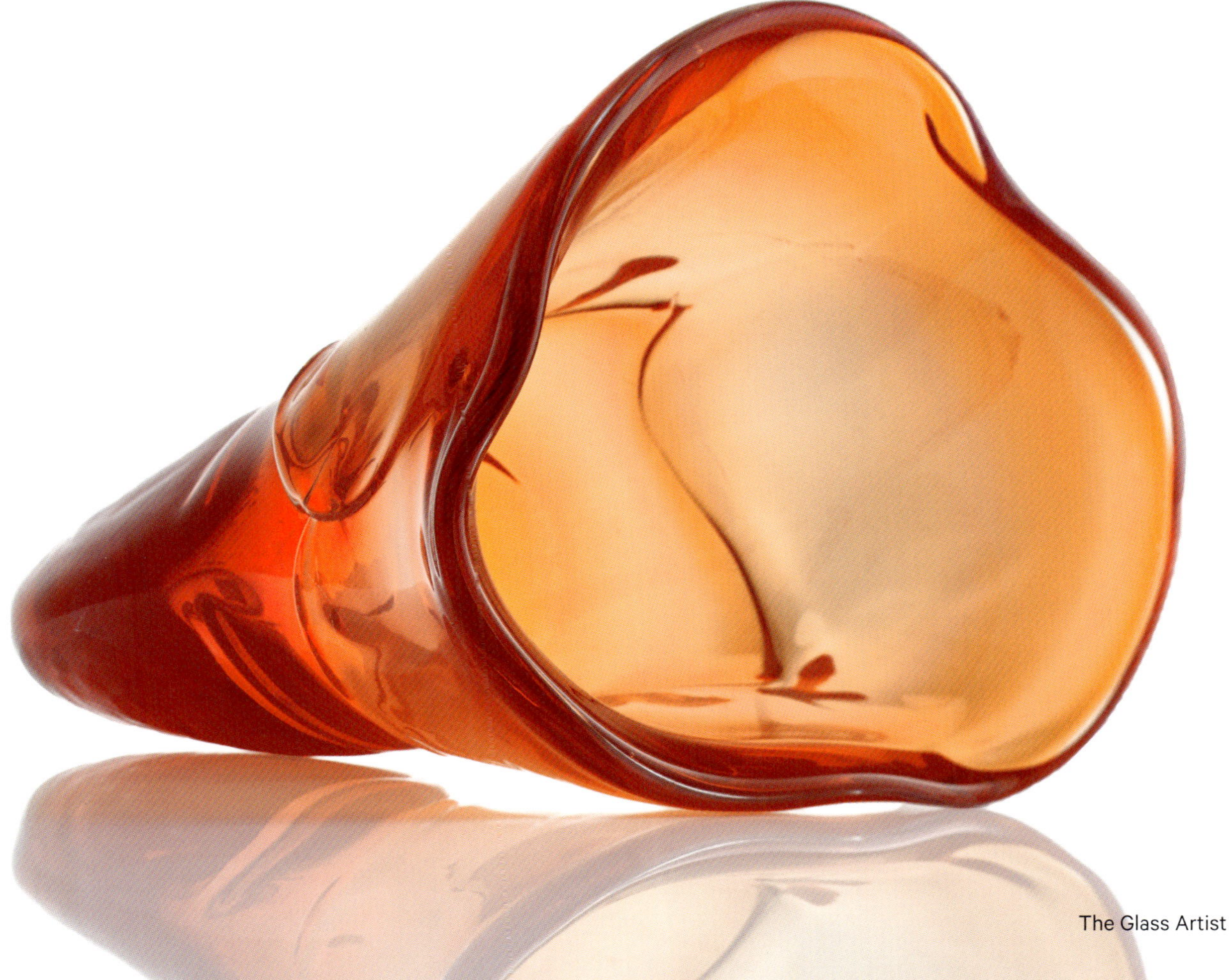

obviously functional, torso-like forms on the same day. Furthermore, on occasion he was more interested in colour than form. The quality of glass at each studio was excellent, so Herman and his various assistants were free to work forms as he wished, given the material's natural limitations.

Colours were bright and jewel-like, as at Lots Road, but the palette changed to vibrant tones of blue, green, yellow, purple and, occasionally, orange. As he worked sporadically, for only a day or a few days at each studio across nearly a decade, time to build experience in the new working environments and materials was limited. Moreover, he had not handled hot glass for over two decades. This all compounded to cause concerns over colour and his working relationship with the different glassmakers assisting him.

Herman could only see the results of adding an amount of colour to a gather of glass when the piece had cooled in the lehr. Therefore, he had to estimate how much colour to use each time, as he could not learn properly from previous work that had been made months or even years earlier. These wide gaps in time also made the development of a close working relationship with a glassmaker difficult and less fruitful than it may have been had the contact been more regular and consistent. Nevertheless, his lifetime of experience and honed artistic direction combined with the skills of the glassmakers, who were keen to work with and learn from Herman, resulted in pieces that many see as among the most successful, appealing and mature examples of his work.

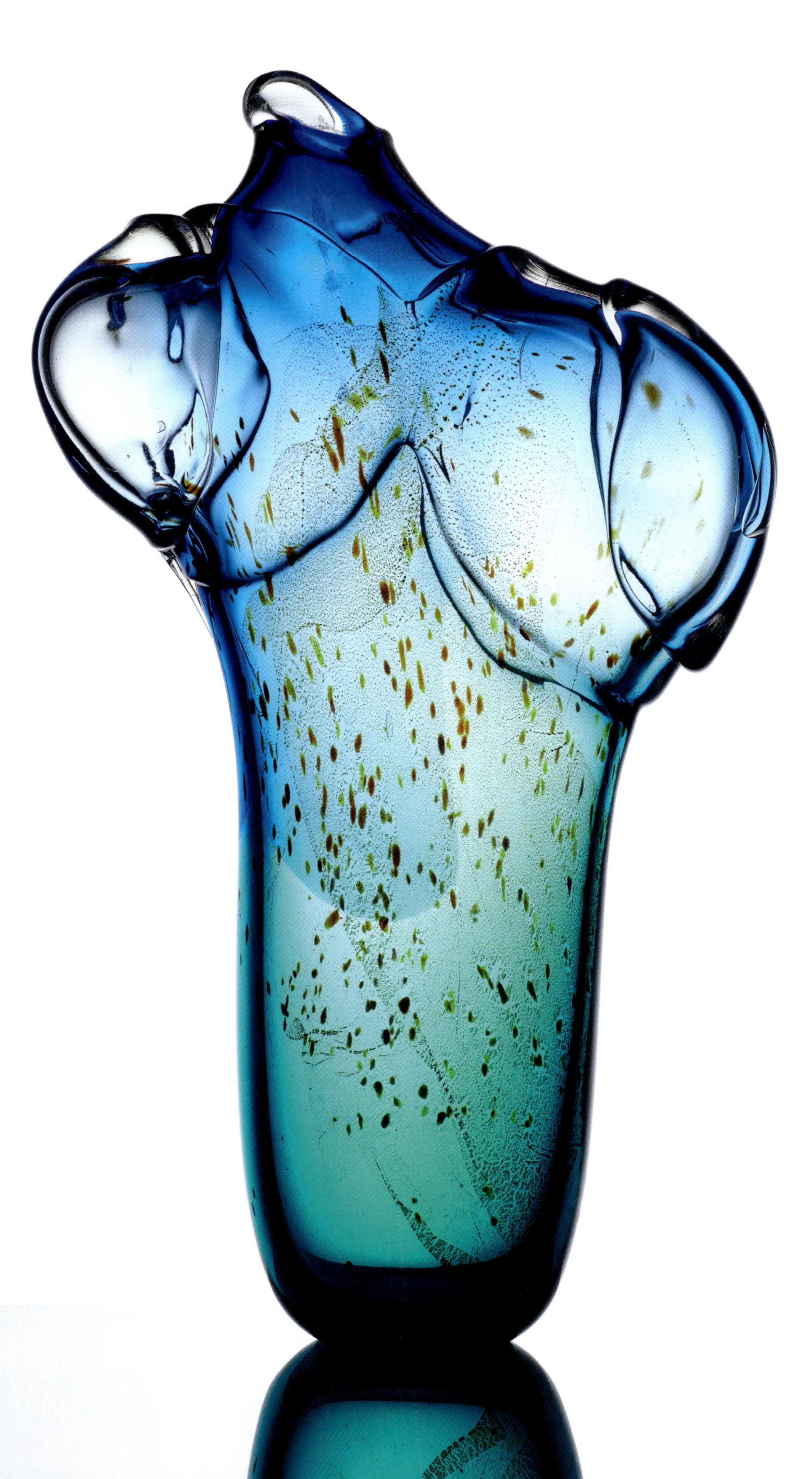

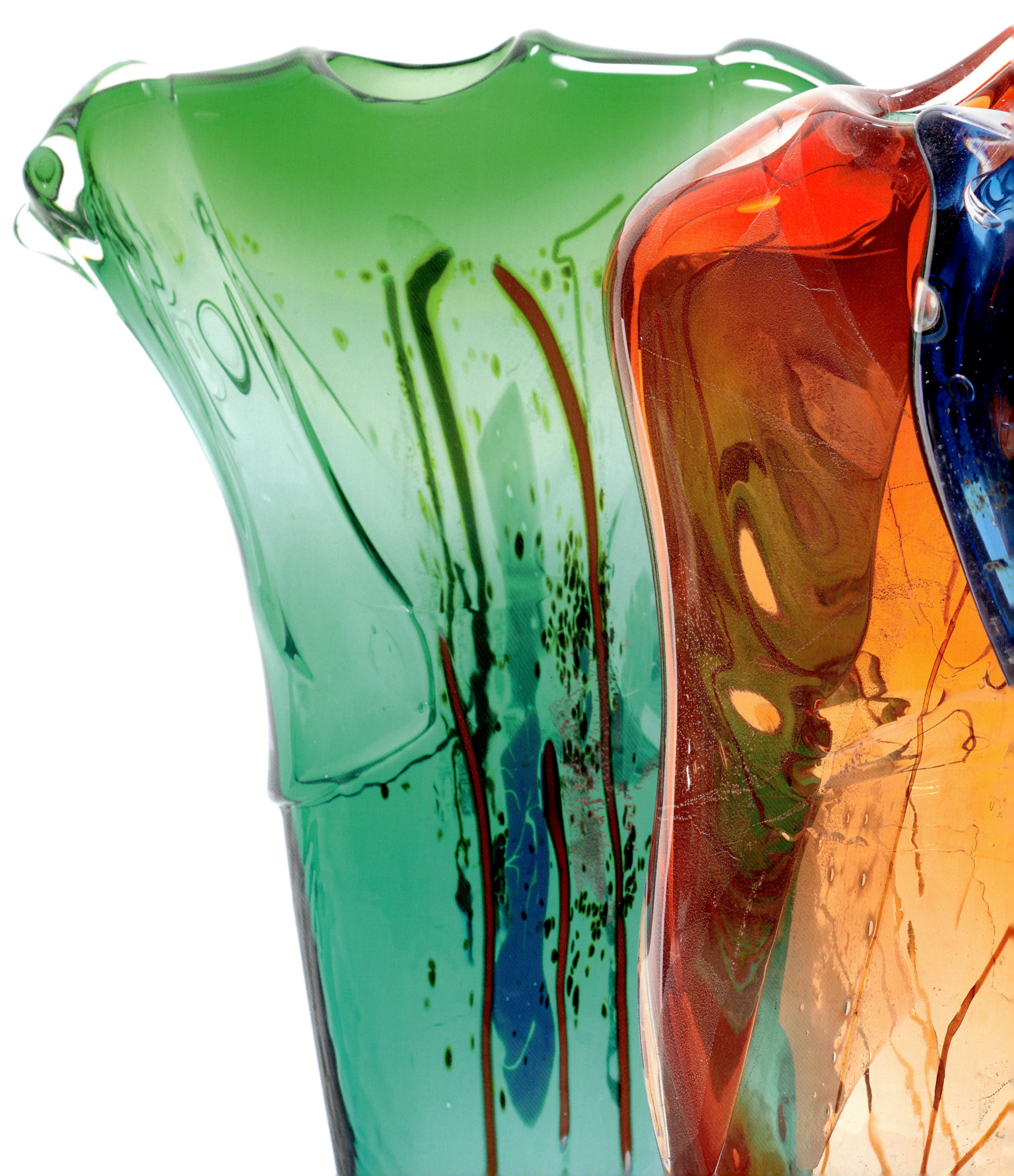

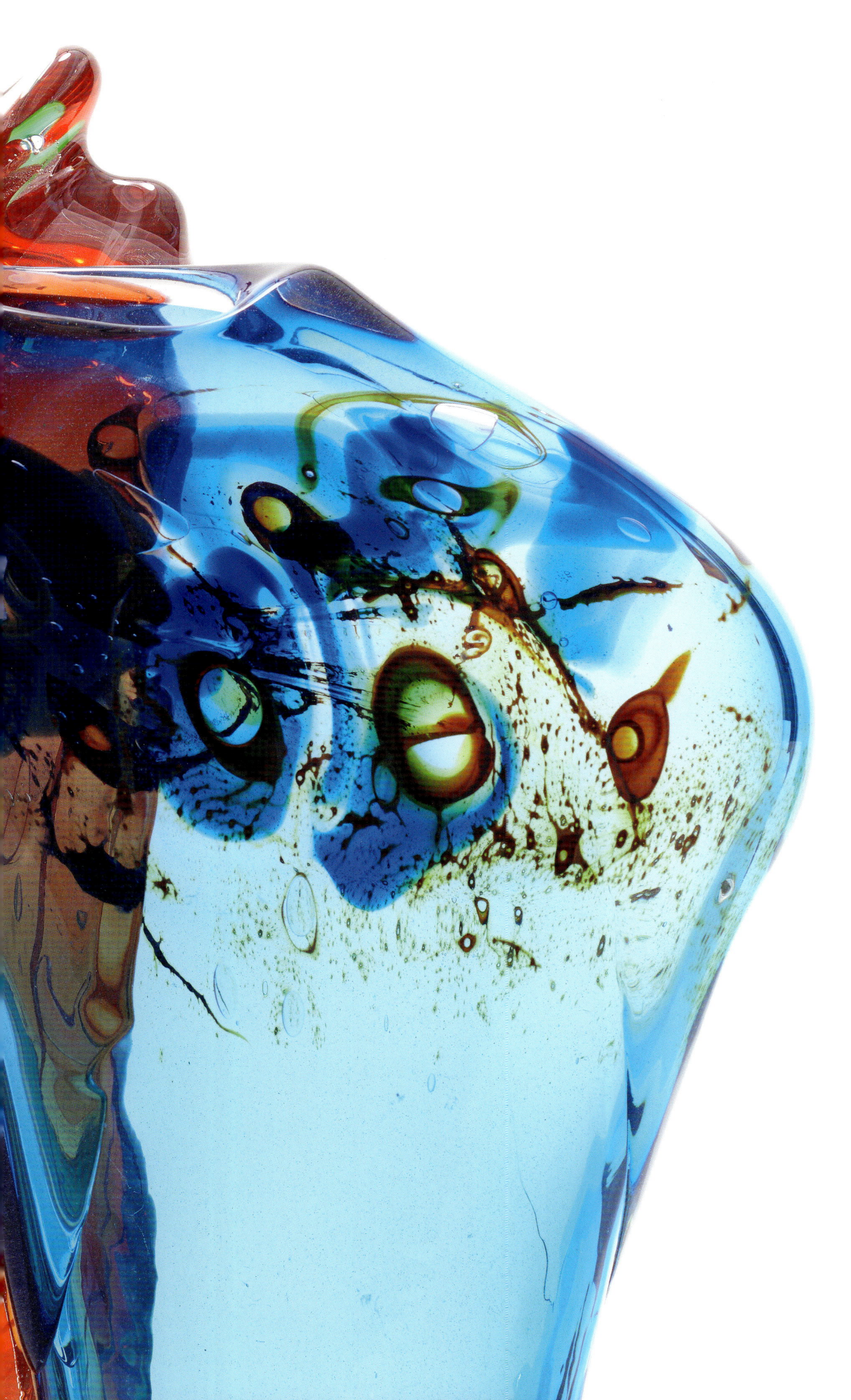

Untitled, 2012, 2008, 2014
blown glass, details,
Private Collection

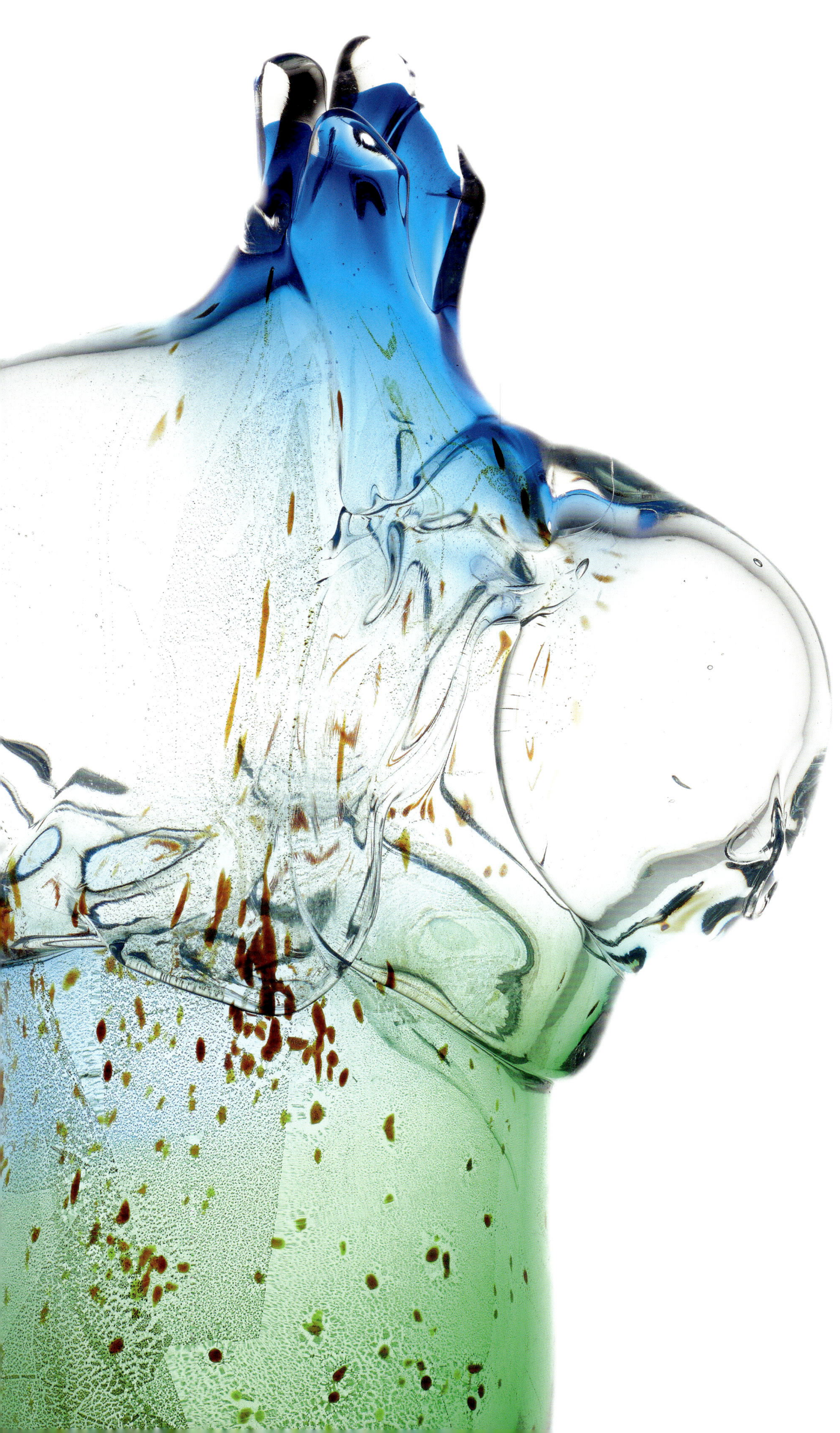

Left
Untitled, 2013
blown glass, 37cm (14½in),
Private Collection

Opposite
Untitled, 2012
blown glass, 50cm (19¾in),
Private Collection

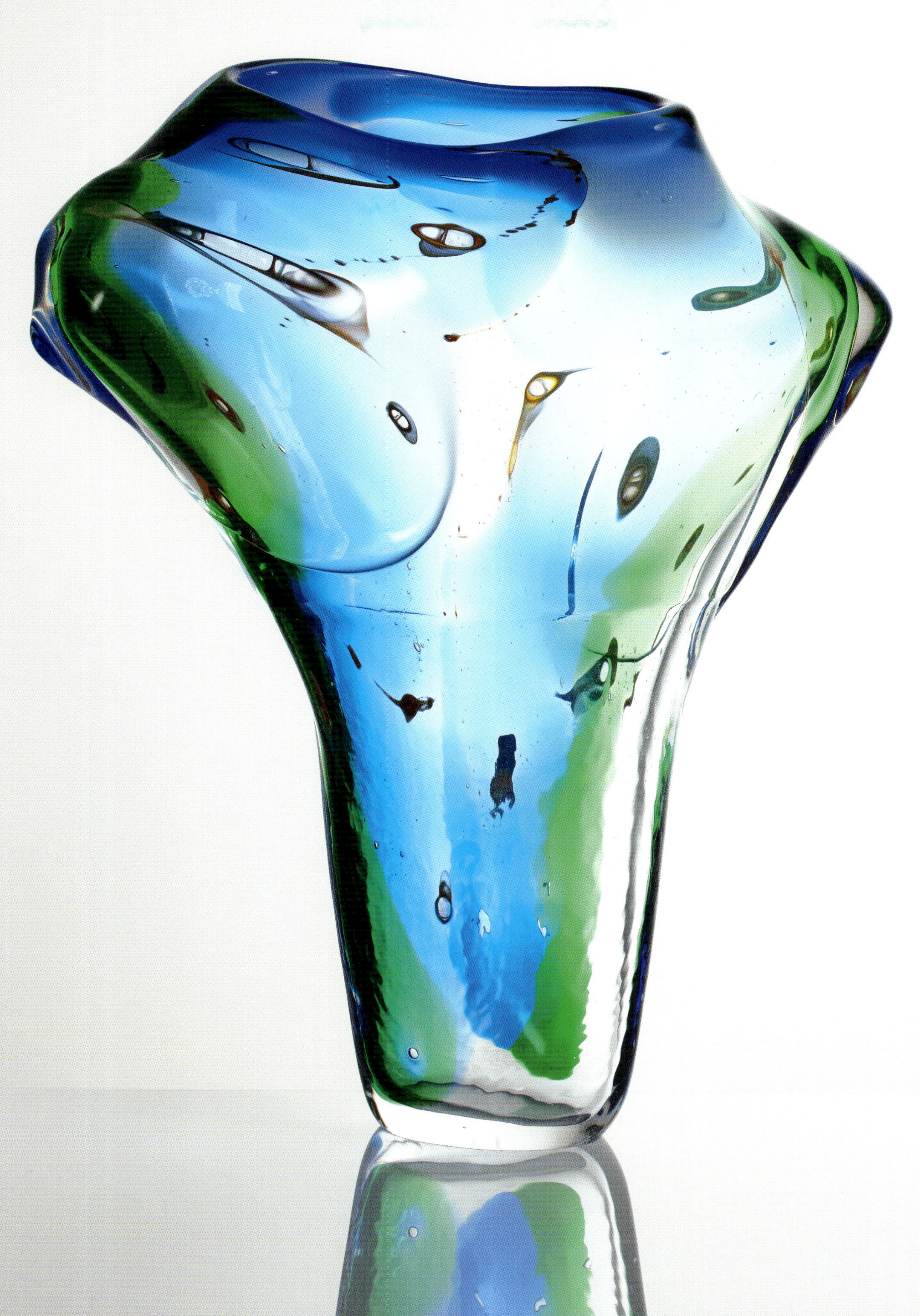

Untitled, 2014
blown glass, 39cm (15¼in),
Private Collection

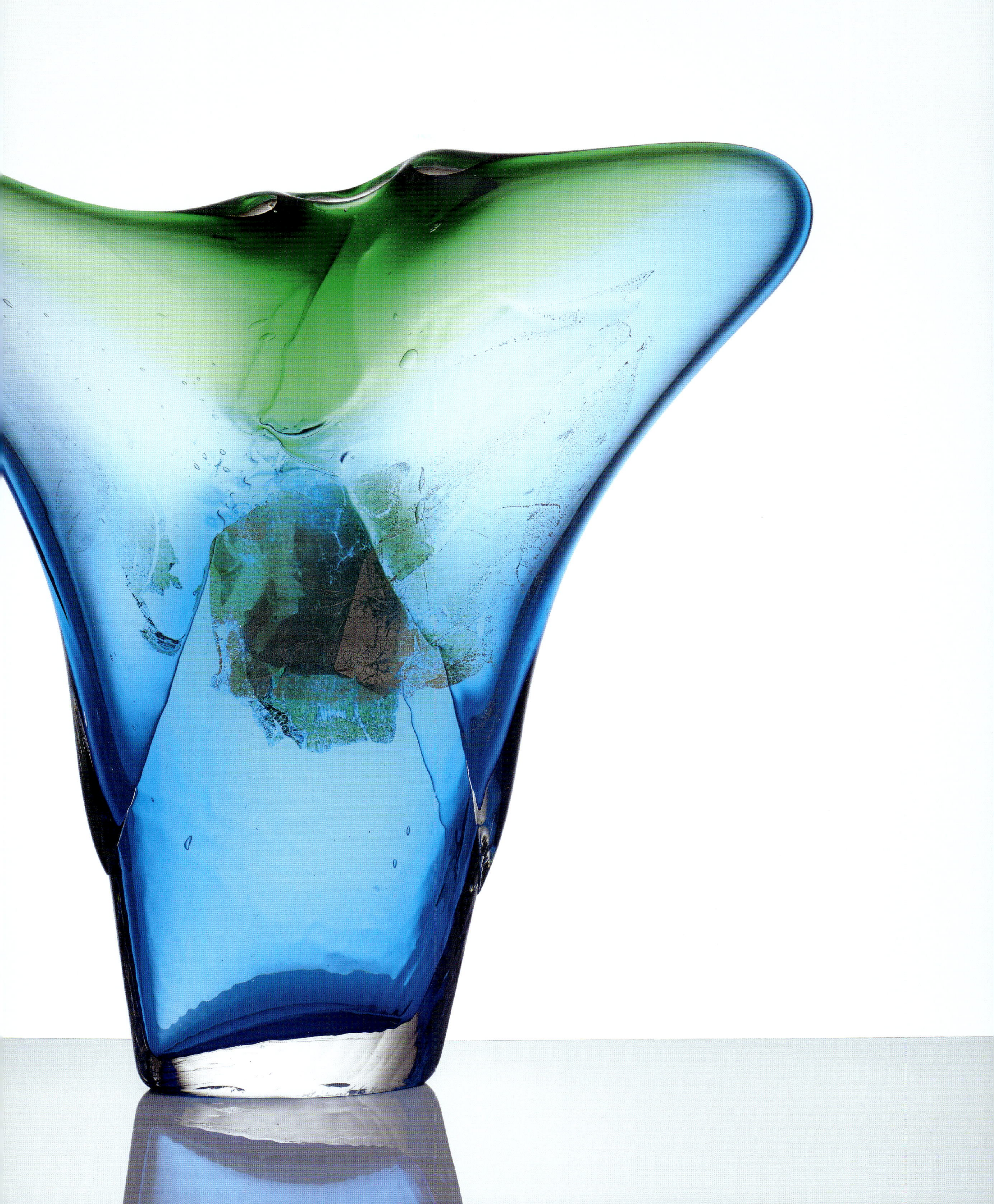

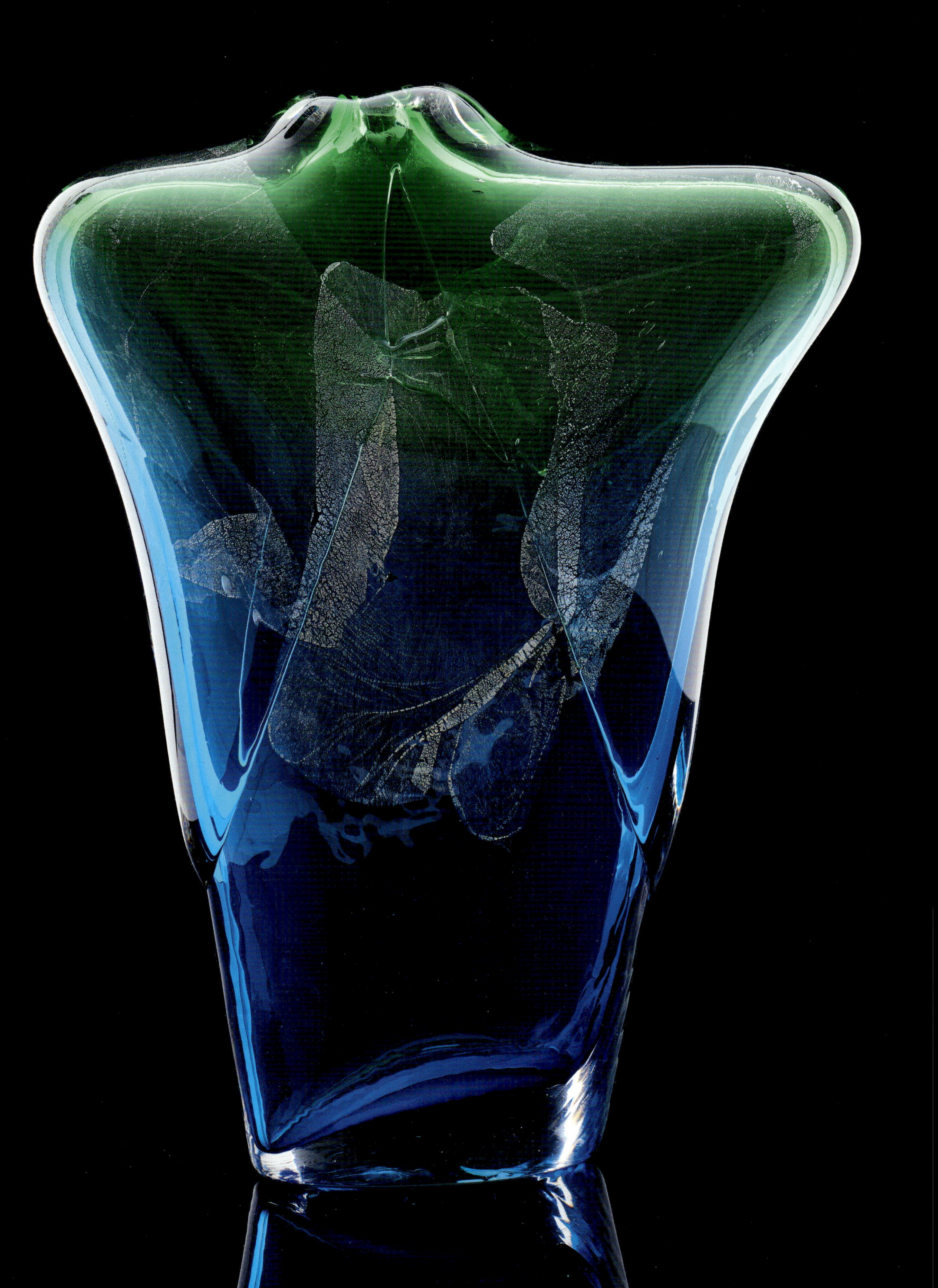

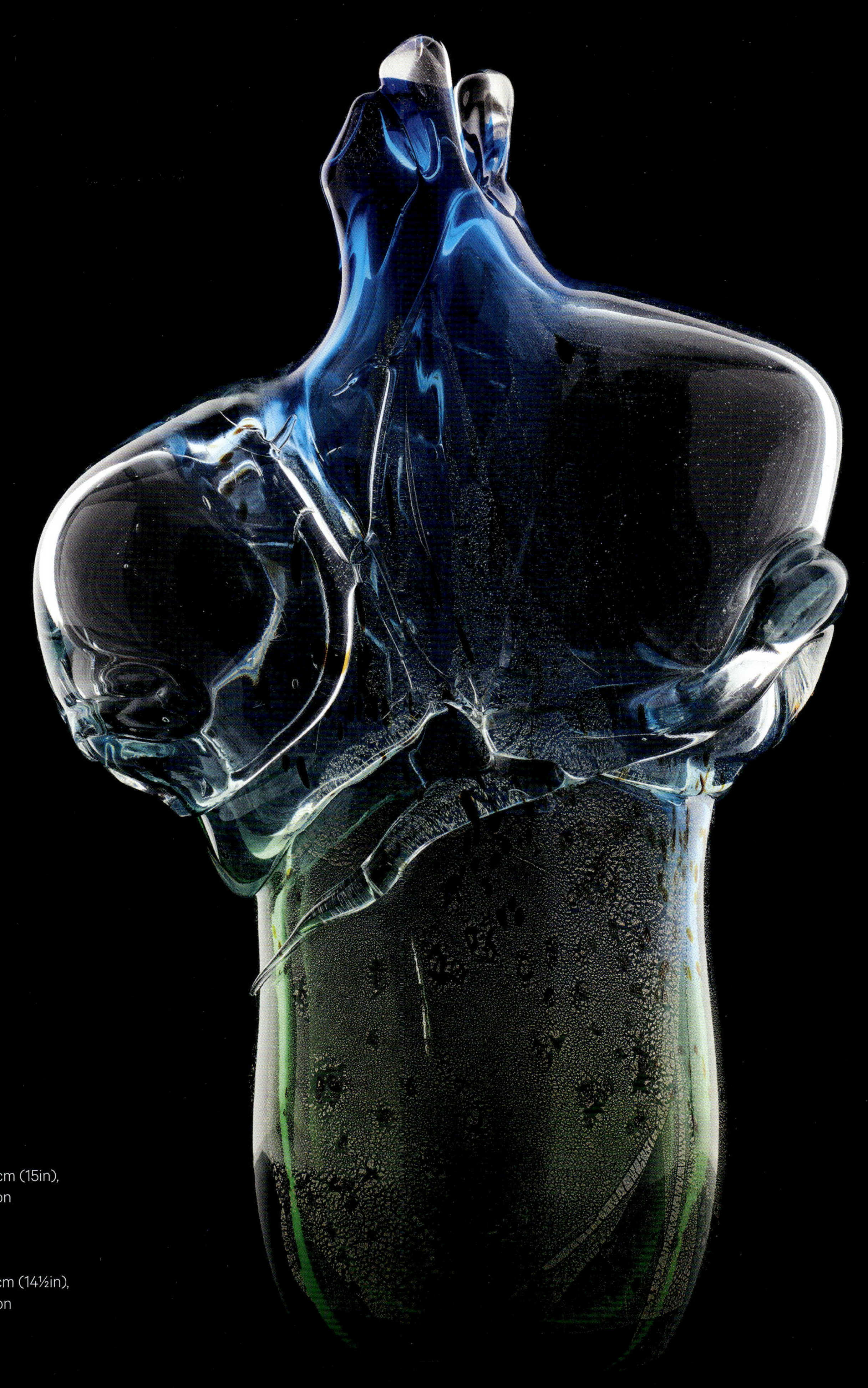

Opposite
Untitled, 2014
blown glass, 38cm (15in),
Private Collection

Right
Untitled, 2013
blown glass, 37cm (14½in),
Private Collection

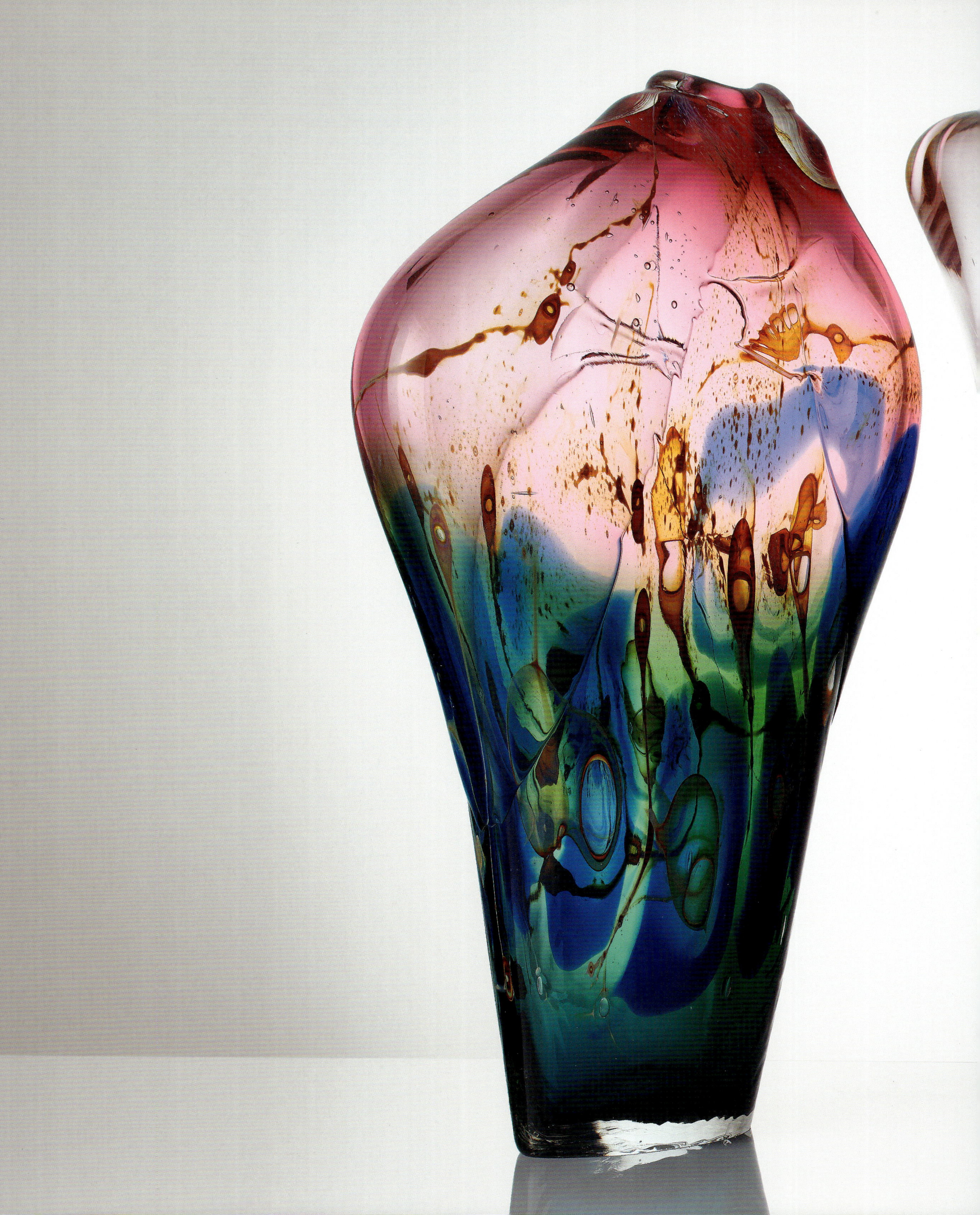

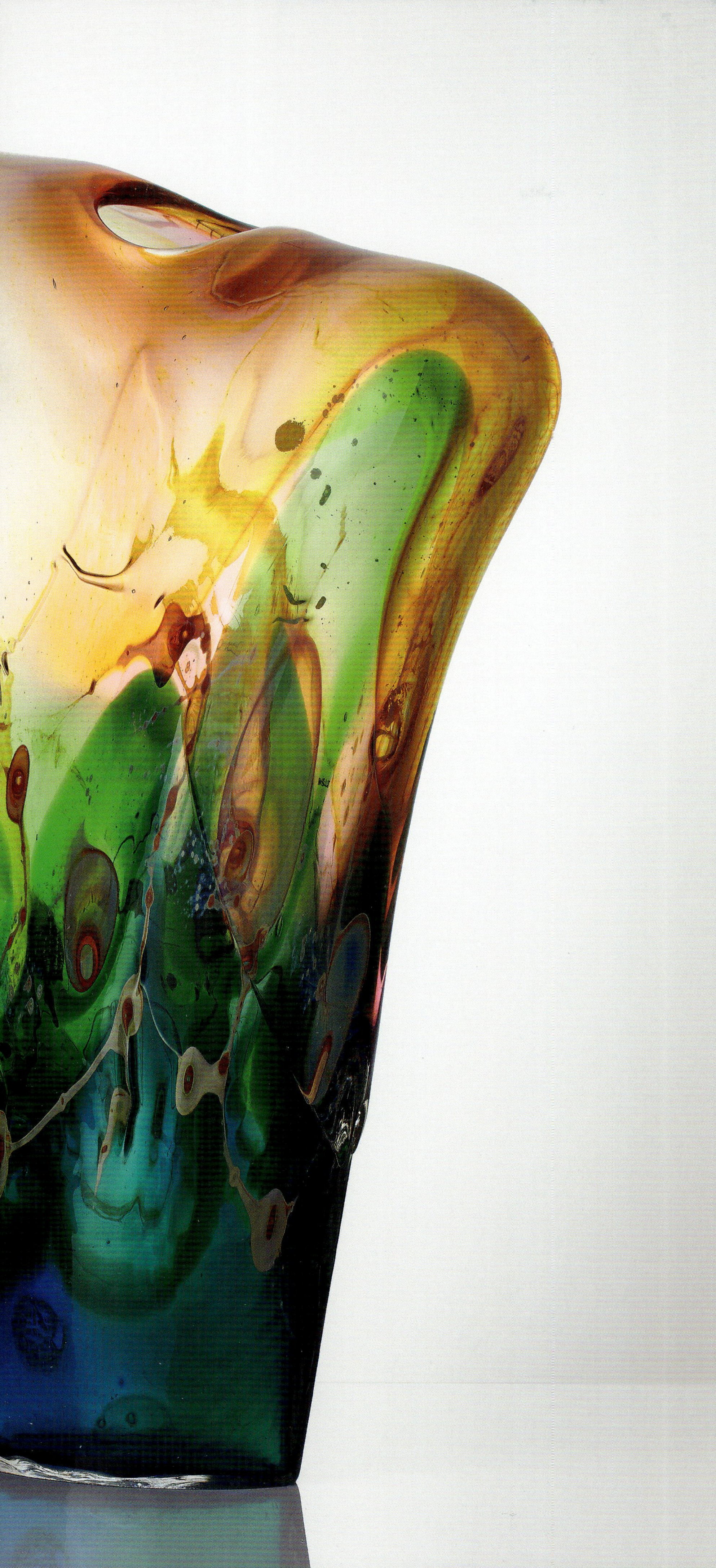

Untitled, 2013, 2014
blown glass, 47cm (18½in),
Private Collection

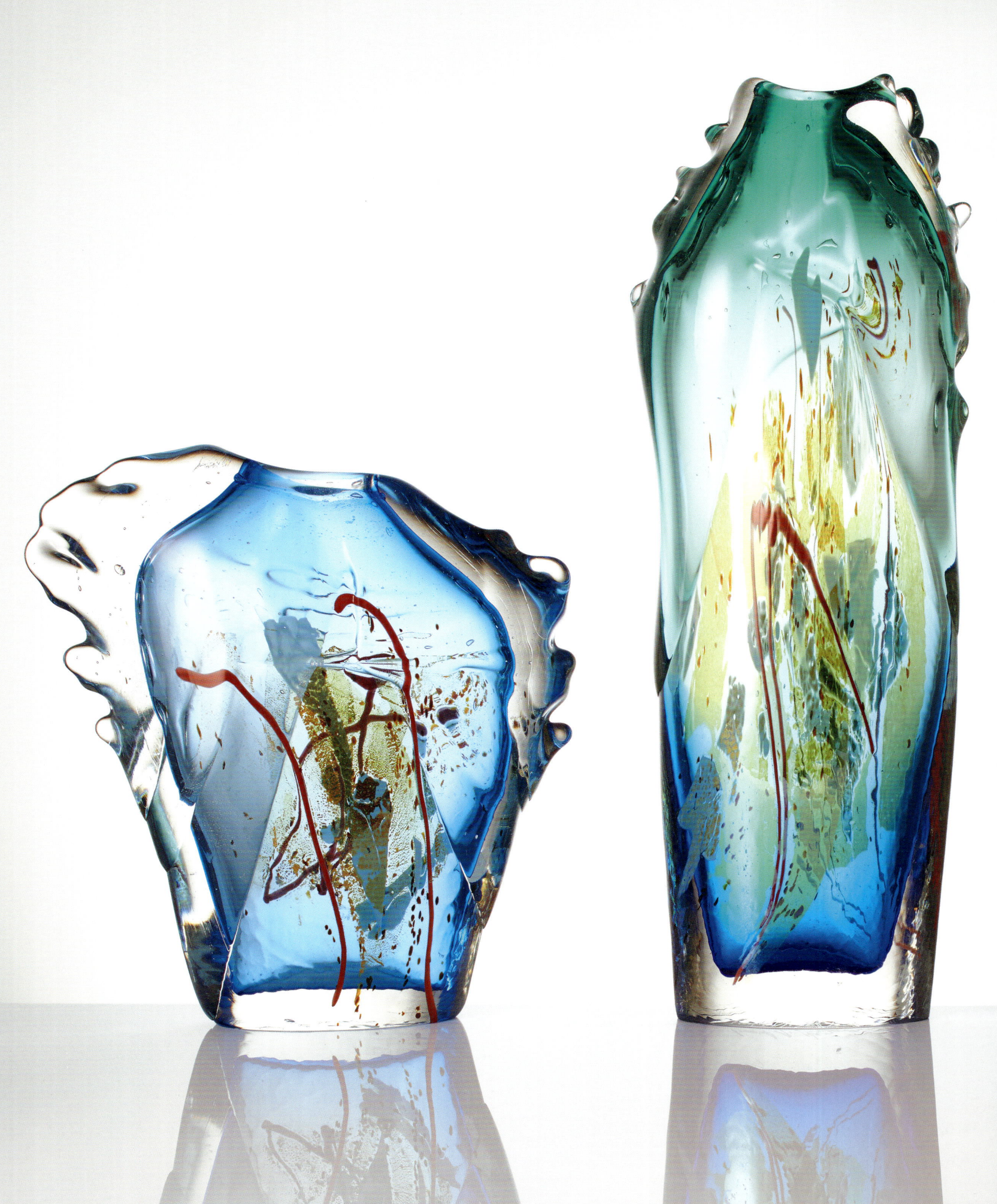

Opposite
Untitled, 2013, 2014
blown glass, 28cm (11in) and
46cm (18in), Private Collection

Right
Untitled, 2013
blown glass, 34cm (13½in),
Private Collection

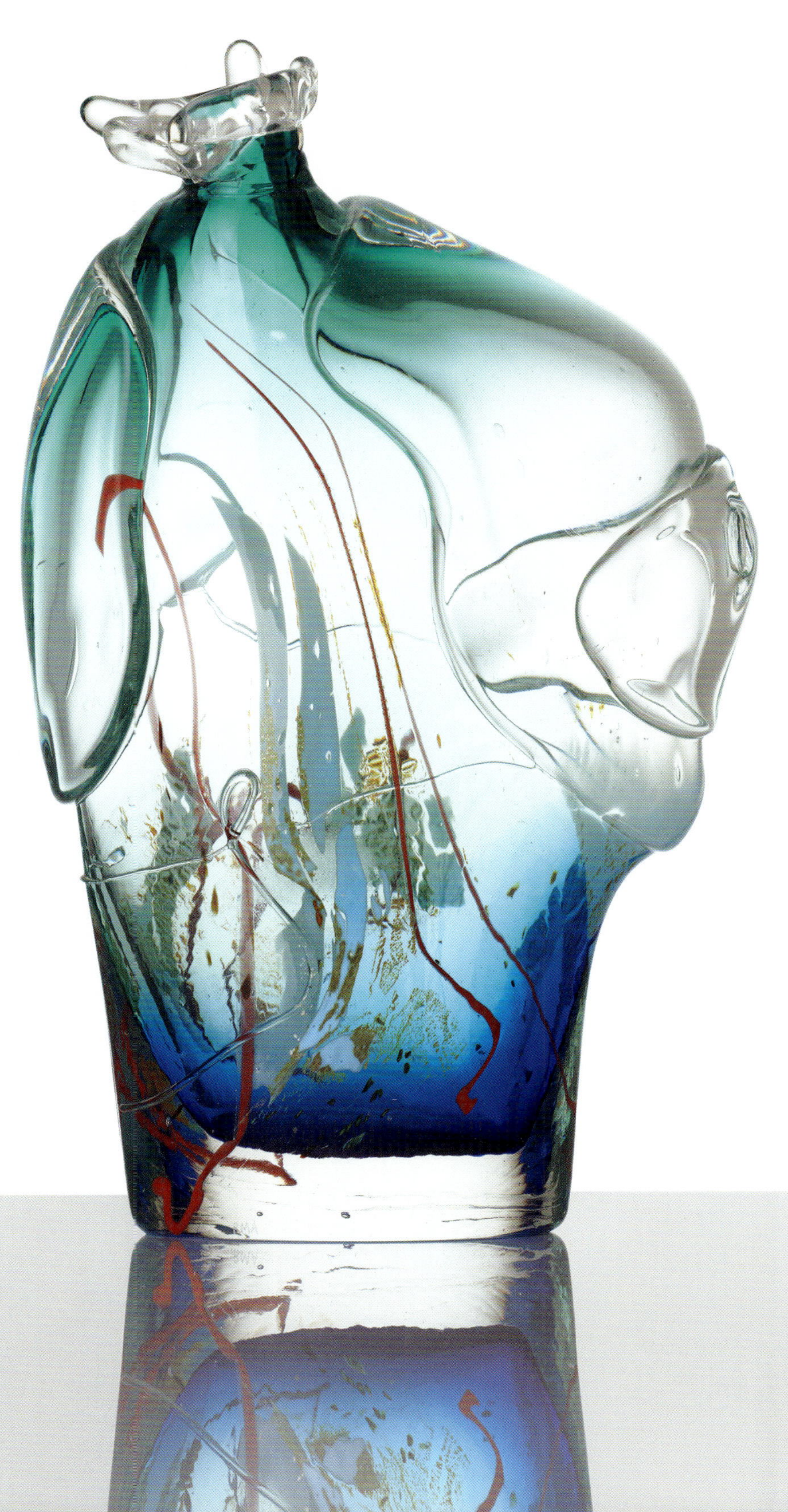

Opposite
Untitled, 2013
blown glass, both 45cm (17¾in),
Private Collection

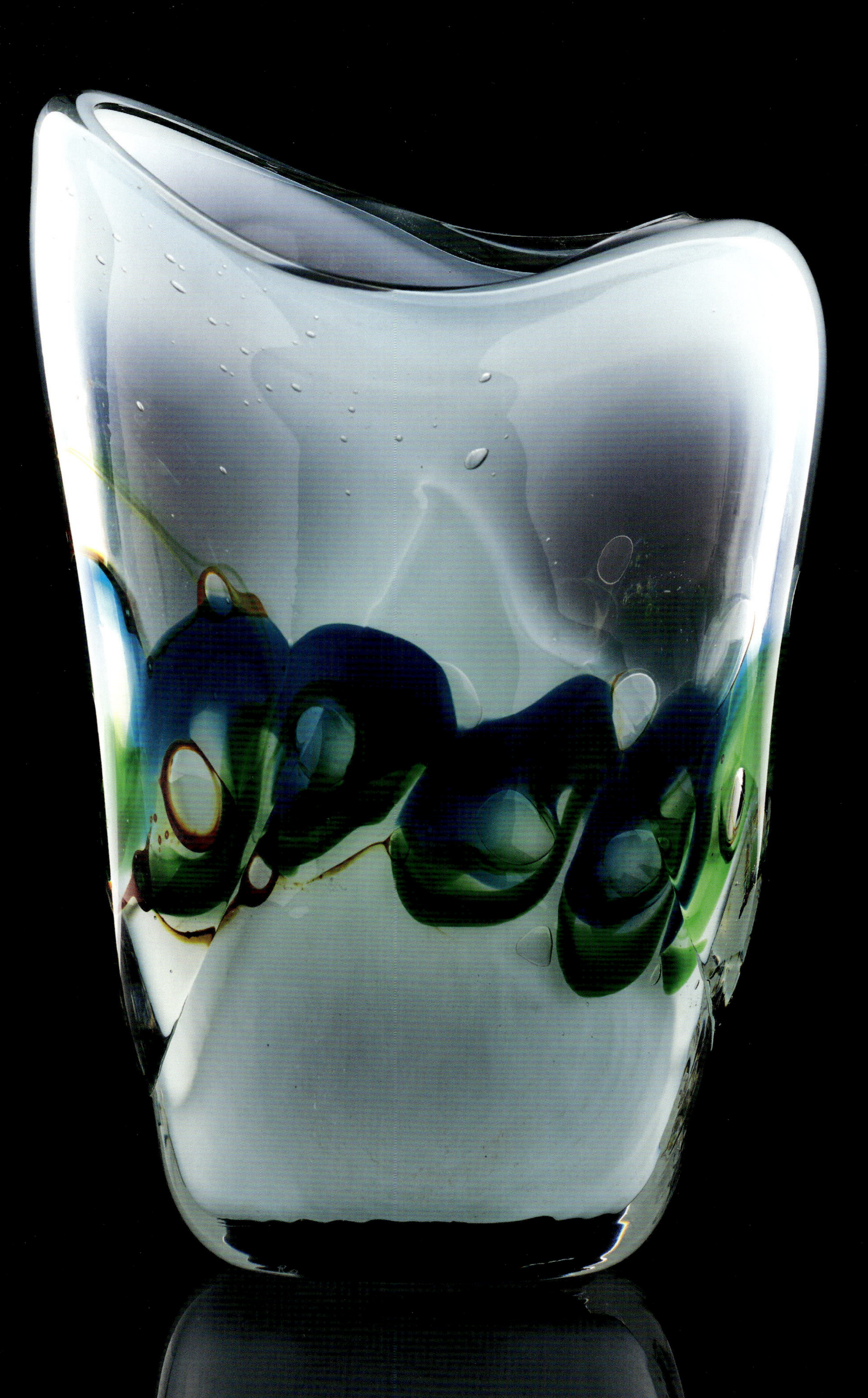

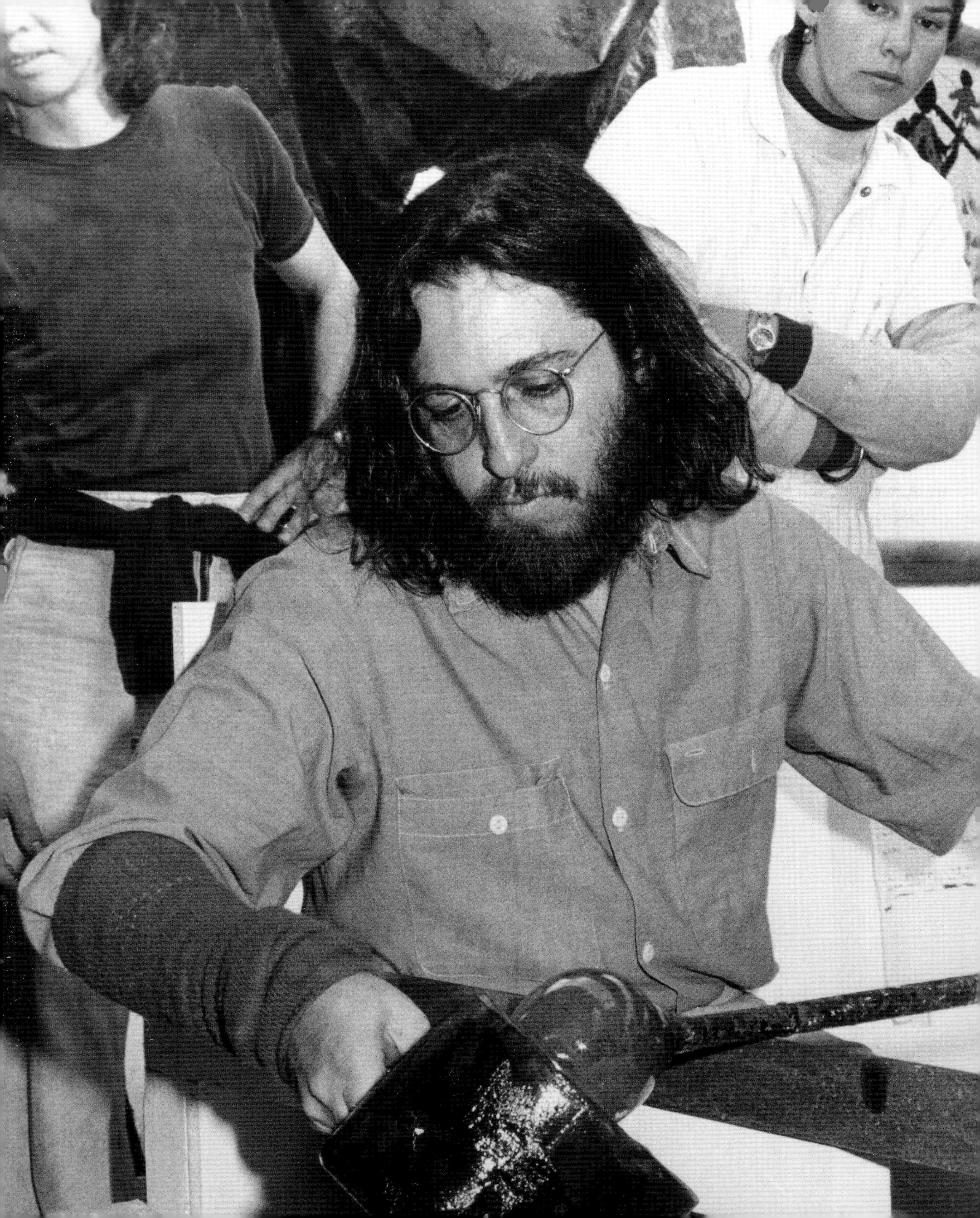

The Educator
Greg Votolato

During the 1960s and 1970s, unlike so much else in culture and society in those turbulent decades, British higher education in the field of art and design was robust. Diploma and degree courses at undergraduate and postgraduate levels were, for those students talented and lucky enough to be admitted, well funded and well accommodated. Students were taught by practising artists and the schools in which they were housed enjoyed the support of local industries. The latter could be a mixed blessing, however, when the conservative objectives of manufacturers came into conflict with the increasingly experimental nature of much art and design practice in the explosive climate of intellectual and aesthetic change at the time, sparked by political unrest on both sides of the Atlantic, economic prosperity, rapidly advancing technologies, new materials and a youthful demographic bulge. From today's perspective of unlimited growth and corporatisation, however, t was a good time to study art in the UK.

In the midst of such large forces, equally radical developments were underway in the tiny world of glass design and production, beginning at the University of Wisconsin in the USA. There, Herman was among the first generation of students to work directly with molten glass using small new tank furnaces developed by Harvey Littleton and Dominick 'Nick' Labino. This technology enabled artists to work in creative directions outside the commercial constraints of the glass industry. Recognising the potential in this new approach to enable students to broaden the expressive qualities of modern glass, David Queensberry, Professor of Ceramics at London's Royal College of Art (RCA), appointed Herman to achieve that aim by transforming the RCA's Industrial Glass Programme into a new and experimental Glass Department. And so, with Herman, the American Studio Glass Movement entered British art education.

Glass students at the RCA had previously worked in the manner of industrial designers, producing design drawings, which were then executed in clear lead glass by the school's expert technician, Bill Heaton, using an industrial furnace. Once equipped with small tank furnaces, and with Fred Daden assisting Herman as a demonstrator, students began to master the difficult skill of glass-blowing, learning by watching and doing, through trial and error. For the first time, they could introduce colour more freely and experiment with forms.

Clifford Rainey (b.1948), Herman's student from 1971 to 1973, explained that Sam ran a tight ship at the College:

He had high expectations and demanded serious
commitment. Sam practised tough love. He could
be absolutely charming until your artistic efforts
did not rise to a level for serious critique. Then you
experienced his darker side. The critiques could
be cutting and gut-wrenching but honest and well-
considered because he always had your best interest
at heart. In the studio he expected conceptual rigour,
technical expertise and material investigation. He
would teach by example demonstrating the ability to
think ideas through with the process of making. I would
be in awe, watching him at the bench balancing large
gobs of molten glass on a blow pipe, adding colours
and minerals, not unlike how an abstract expressionist
would, then working the mass to give it a sculptural
form. It was inspirational. He taught us creativity
that embraced open-mindedness, experimentation,
risk-taking and innovation. His approach allowed his
students the time, space and intellectual freedom to
develop unique, knowledgeable, individual voices.[54]

This apparently relaxed, American-type attitude to
learning in the creative arts masked an underlying control
and resolve under Herman's leadership. Students of the
period cite the free approach Herman took in encouraging
them to develop their work by taking risks and making
mistakes, finding their own way to a personal strategy
through rigorous self-examination and questioning. Peter
Aldridge (b.1947), a student between 1968 and 1969, recalled
that Herman 'did not judge or criticise . . . but there was
an atmosphere created where one ended up rigorously
questioning one's own motives. There were no rules, we were
buoyed along in an atmosphere of inquisitive enthusiasm
and hard work. We came up with our own techniques and
processes and that is my personal debt to Sam.'

Afterall, this was postgraduate education at the
premier art school in the country and mediocrity was not
tolerated. Yet the same high standards, appropriate to
the level, were also essential to Herman's approach to his
teaching on undergraduate art and design courses in such
places as Stourbridge (West Midlands), where he was a
visiting tutor, and High Wycombe (Buckinghamshire), where
I met and worked with him in the 1980s when he headed the
Glass and Ceramics Programme. These standards were also
applied when teaching and demonstrating to students and

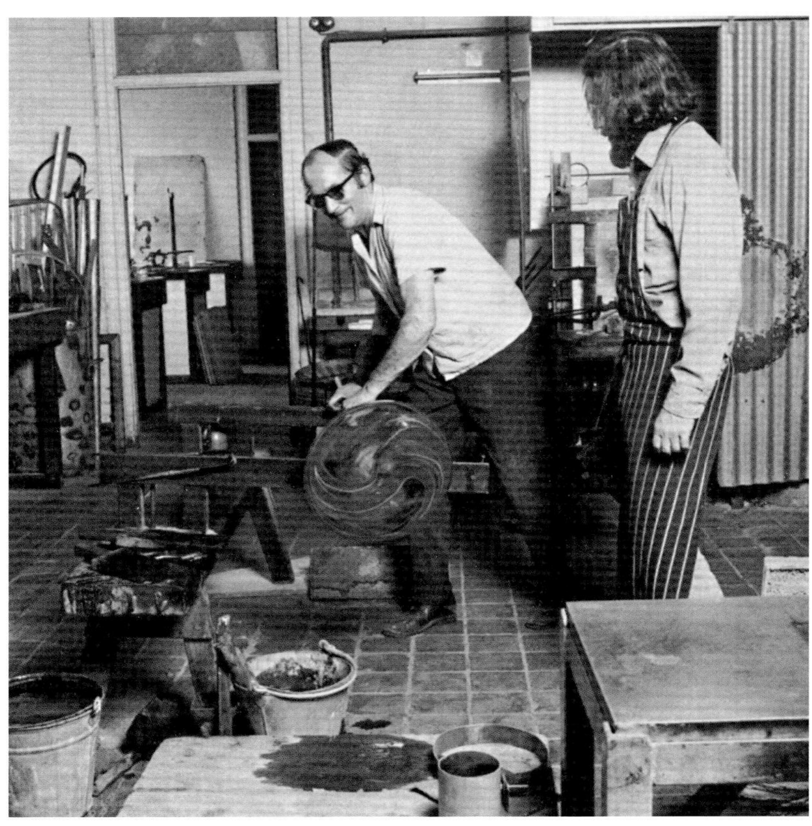

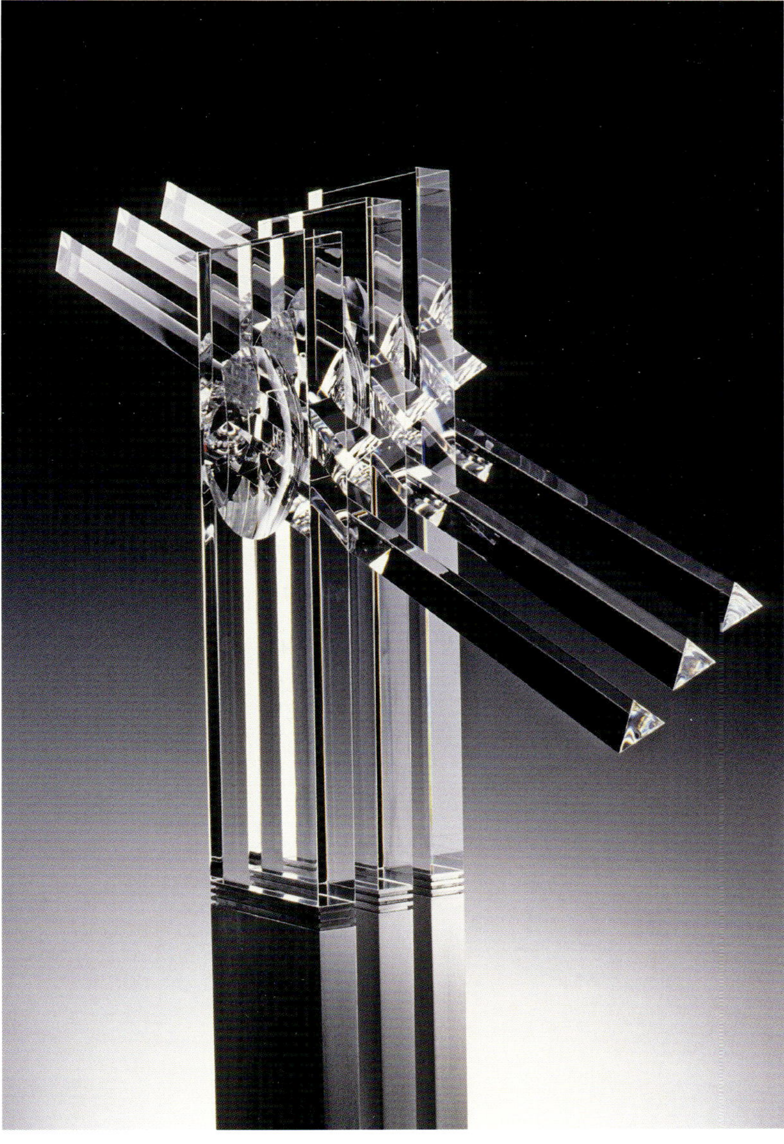

Below

Peter Aldridge, detail of glass sculpture *Echoe*, **1988, 195cm (76¾in), cast in Steuben crystal, precision ground, cut and polished.**

apprentices in Australia during his time in charge of the glass studio at The Jam Factory in Adelaide.

In those bygone days, student numbers in material-based courses were small, allowing for a relatively loose interpretation of 'curriculum', with demonstrations, individual tutorials, group critiques and assessment exhibitions the primary methods of teaching and of examining learning and achievement. Herman's teaching was appropriately tailored to individuals and their particular talents and ambitions. Their aims ranged from working as designers for industry to conceiving and making their work in studios or small factories. As a result, particular importance was placed on demonstrations by Herman and his glass technician to show each student what he or she needed to know in order to achieve their specific objectives. They also assisted individual students in hands-on exercises using the material and techniques of glass forming.

Some students emulated Herman's personal aesthetic and technique, reflecting what has always been an important and valued method of learning in art schools and ateliers. But Herman encouraged his students to search for their own direction. As Peter Aldridge discovered,

It turned out I was not a glass blower . . . I was attracted to the optical properties of glass. With Sam's encouragement, I built a furnace to cast glass. I flourished in this newly found freedom to innovate . . . Sam encouraged the vision and confidence in me to go my own way in total contrast to his own path. For that I will always be grateful.[55]

One of Herman's more unusual teaching methods was particularly suited to those students who wanted to pursue careers designing for industry. For all glass designers, Herman emphasised the importance of understanding the ways in which vessels were used and the feel of using them. To do this, he blindfolded students and held handling sessions to test the feel of various vessels (full or empty) and to promote a haptic understanding of weight, balance and form in relation to the human hand. A further objective of this exercise was to appreciate that designing a functional object was as much about the experience of using it as about its appearance or style.

Preparing students for the world of professional practice beyond their academic degree has always been a problem on creative courses in which students are deeply involved in the immediate task of mastering materials and techniques. The artificiality and apparent disconnectedness of many professional practice elements of studio courses remain an issue for teachers and students alike. Such a syllabus, involving balance sheets and formal letter writing, often seems at odds with the imaginative and physical activities at the heart of such an education. Understanding this, Herman found a better way, asking students to consider what they wanted to do professionally, where they wanted to work, how much they aimed to earn. He wanted to communicate a sense of realism regarding the costs of establishing independent studios and workshops, how they could sell their work and what the marketing of their work entailed. Of course, this was more achievable when student numbers were small and studio staff and students knew each other well.

In addition to this personal and intuitive approach to professionalism, Herman established The Glasshouse in Covent Garden as a testbed for the transition from education to practice. A graduate from one of Herman's early cohorts of RCA students, Pauline Solven, remembers her excitement when Sam offered her the job of assisting him in setting up The Glasshouse and managing it:

> The novelty of glassblowing in central London resulted in plenty of press and TV coverage . . . The public, drawn in by the action, became enthusiastic about the new art form, inspiring some to become glass collectors – and great for us young blowers to see our work selling so well. The pieces were as varied as their artistic makers – mine, inspired by natural forms, were organic and colourful. I looked forward to the students coming for their work sessions, making for a lively atmosphere . . . My duties included seeing to the furnace, producing a quota of blown pieces every week, display, dealing with the public, and selling – challenging to say the least![56]

Pauline Solven, three-cornered bowl, free-blown glass, 1992, 18cm (7in)

Clifford Rainey, *Shy Boy*, from Boyhood series, 2005, glass pigment, gold leafed bottle, 106.5cm (42in)

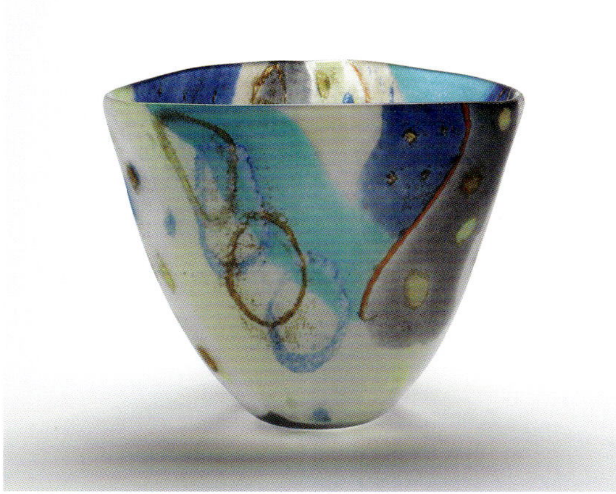

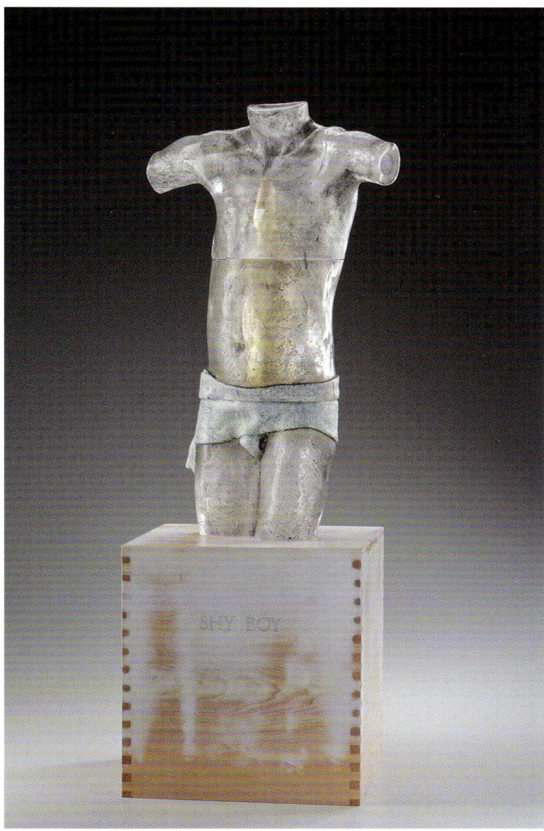

It would be difficult to imagine a more useful challenge for a freshly minted art graduate crossing over into the professional world. And so, Herman's approach to instilling the principles, responsibilities and opportunities of professional practice were as organic to the study of art as his methods of imparting aesthetics or material techniques to his students.

Many of Herman's early students went on to achieve international recognition for their work in glass. Peter Aldridge, Clifford Rainey and Jane Bruce went to the USA to very successfully pursue their art on the East and West coasts. Pauline Solven, Dillon Clarke (b.1946), Steven Newell and Annette Meech all had successful studios in the UK. Åsa Brandt (b.1950) returned to Sweden, Jiří Šuhájek and Ivan Kolman (b.1944) to the Czech Republic and Yoshio Hamada (1944–2011) to Japan, where they all continued to develop, flourish and spread the word of the Studio Glass Movement.

Above all, Herman has been an inspirational force through his teaching, redefining the medium of glass and encouraging a generation of students to push the boundaries of the medium in new directions and to spread the aims of studio glass around the world. The experience he offered those students by his example is well summed up by Peter Aldridge, who remembers, 'Sam, always smiling, twirling his blowpipe, running out seemingly impossible forms, picking up glass canes and rolling in oxides of every colour in a flurry of activity only brought to an abrupt end as the lehr door closed. Oh . . . then we all cheered!'[57]

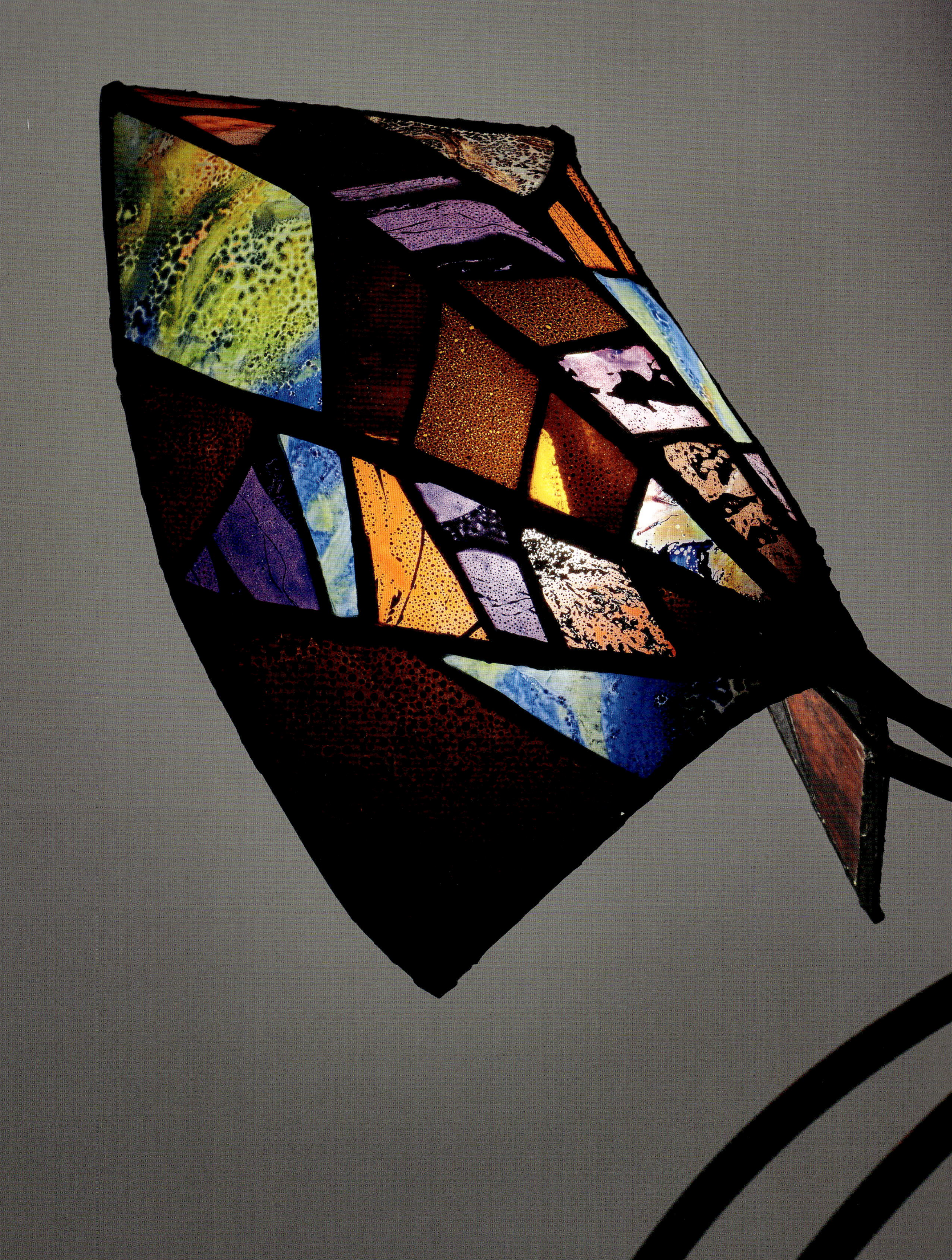

The Sculptor and Painter

Michael Regan

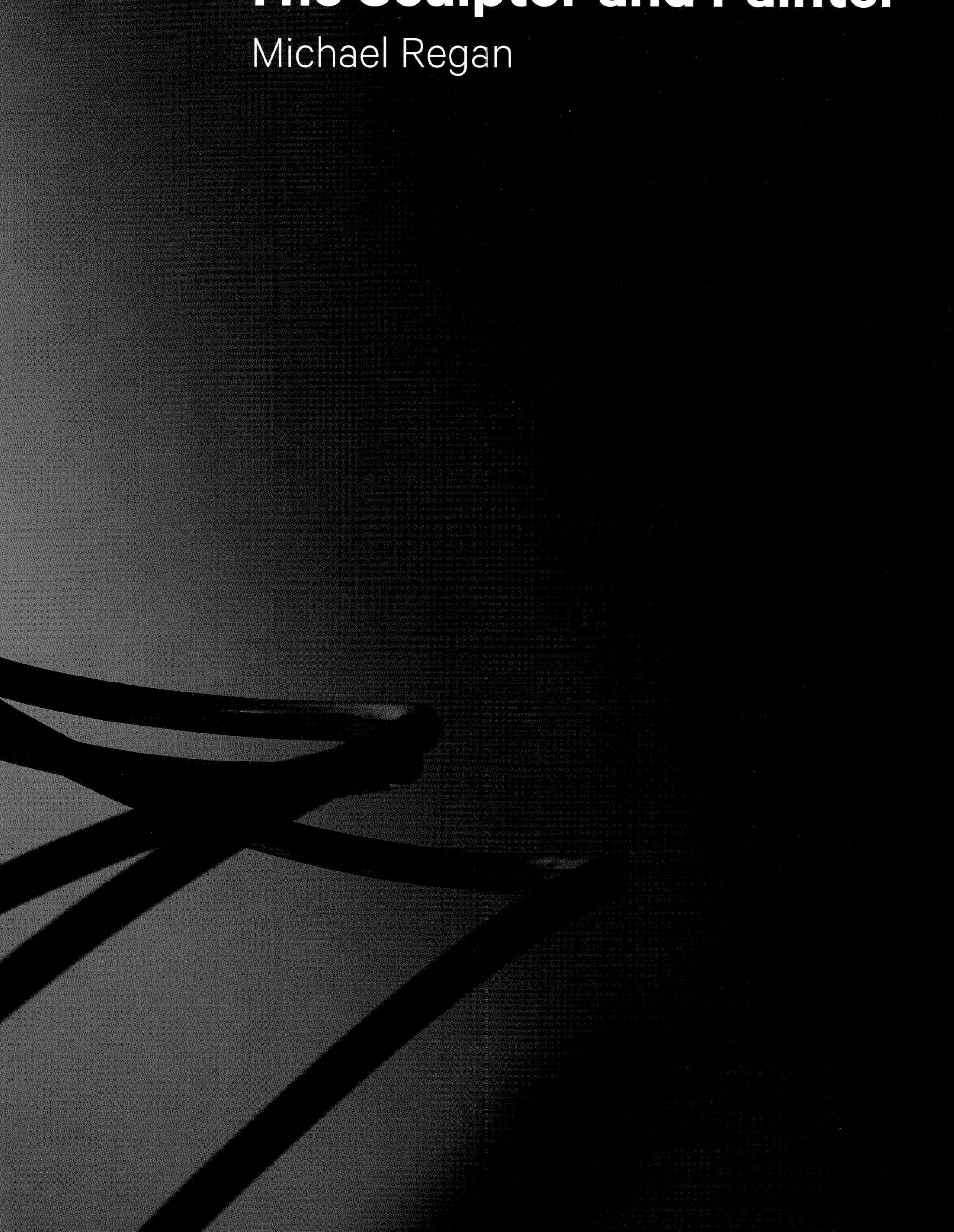

It is perhaps inevitable that any study of Sam Herman's creative oeuvre raises the question of how to categorise his work: is it that of a painter, sculptor, metalsmith or glass artist? These disciplines all feature in his output but none solely describes his total activity. In this sense, Herman belongs to an earlier generation, before the separation took place between the arts and crafts. Nowadays, few can handle all of these differing activities, but this prolific man does so in an individualistic and provocative manner. Herman's spontaneity does not allow him to stay put in any of our indexed cataloguing. Is he a sculptor – a craftsman – or what?

In the early 1960s, while studying for a BA in Anthropology and Sociology at Western Washington State College in Bellingham, Herman also took up art classes at the college on a part-time basis. The period spent at Bellingham thus gave him the opportunity to come to grips with artistic ideas that were taking shape in his mind. His interest in art and his particular interest in materials and techniques developed to such an extent that, on completing his undergraduate studies at Bellingham in 1965, Herman decided to undertake a Master of Fine Arts at the University of Wisconsin in Madison, under the tutelage of Leo Steppat

who also ran the sculpture course there. Steppat had fled Nazi persecution in Austria and had made a new home for himself in the USA, taking up various teaching positions, including this, his last appointment, at Wisconsin. Herman's brush with Steppat was unfortunately brief, but it was significant enough to have a lasting impression on the young artist. Steppat, a sculptor in his own right, was one of the first artists in the USA to sculpt welded metal, and he introduced Herman to the technique. Welding had been used extensively in industry since the 1800s, but it was only following the advances in technique and equipment in the 1940s and 1950s that it became a viable and economical option for sculptors.

Steppat also exposed Herman to the post-war brutalist sculptors and painters and to the kitchen sink realists.[58] Herman became aware of the work of a younger generation of British sculptors who had burst on to an international stage, including Reg Butler (1913–81), Lynn Chadwick (1914–2003), Kenneth Armitage (1916–2002) and Geoffrey Clarke (1924–2014). Their work was stylistically summed up in the often-quoted phrase by the British art critic Herbert Read (1893–1968) as the 'Geometry of Fear'.[59] Another young Scottish sculptor admired by Herman was Eduardo Paolozzi

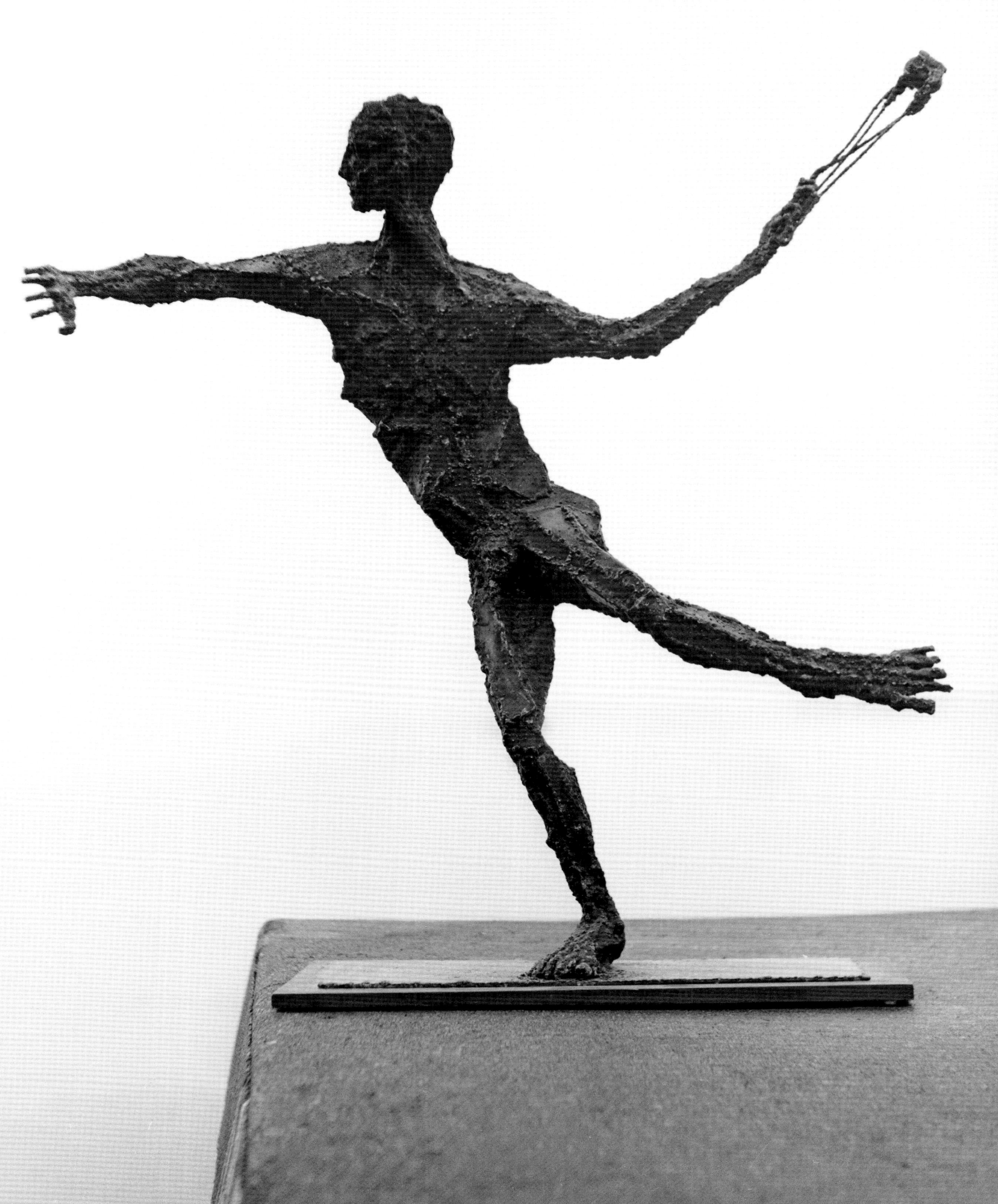

(1924–2005), one of the pioneers of pop art, who had found an effective way of escaping the constraints of traditional sculptural methods by working in concrete. Herman also developed a deep appreciation of the work of Henry Moore (1898–1986) and his belief in 'truth to materials',[60] solid organic forms and monumentality. And in Italy he was attracted by the taut neo-primitivism of Marino Marini's figurative equestrian sculptures and circus figures. Nearer to home, Herman was fascinated by the work of American sculptor David Smith (1906–65) who often incorporated 'found objects' into his large-scale abstract, geometric sculptures. At Wisconsin, Herman first became exposed to the worlds of art history and aesthetics, and this wider access to works of art was also instrumental.

Steppat, Moore and the younger generation of British artists exerted a strong influence on Herman's formative years at Wisconsin as he began quickly to establish a visual language of his own. The ability of these artists to successfully combine semi-abstract or semi-figurative elements in the same moment in a single piece was adopted by Herman in the series of confident, large table pieces he produced between 1963 and 1965. He adopted Steppat's technique of working in welded metal, which allowed him to sketch an outline in space and rapidly build up a three-dimensional form of substantial scale from scrap or cheap materials without the labour-intensive and time-

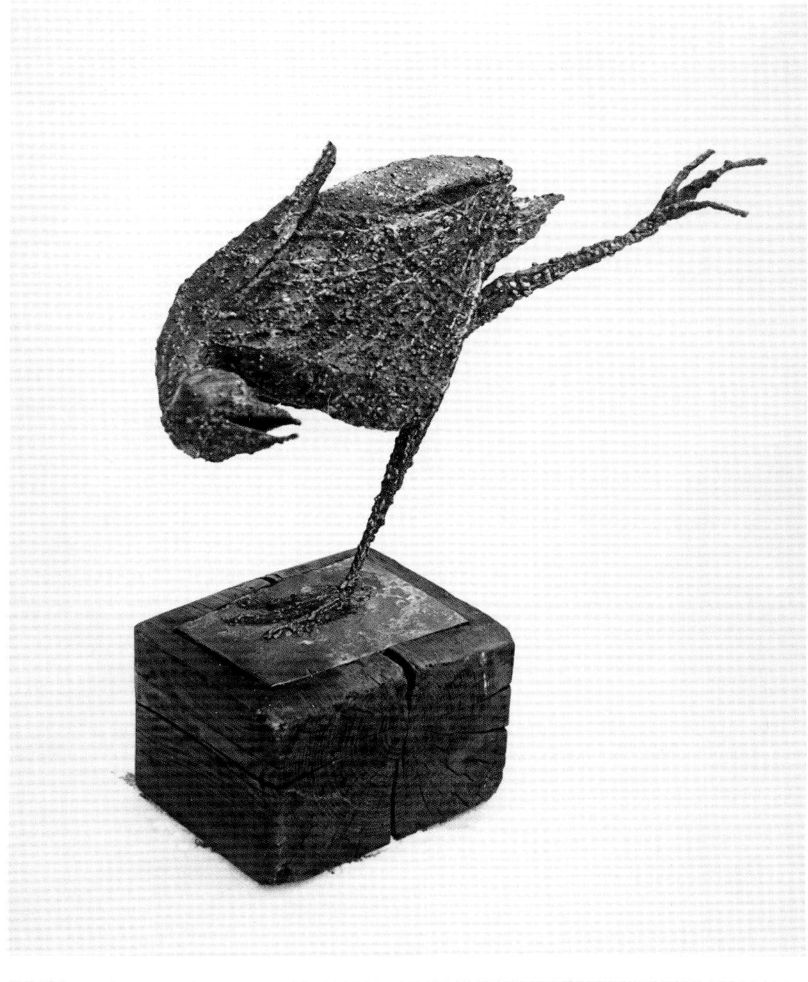

Above right
Bird, 1963
welded steel, 55cm (21¾in),
Private Collection

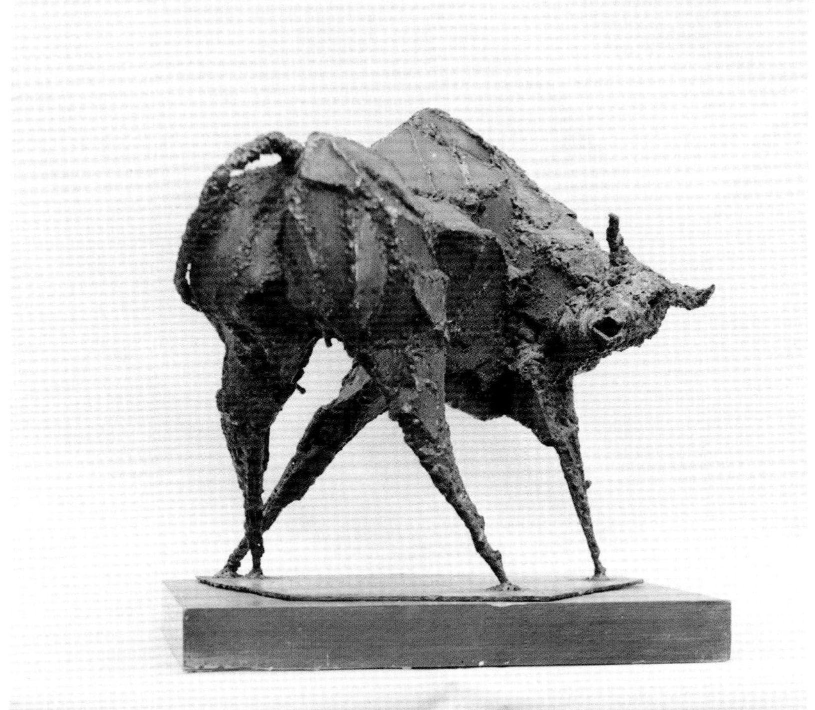

Right
Bull, 1964
welded steel, 38cm (15in),
Private Collection

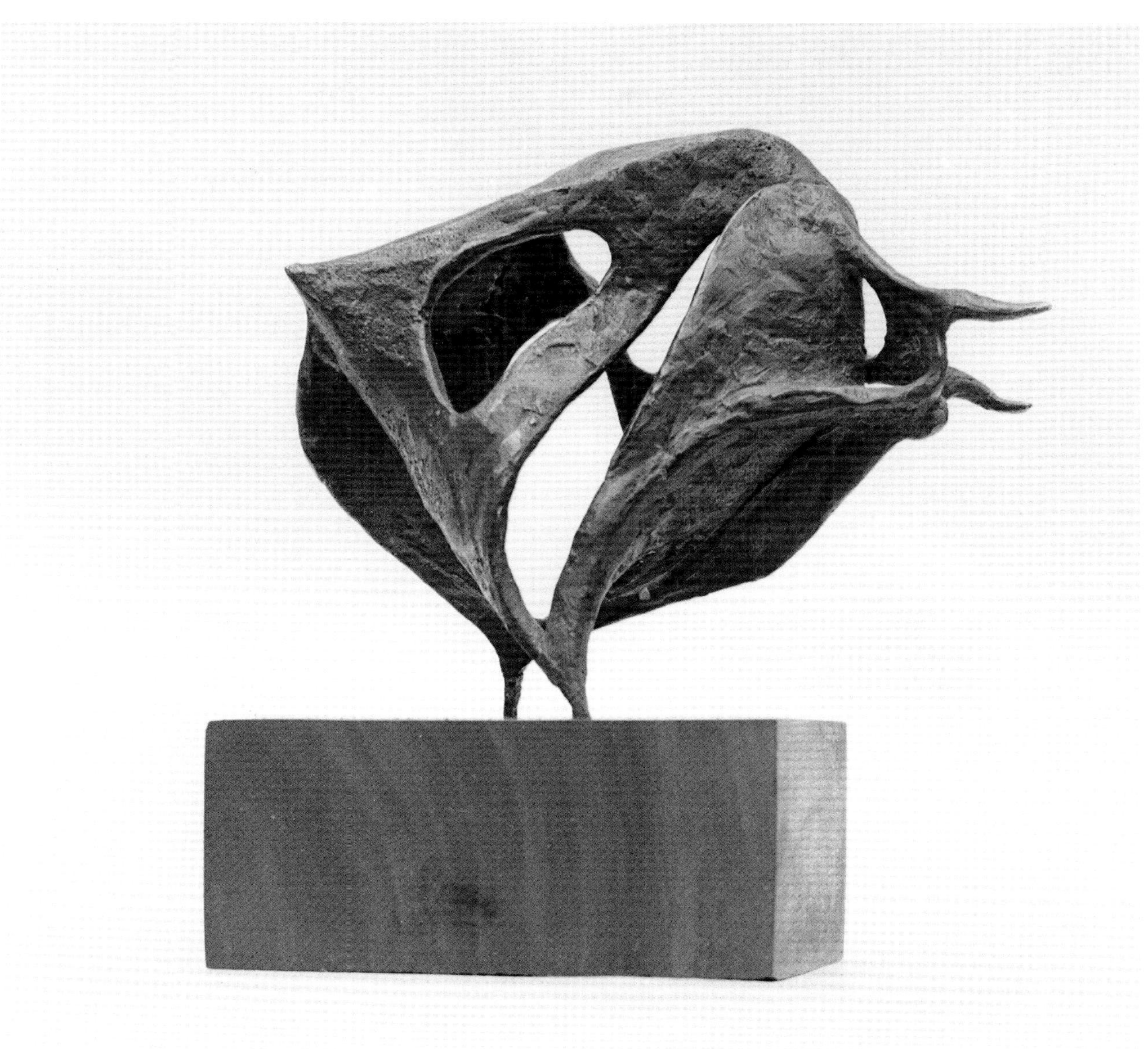

consuming process of carving or casting. It also meant that he maintained sole control. Herman created brutal surface textures, giving a spiky, jagged appearance to the sculptures he created in the mid 1960s, which were of semi-figurative animal or human forms, with titles such as *Bird*, *Cat*, *Bull* and *David*. Like many of his contemporaries working in sculpture, he chose the animal world as a metaphor for the inherent vulnerability of the human condition – stripped of cultural overlay and pretence. Later, he derived the imagery for his sculptures from a combination of his imagination and observed sources.

Herman also arrived at independent solutions for modelling, construction, welding and forging, using found objects and waste materials to create new forms. He imposed no boundaries in terms of materials and techniques, and he was attracted to the creative processes developed by Harvey Littleton, Professor of Glass at Wisconsin, who was building the first small furnaces capable of producing blown glass (designed by Dominick 'Nick' Labino). Herman, always willing to take a hands-on approach, volunteered to join a small team to help build the glass furnace and in the process learned how to manipulate

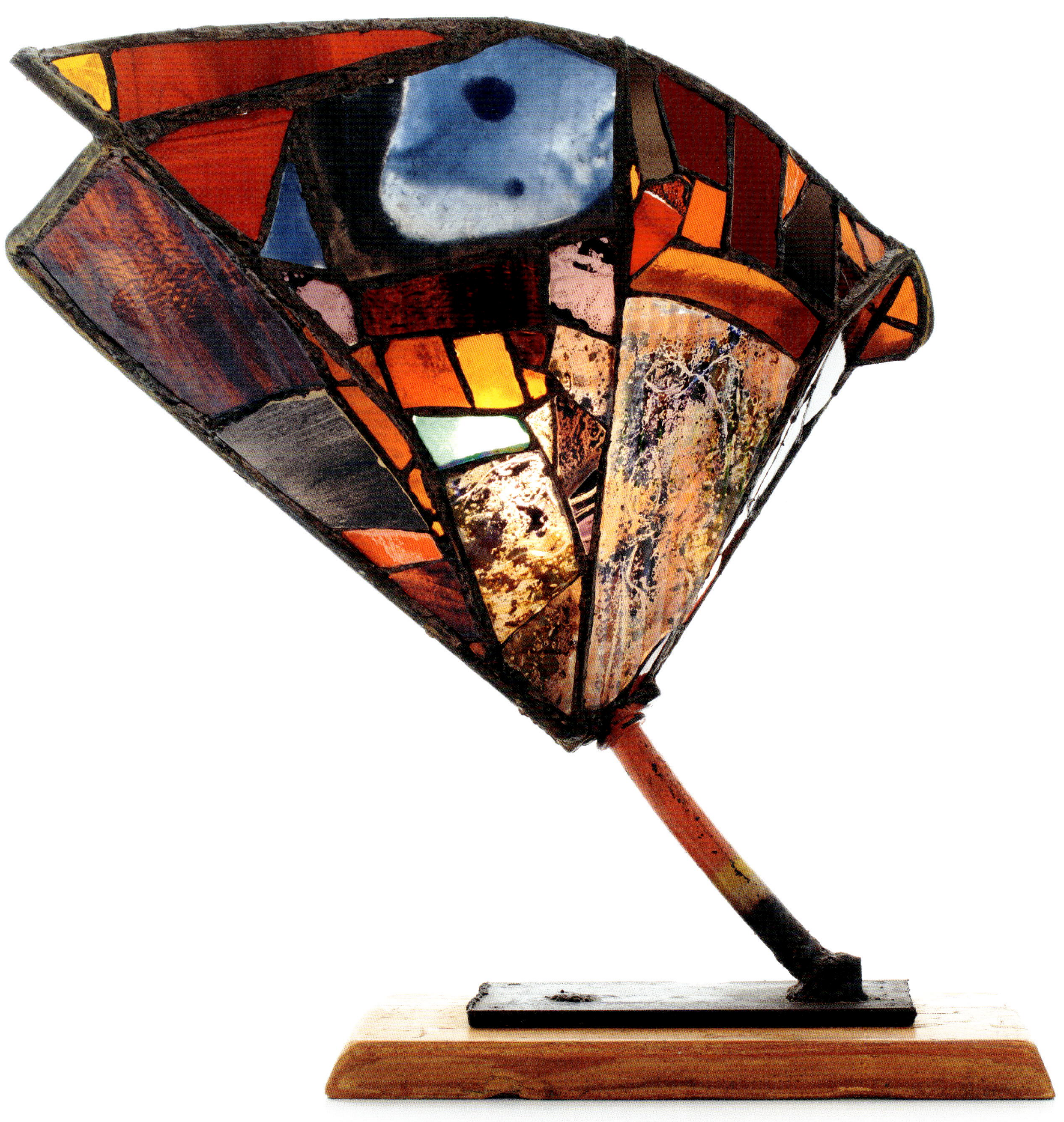

the material. He began to incorporate pieces of glass that he had made into his sculptural works, formed as cullet-like gobbets of glass, as organically misshapen as natural pearls, their surfaces deliberately juxtaposed with the rugged texture of another material. His imagination was sparked by the way in which metal and glass could work together even though one is inherently strong and the other is inherently weak. He turned to modernist architecture for inspiration, looking at buildings that incorporated both materials, fascinated by the way they were used to support a building's inherent structure, both internally and externally.

Herman became ever more involved in developing his skills in creating pieces of blown glass, but his intent was always to work towards making sculptural forms – abstracted human forms – and this intent has always remained the same. If a piece was viewed as 'tableware' (being functional or semi-functional), at its heart it was a sculptural piece, and to Herman its shape represented a human 'torso'. Steppat had encouraged Herman to make sculpture that made you want to walk around it, and he applied exactly the same principles to making a piece of blown glass. Herman is that comparatively rare being, an artist whose conceptual and technical strengths are in perfect balance.

His technical expertise can be seen in his use of light as a raw material, just as he might use metal, ceramic or pigment. His sculptures, made of glass or combining glass elements, are light-receiving objects that concretise light, or make it 'objectively' accessible; he creates energy, an invisible energy. In order to make light entirely visible it is

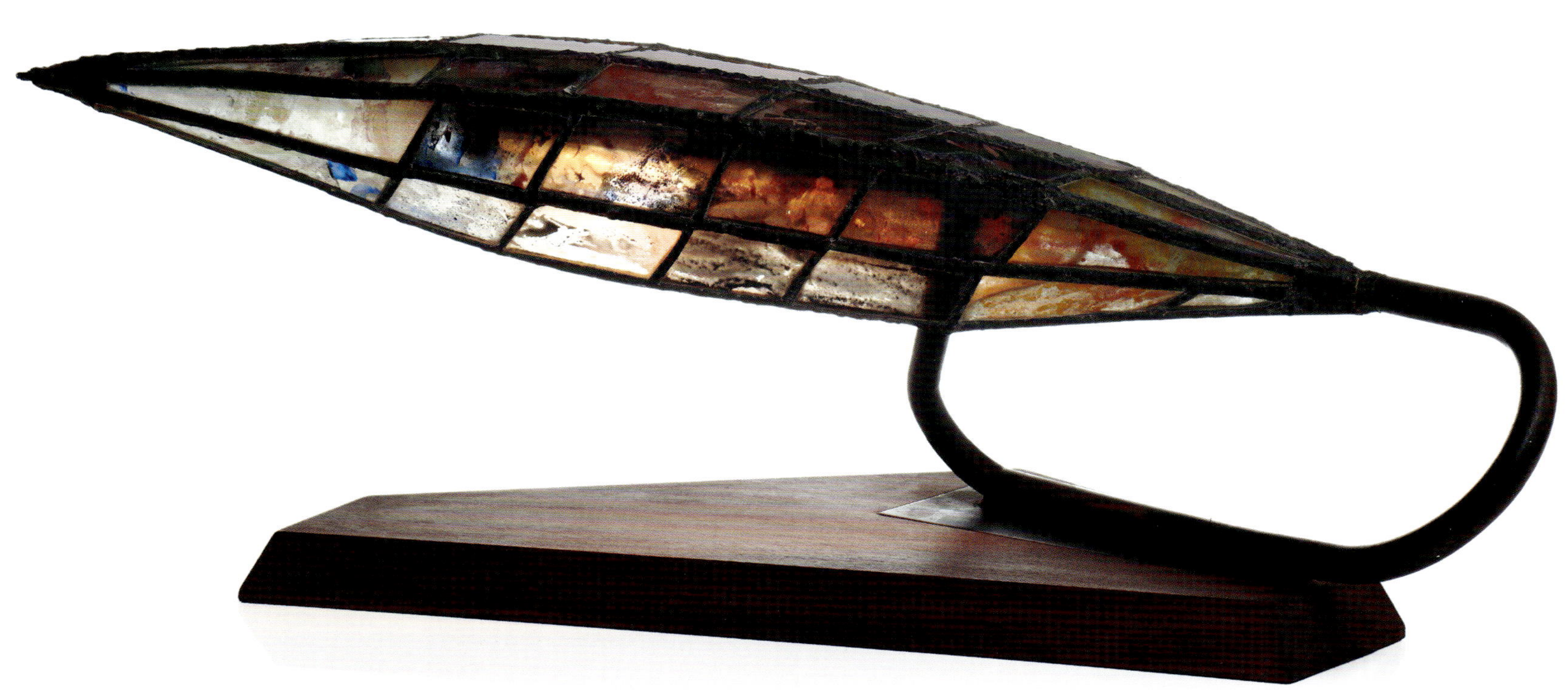

Below
Untitled, 1985
mild steel and glass, 38cm
(15in), Private Collection

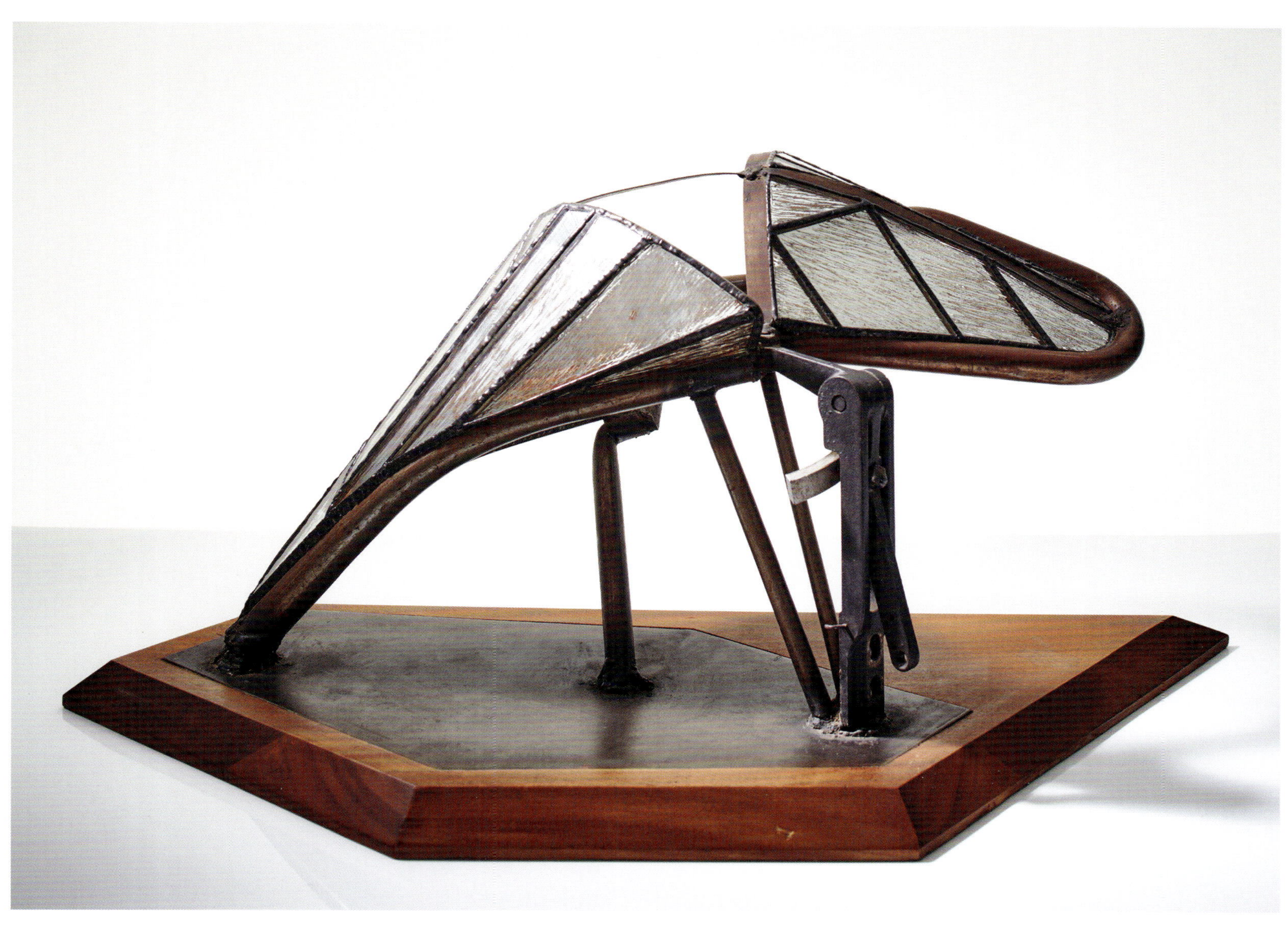

Opposite
Untitled, 1991
mild steel and g ass, 62cm
(24½in), Private Collection

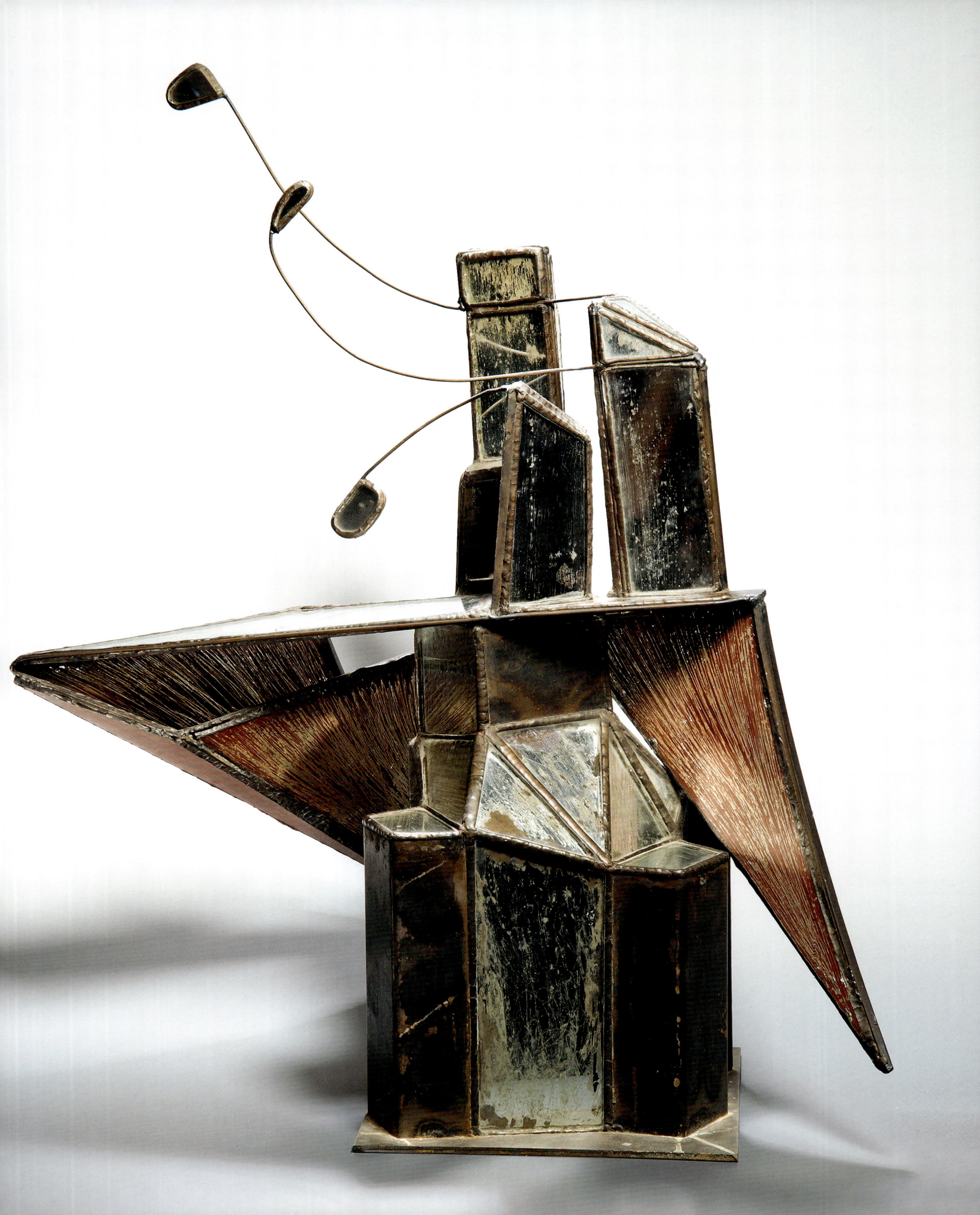

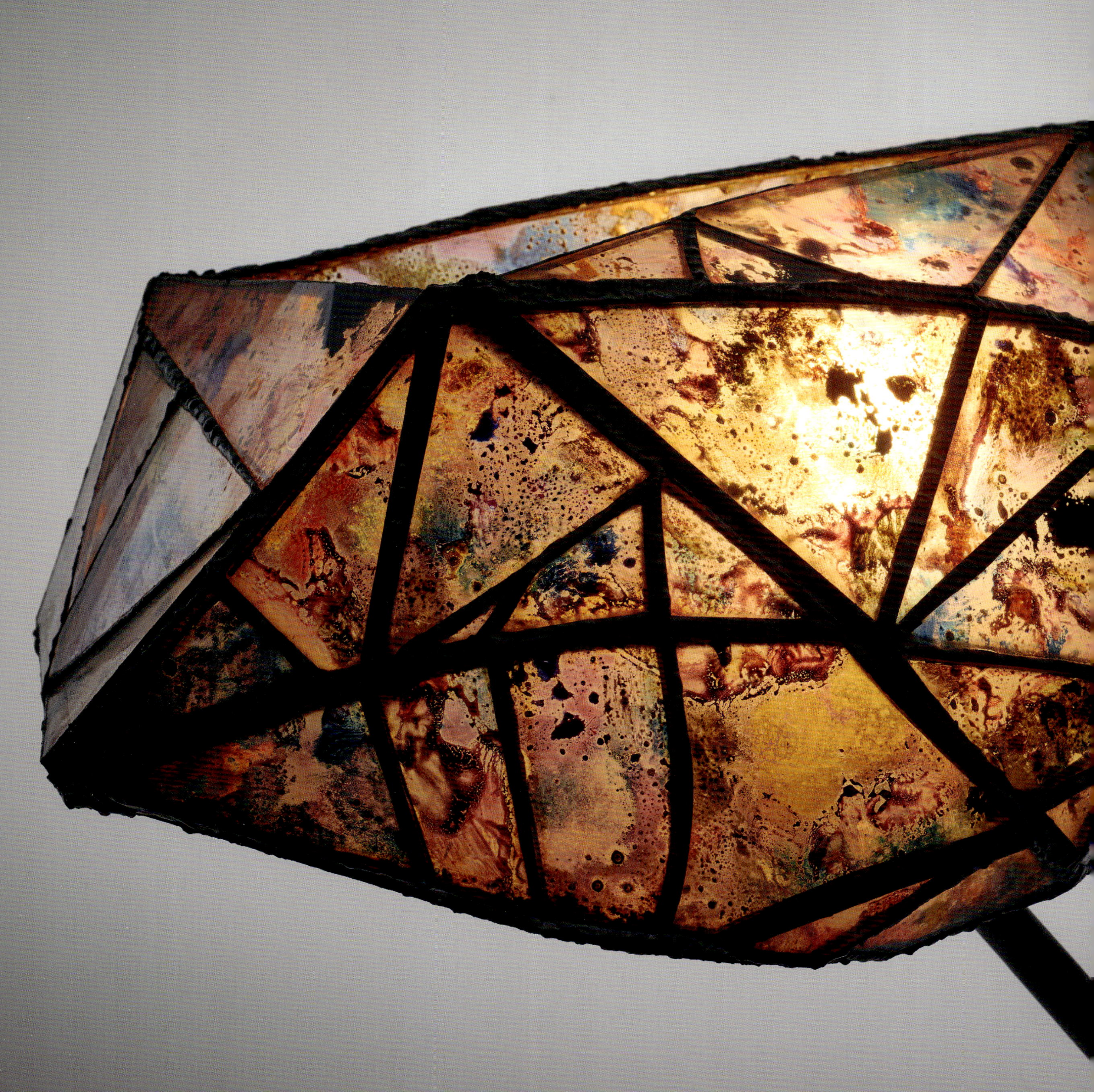

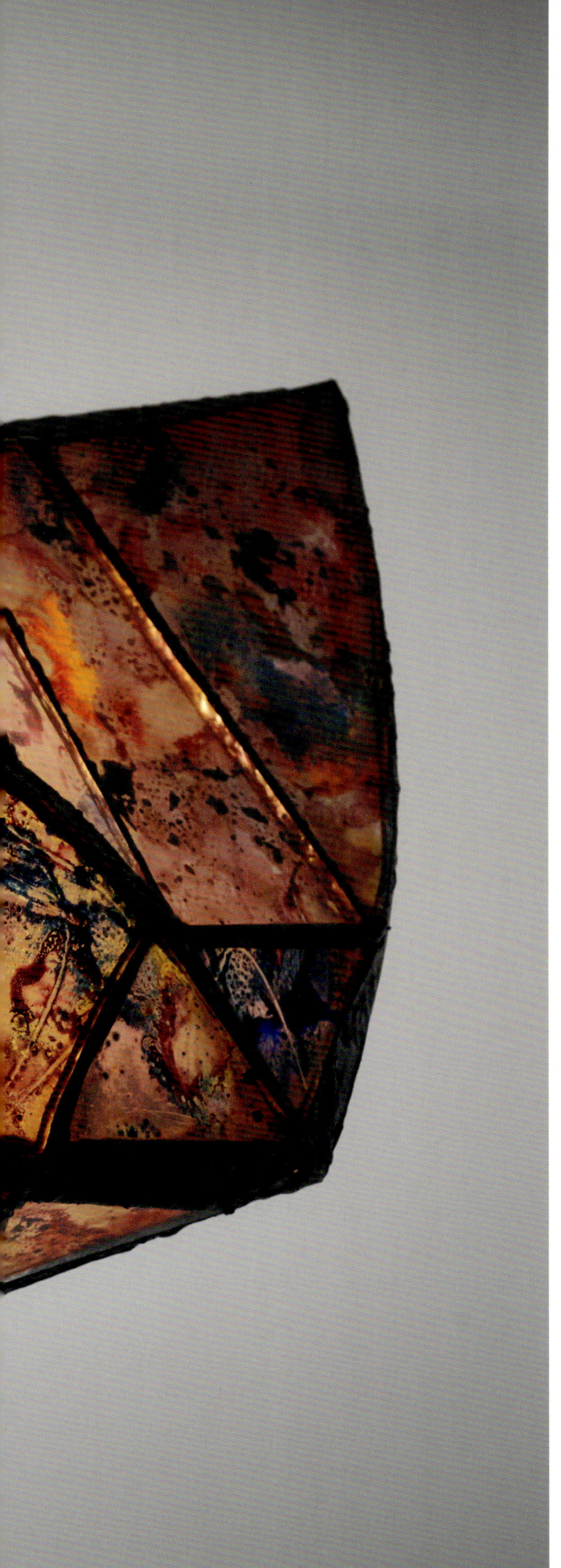

necessary to exploit not only our everyday visual experience of light, but also the realms of physics and the chemistry of glass making. Herman exploits the inherent transparency of glass and its capacity to act as a lens or a mirror, enabling the spectator to discover light as a 'trans-optical' reality.

More recently, Herman has experimented by combining pieces of hand-blown glass, transparent painted, mirrored and inked glass, incorporating these elements into his sculpture. In some instances they are used as fragmented pieces, where jewel-like colours are assembled to form shapes reminiscent of medieval stained glass; in others they are less tightly packed and there is more emphasis on the broader gestural quality of the mark-making of the individual pieces of painted glass. Like some of his more recent bronzes, several of these works sit on specially designed and hand-crafted plinths. For Herman, the plinth itself becomes a way of controlling how the viewer looks at a piece, the element that essentially elevates a sculpture from the space in which the viewer stands.

From the mid-1980s onwards, Herman has experimented with making a series of sculptures that combine pieces of hand-coloured glass with fragments of mirrored glass to create works whose shapes are derived from organic living forms such as mussel shells, flowers, butterflies and dragonflies. In these sculptures, Herman also uses artificial light sources to enhance the colours of the glass pieces, producing luminous, chromatic effects that play with the interception, reflection, transmission and interference of light. The pieces often incorporate incongruous-looking found objects, such as recycled farm implements or old car parts, which also function as supports for the glass elements of the works. They are chosen not because they refer to their previous function but because they simply appeal as shapes.

Untitled, 1987
mild steel and glass, detail,
Private Collection

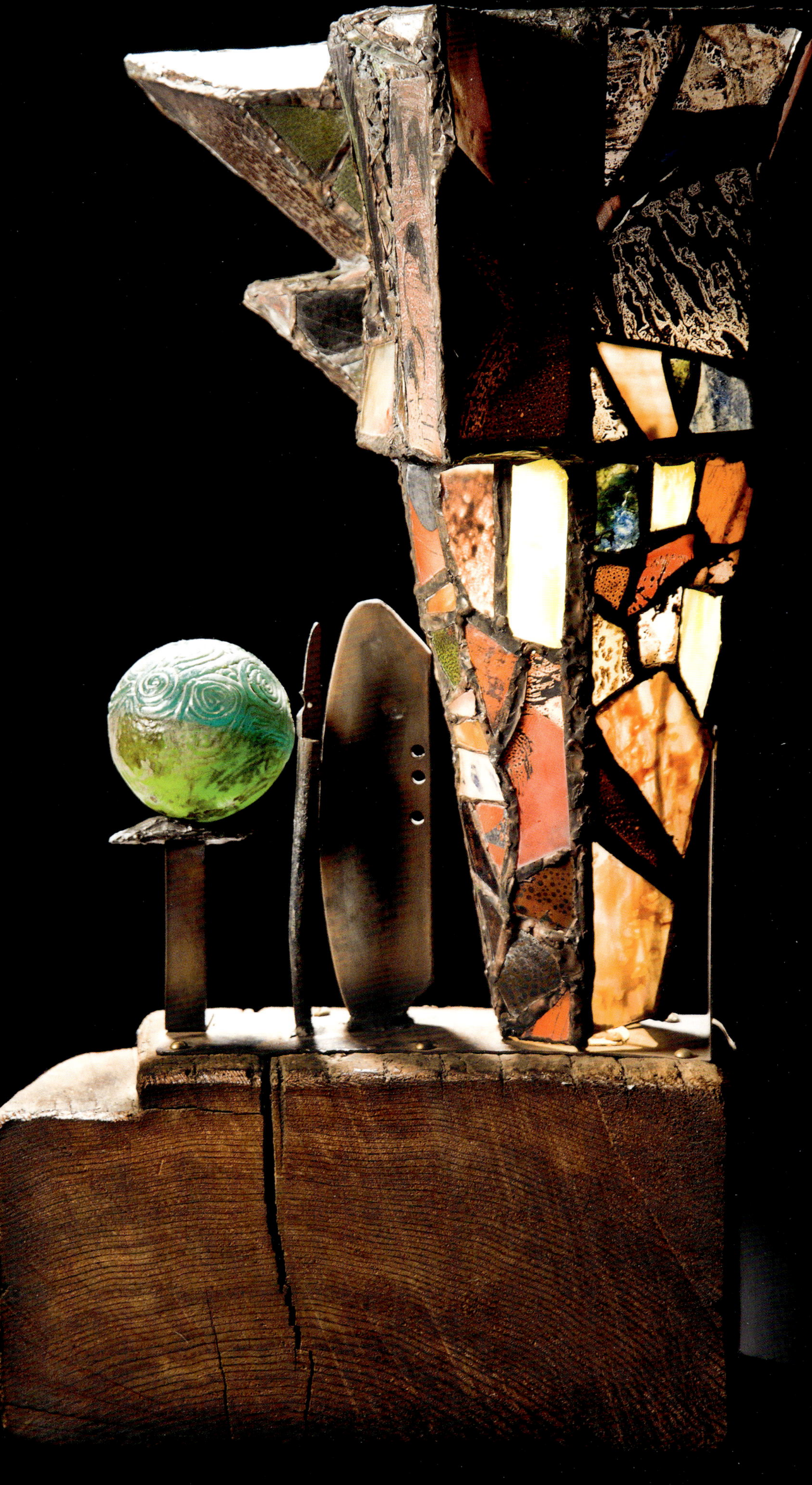

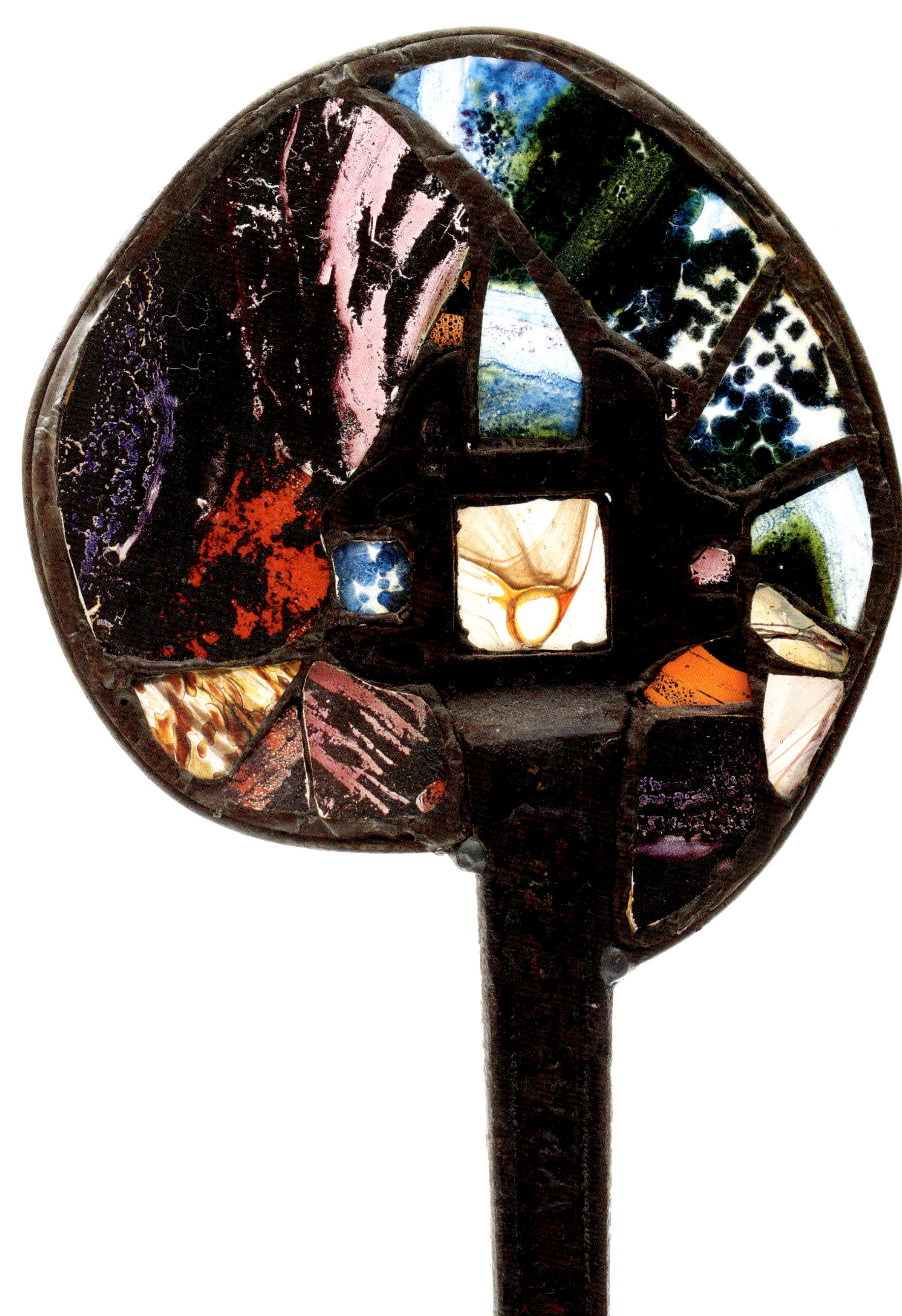

Opposite
Untitled, 1991
mild steel and glass, 57cm
(22½in), Private Collection

Right
Untitled (detail), 2012
mild steel and glass, 74cm
(29in), Private Collection

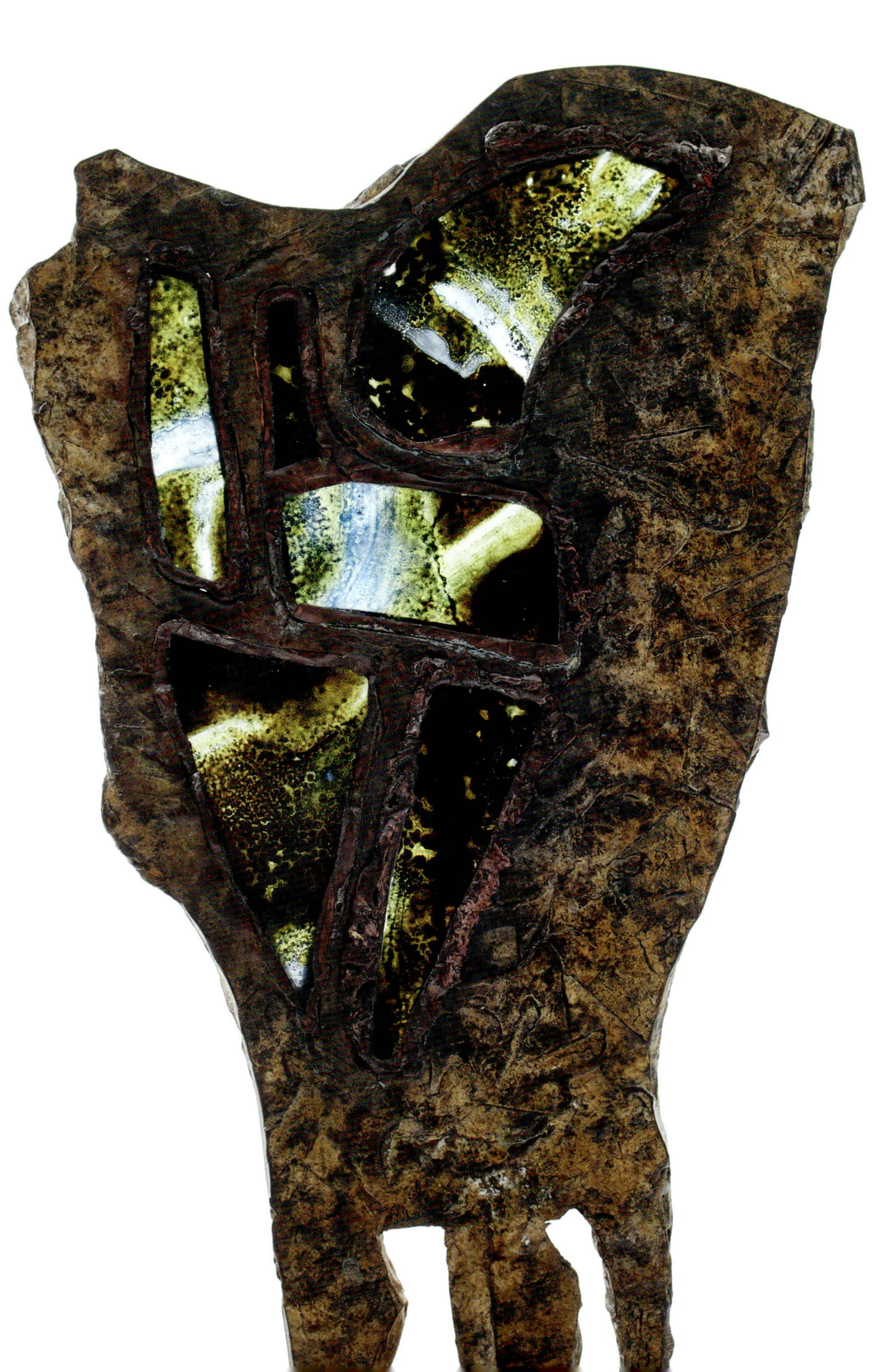

Below
Untitled, 2012
bronze and glass, 31cm
(12in), Private Collection

Opposite
Untitled, 2012
mild steel and glass, 74cm
(29in), Private Collection

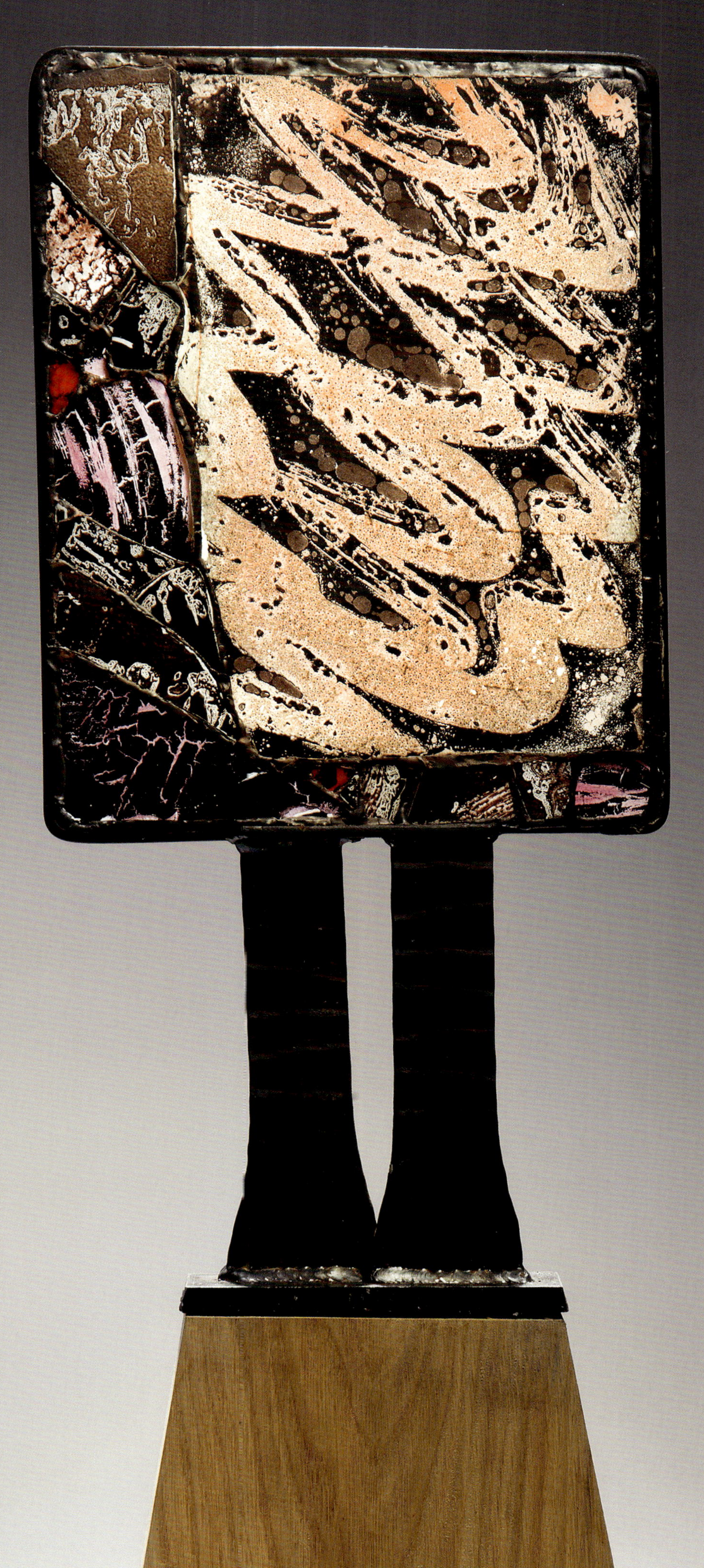

Contemporaneous with these works are smaller cast
bronze sculptures, single or grouped compositions that
are fully active, upright, headless pieces with outstretched
'wings' or arms. Despite the anthropomorphic undertones
of these extended figure fragments, less aggressive than
Herman's earlier non-glass depictions of the human form,
the works contain the living presence and vital animation
sought by the artist. Not only do they signal Herman's
return to using solid volume and conscious allusion to
the human figure, but they also reflect a confidence in the
continuing relevance of sculpture's most enduring themes.

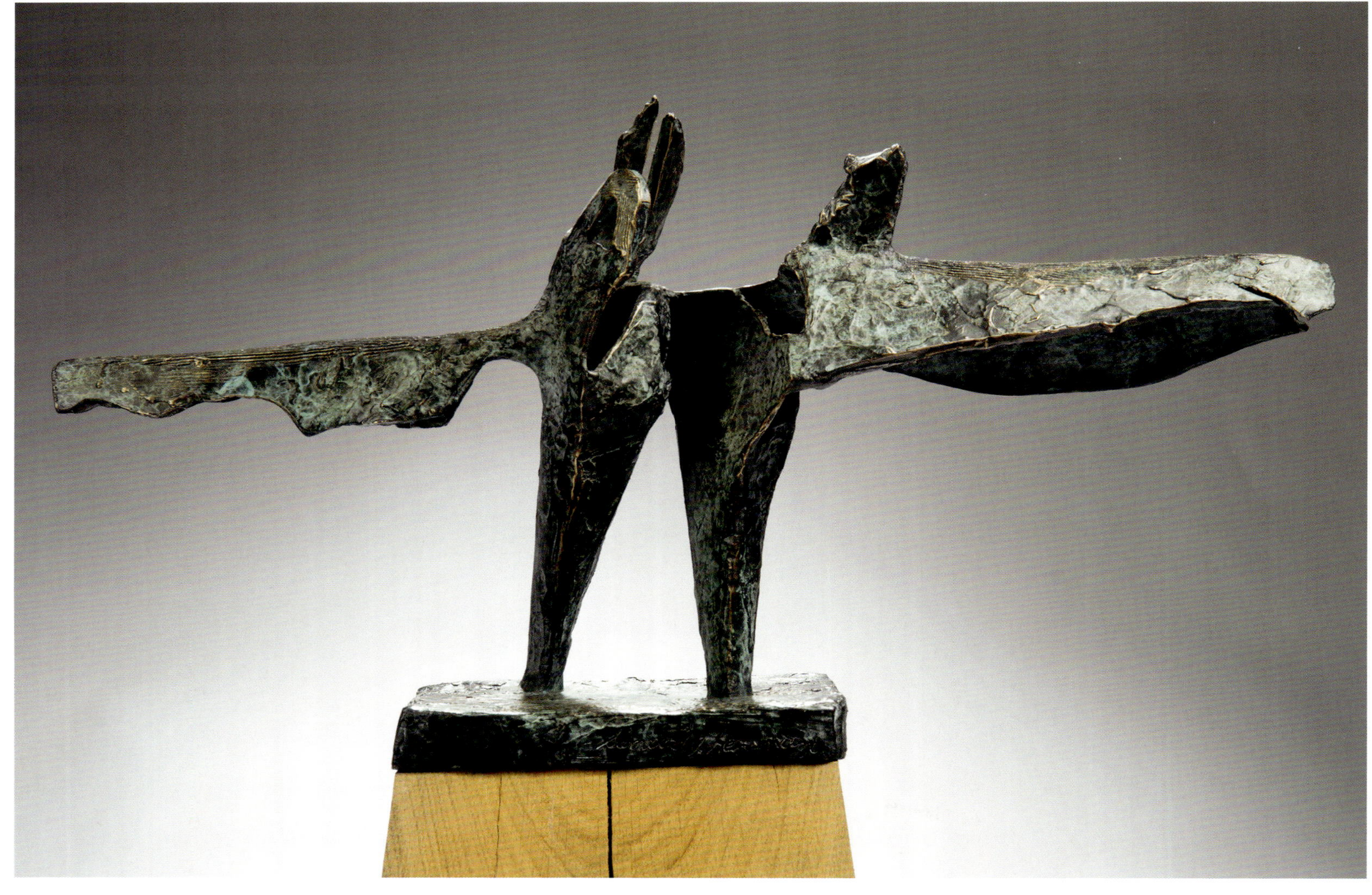

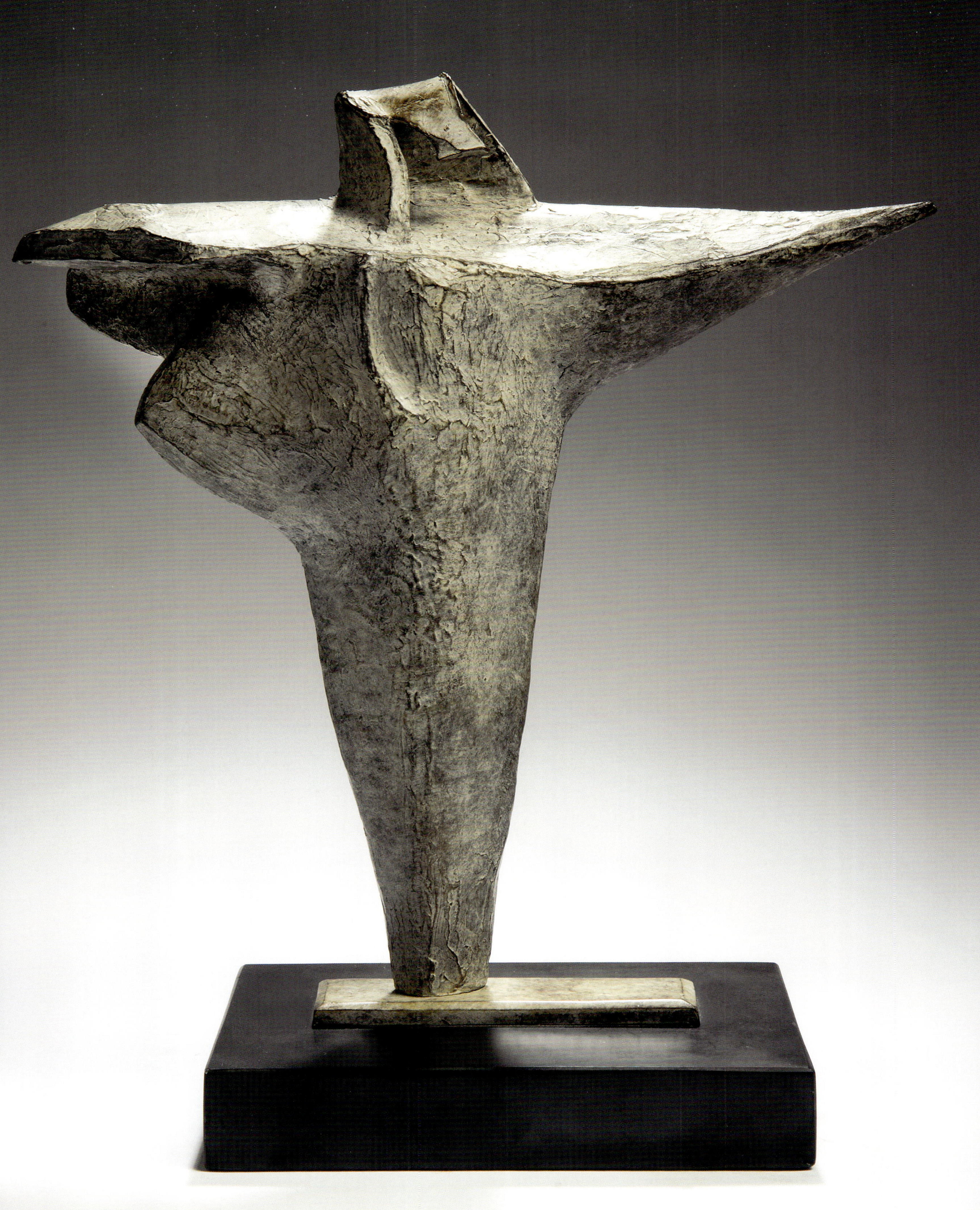

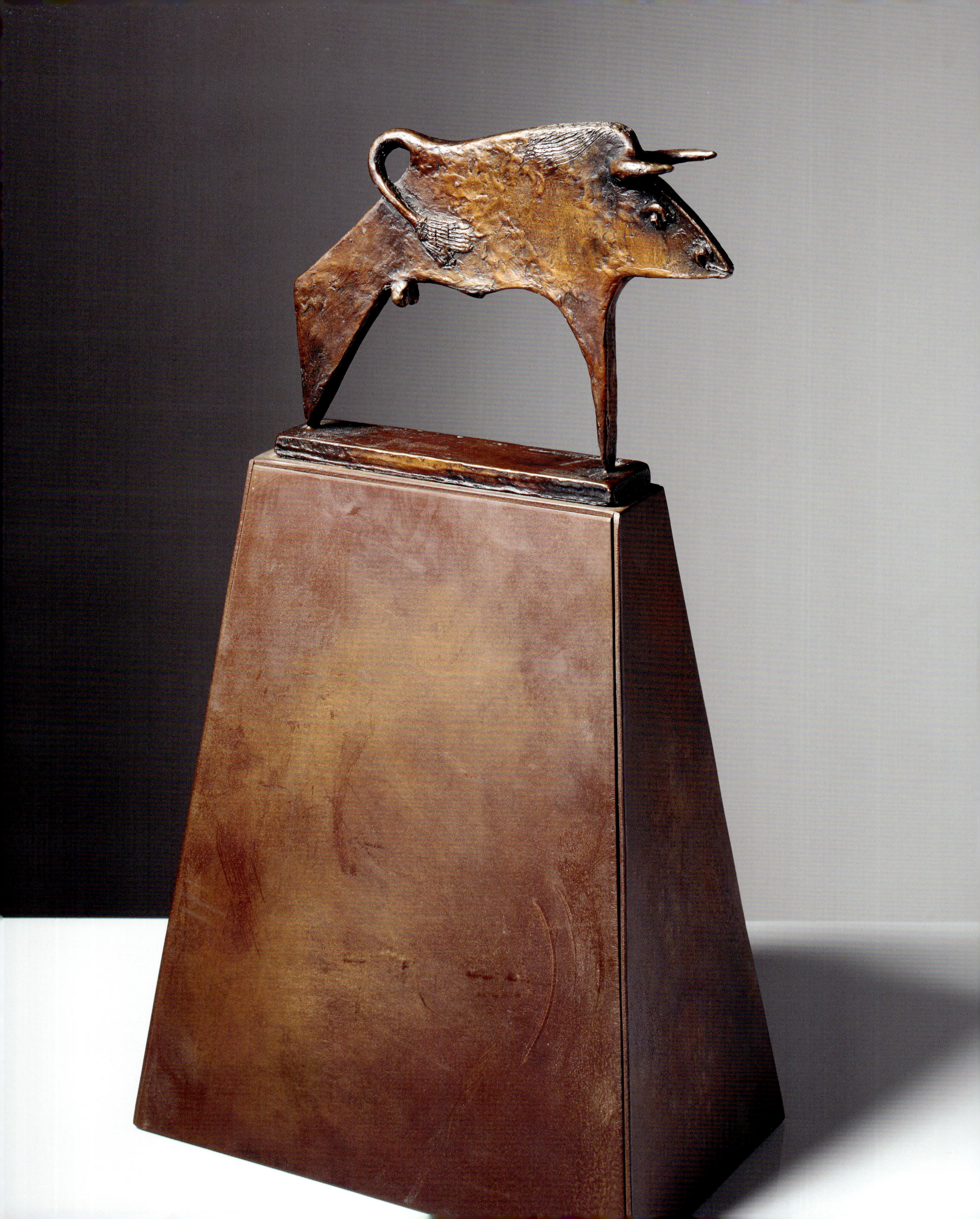

Below
Gossiping Neighbours, 1963
bronze, 6.5cm (2½in),
Private Collection

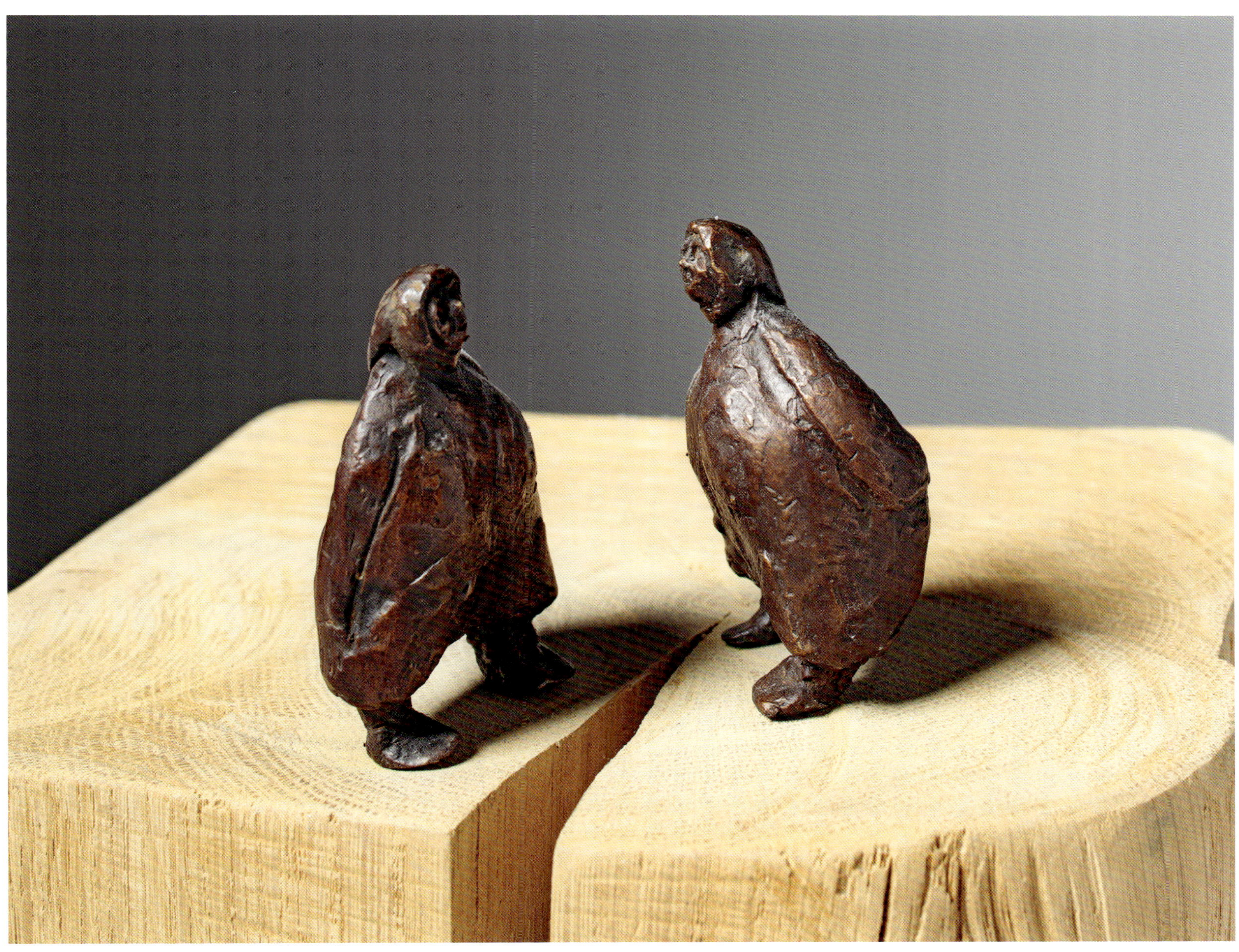

Opposite
Bull, 2013
bronze, 25cm (9¾in),
Private Collection

Around 1984, Herman closed his glass studio and
established a much smaller studio in which to work. This
prompted him to take up painting, an interest he had
always held and which had the added attraction of being
an activity that did not require any special equipment,
such as a glass furnace. He also saw painting as a medium
with the potential to be more controllable. Blown glass has
its own 'gravity' and viscosity, and the physical process
of creating juxtapositions of colour and shape is less
controllable and the final outcome less predictable. Herman
was, and continues to be, attracted by the alchemy that
takes place in the furnace and has often incorporated
the accidental into a final piece. He has always taken a
completely experimental approach to both media and loves
to explore different methods that allow for creative input
and controlled output.

In his painting, Herman began by treating space
in a more recessive manner, with any illusion of space
negated by the use of layered vertical brushstrokes and
scrape marks that emphasised the flat surfaces of the
canvas or board. Spatial ambiguity was elicited through
the use of transparent, or film, colour allowing mysterious
overlaps between variously shaped planes. This technique
was combined with a gradual development of a rich but
weathered and textured surface. He mixed paint with wax,
perhaps in an attempt to stimulate the integration of subject
matter, form and execution. Herman was introduced to
many of these techniques by British painter and printmaker

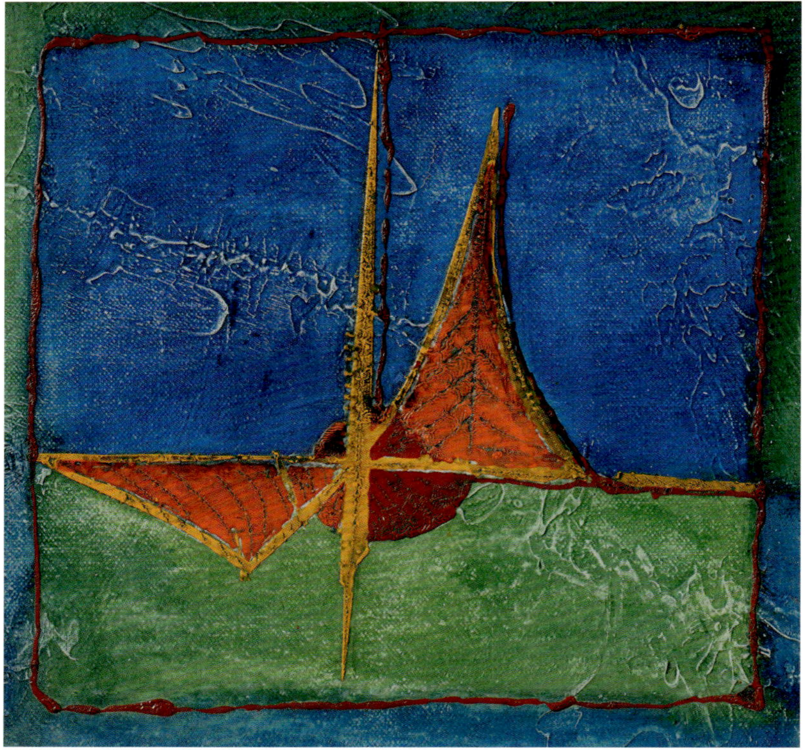

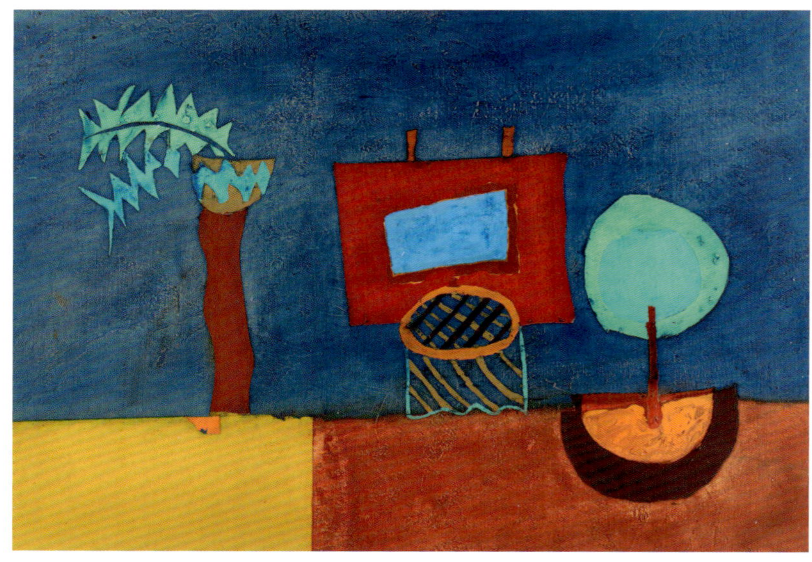

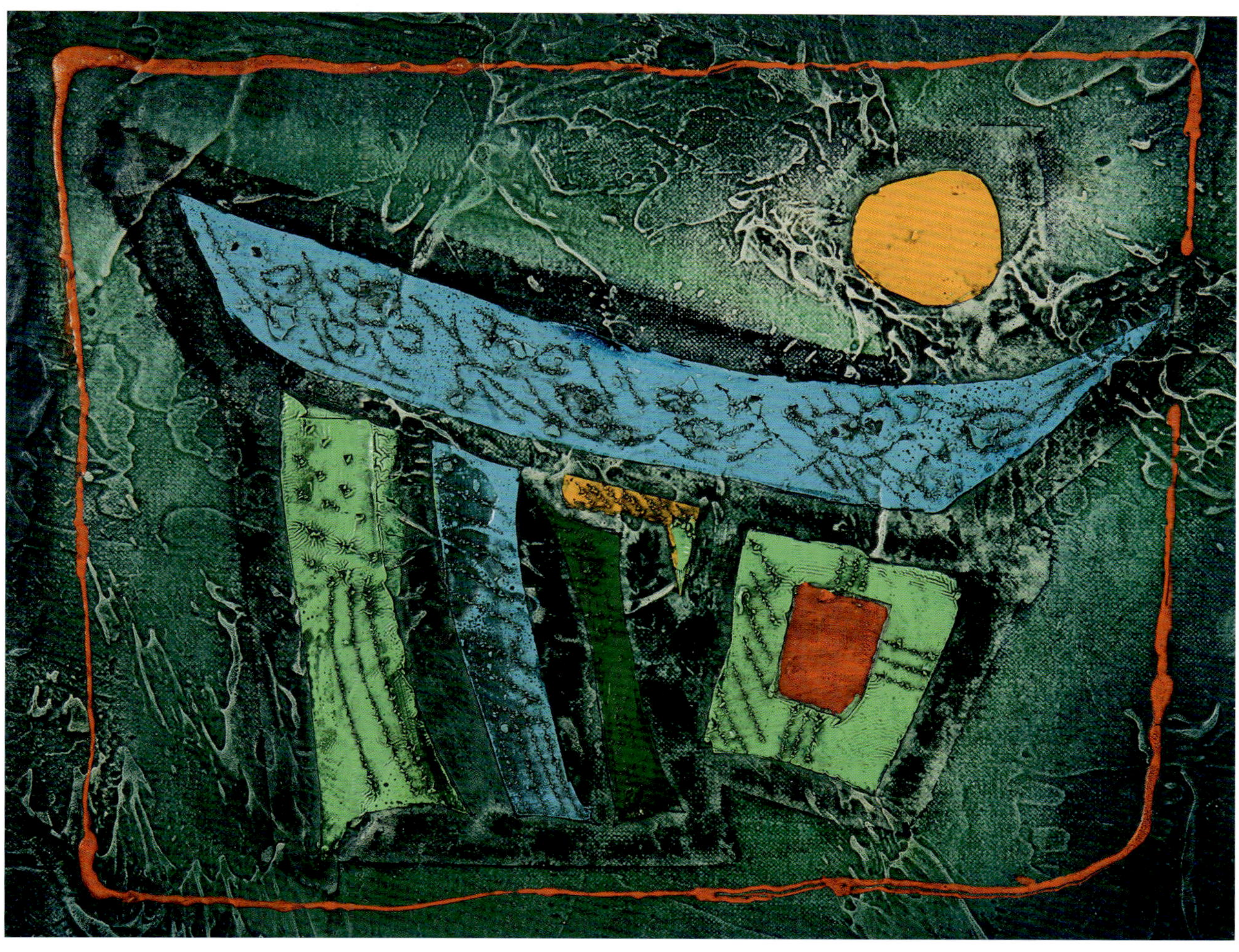

Helen Wilks (b.1950), and she helped him overcome his initial suppositional belief that the materials themselves created boundaries. He found an affinity between making blown glass and making a painting, they shared a visceral quality; for him, both are 'liquid' and both can be made in a relatively short space of time.

Early on, Herman developed an interest in collage and incorporated newspaper clippings, print type, magazine advertisements and found photographs into his picture making. These collaged elements contributed to the flatness of the paintings, and were also a pragmatic way for the artist to instantly create an image through the use of scissors and glue.

Herman's flattening of space and the ideograph c nature of his work could be termed naïve, but it underlines the notion that in a painting the artist seeks an ultimate reality uncomplicated by the associations of life; in other words, an innocent perception. In the paintings, the cesire to achieve flatness is also apparent, with the colour laid out to stress the reality of the picture as a two-dimensional object. This is compatible with Herman's innocent perception and with his sculptural interest in remaining truthful to materials, and is a crossover with the act of creating colours and shapes in his blown glass.

Herman's still-life paintings often refer to vessels he may have made himself, shown against backgrounds that

Below
Cosmos Containers, 2001
oil on canvas, 27 x 34cm
(10½ x 13½ in), Private
Collection

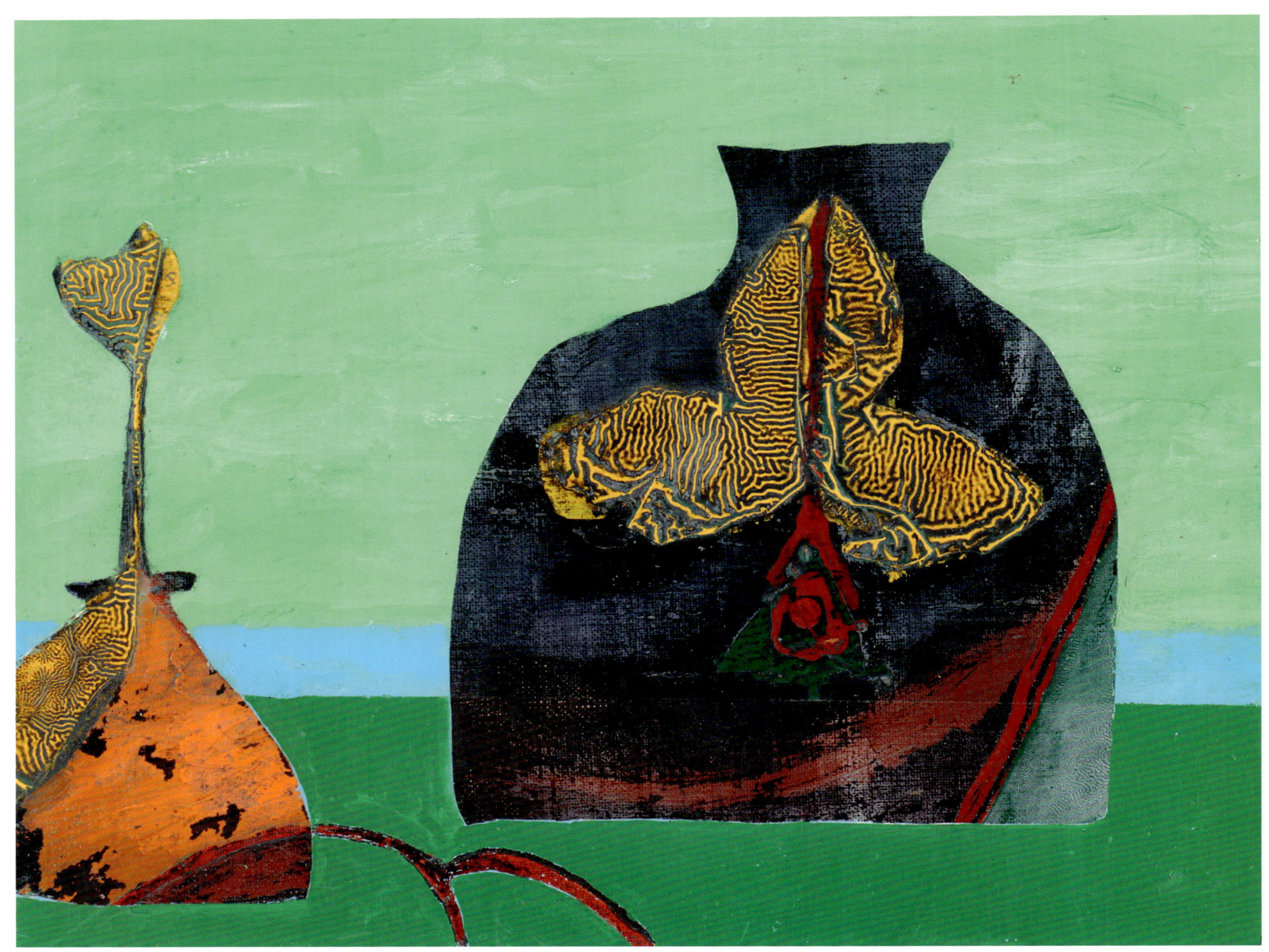

Opposite
Still Life, 2000
oil on canvas, 23 x 24cm
(9 x 9½ in), Private Collection

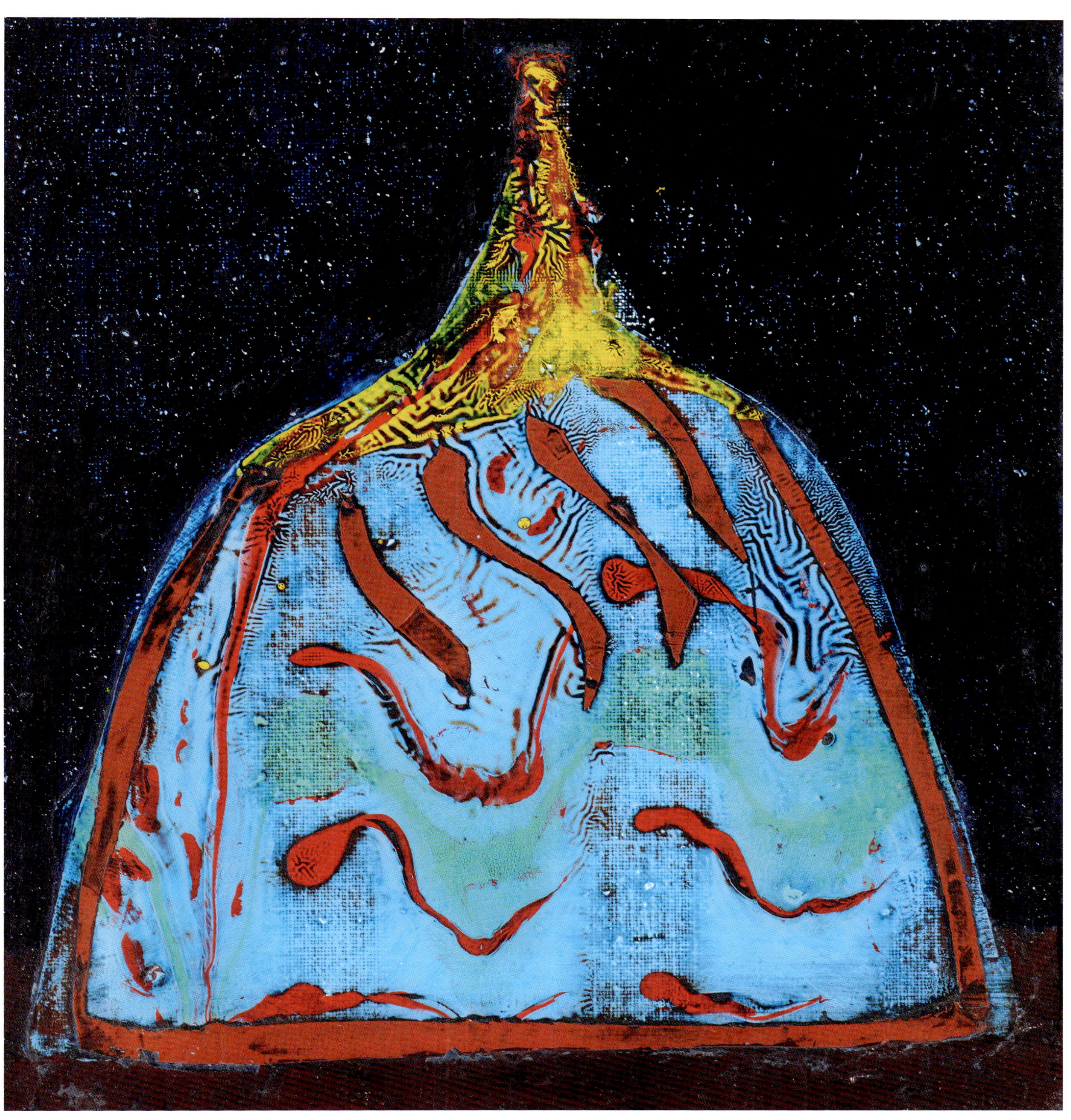

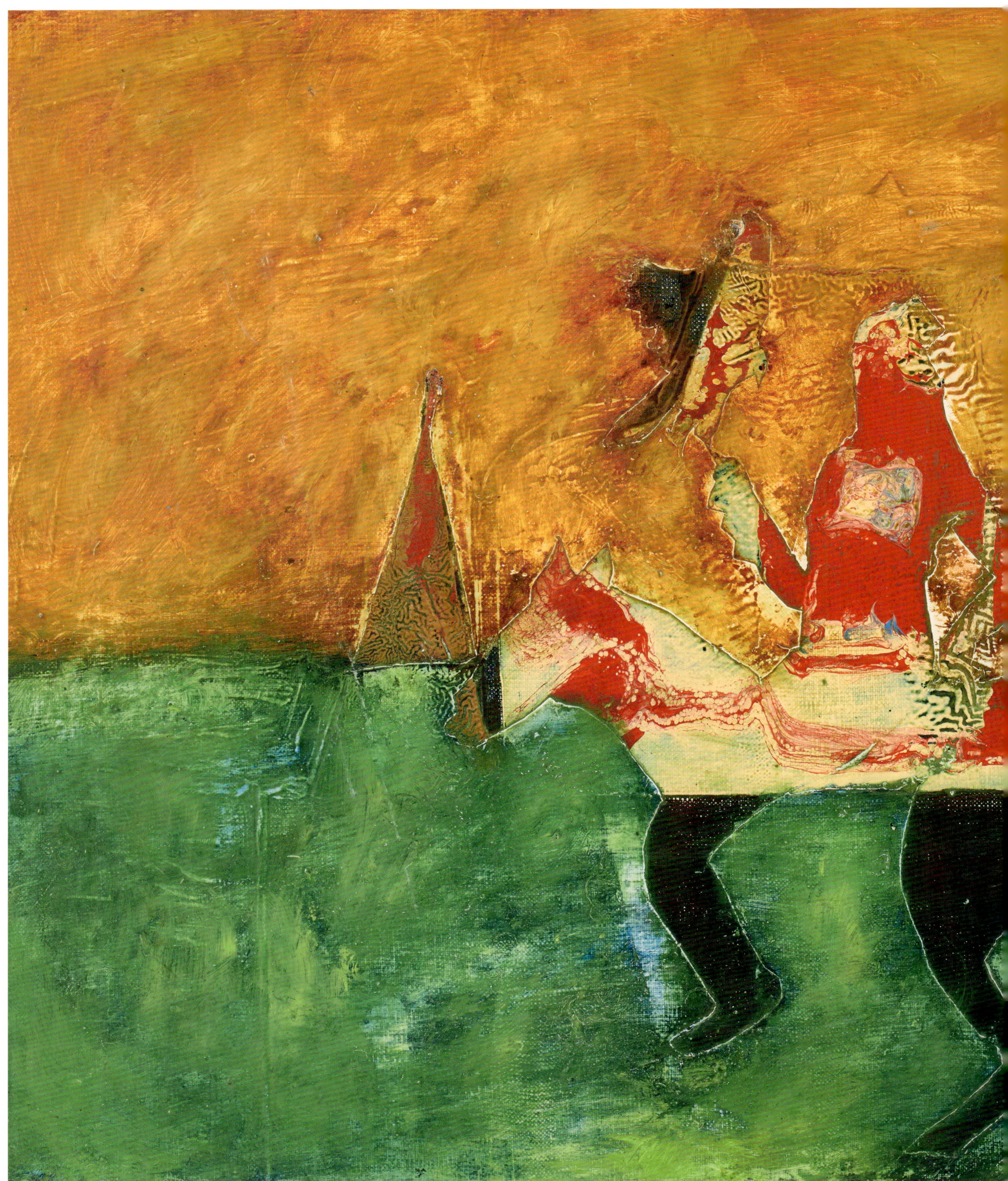

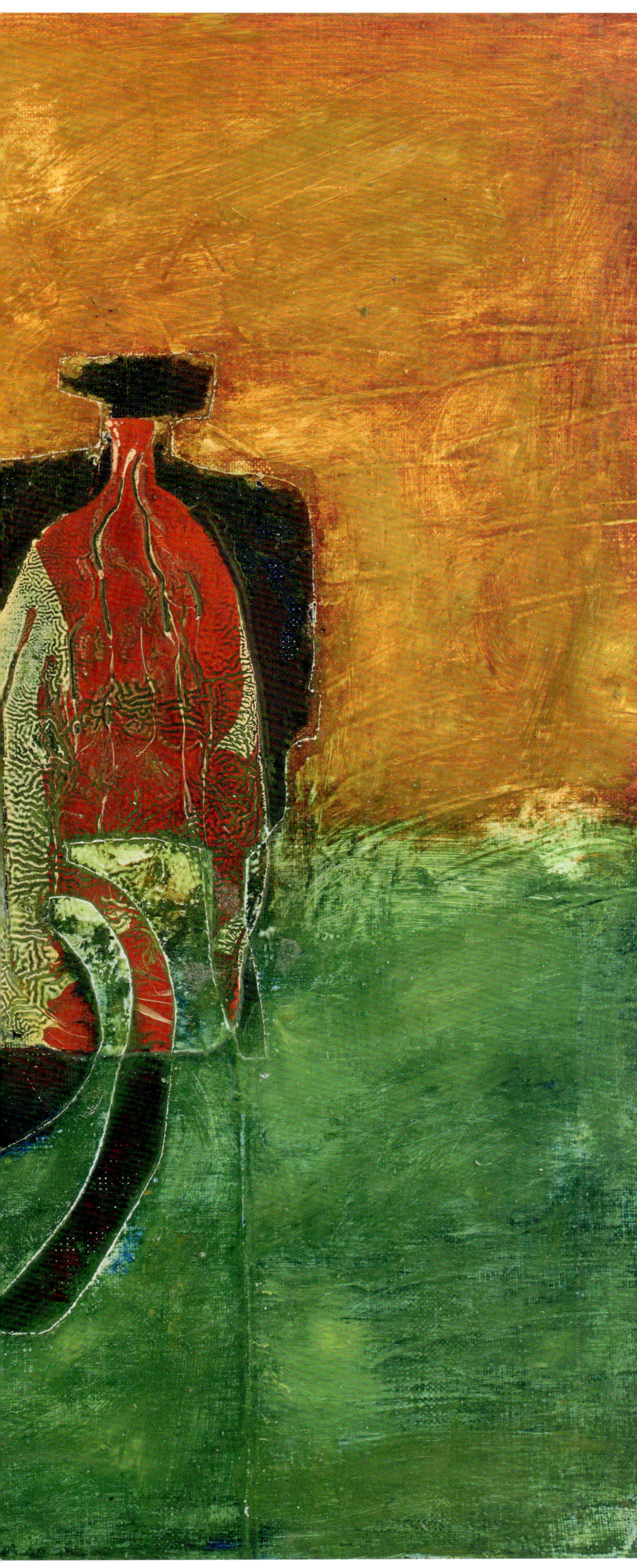

Don Quixote, 2011
oil on canvas, 40 x 55cm
(15¾ x 21¾ in), Private Collection

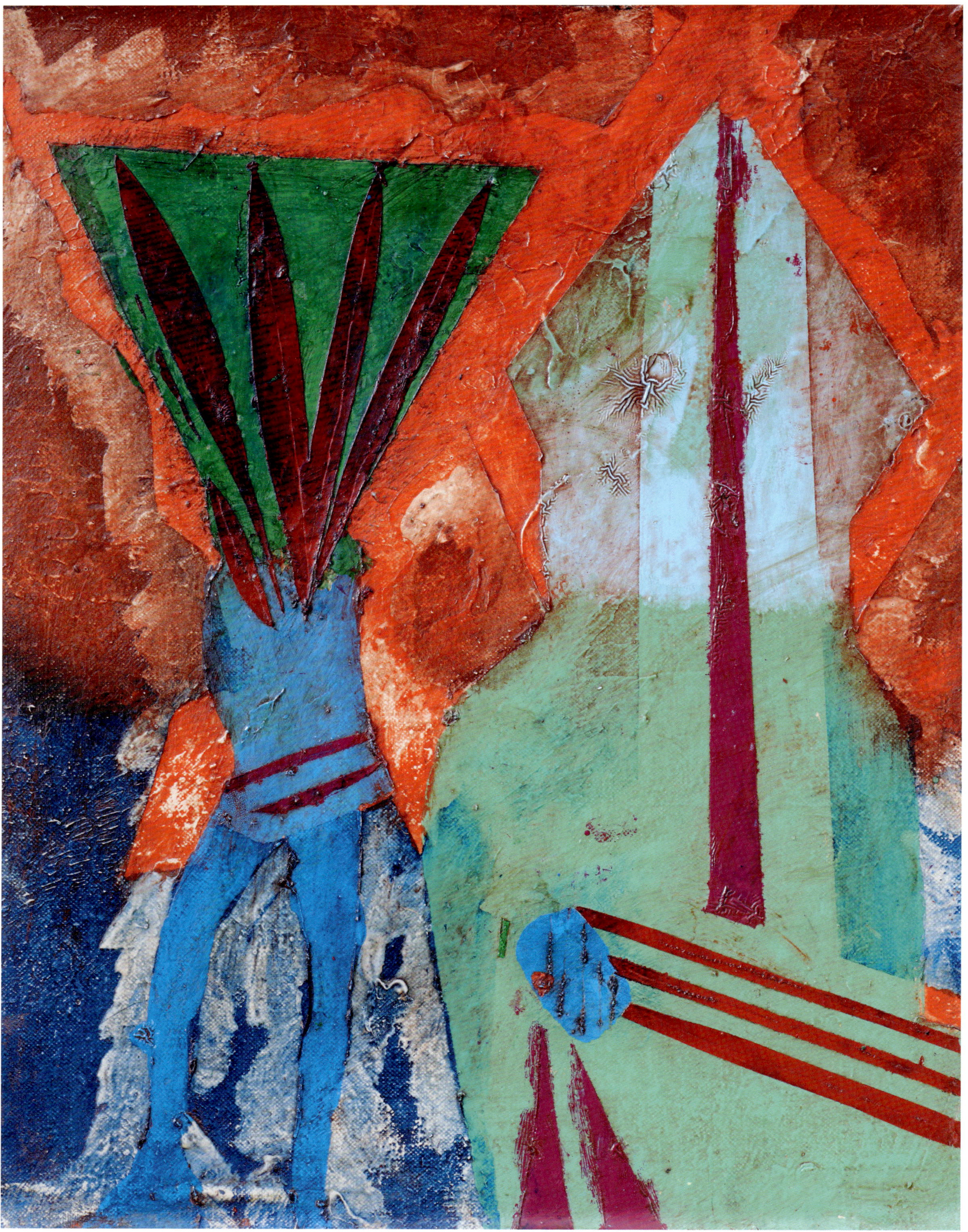

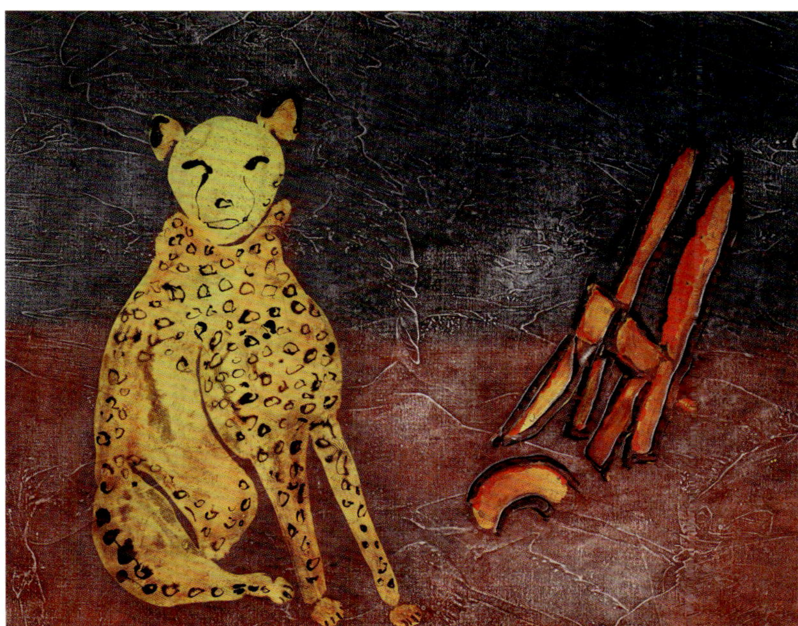

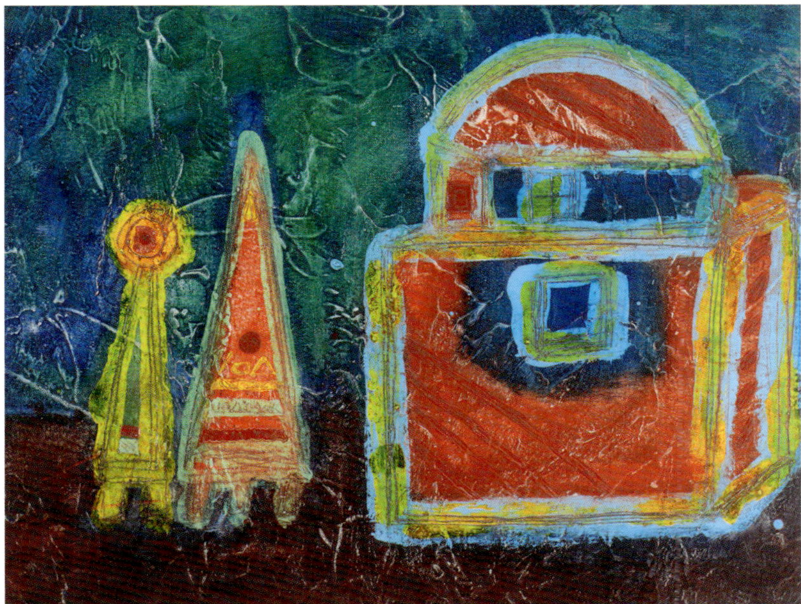

are almost non-referential. The treatment of space and the play between two-and three-dimensionality, and between transparency and opacity, provide many of these pictures with a shallow atmospheric space. Often, their angle of vision and their shallow space are reminiscent of Georges Braque's depiction of still life in his paintings of the late 1920s.

Herman's notion of the inseparable relationship between idea and form is transferred from his sculpture to his painting. They appear to stress imagination and instinct, and the imagery invoked originates from a deeply felt personal involvement with such themes as his continued interest in the human form and subjects that refer to autobiographical incidents and events. Herman also draws on an extensive image bank of visual information, anything from elements of Greek Orthodox Church painting to shattered and discarded Spanish agricultural implements. He often combines abstract and surrealist elements in a single work; for him they are mutually exclusive.

Many pictures are brightly coloured and make you laugh, but what they have to tell you is generally sombre and there is nothing sentimental or childish about their subjects. The defined silhouette of a figure returning home, heroic figures on horseback caught in bizarre dramas referenced from the past, a broken chair symbolising broken society, stiff-winged birds and other creatures whose salient features divide the compass north, east, south and west are forever measuring themselves against nothingness. Humanistic certainties are replaced by something closer to the anguish of Existentialism. The joke can be bleak.

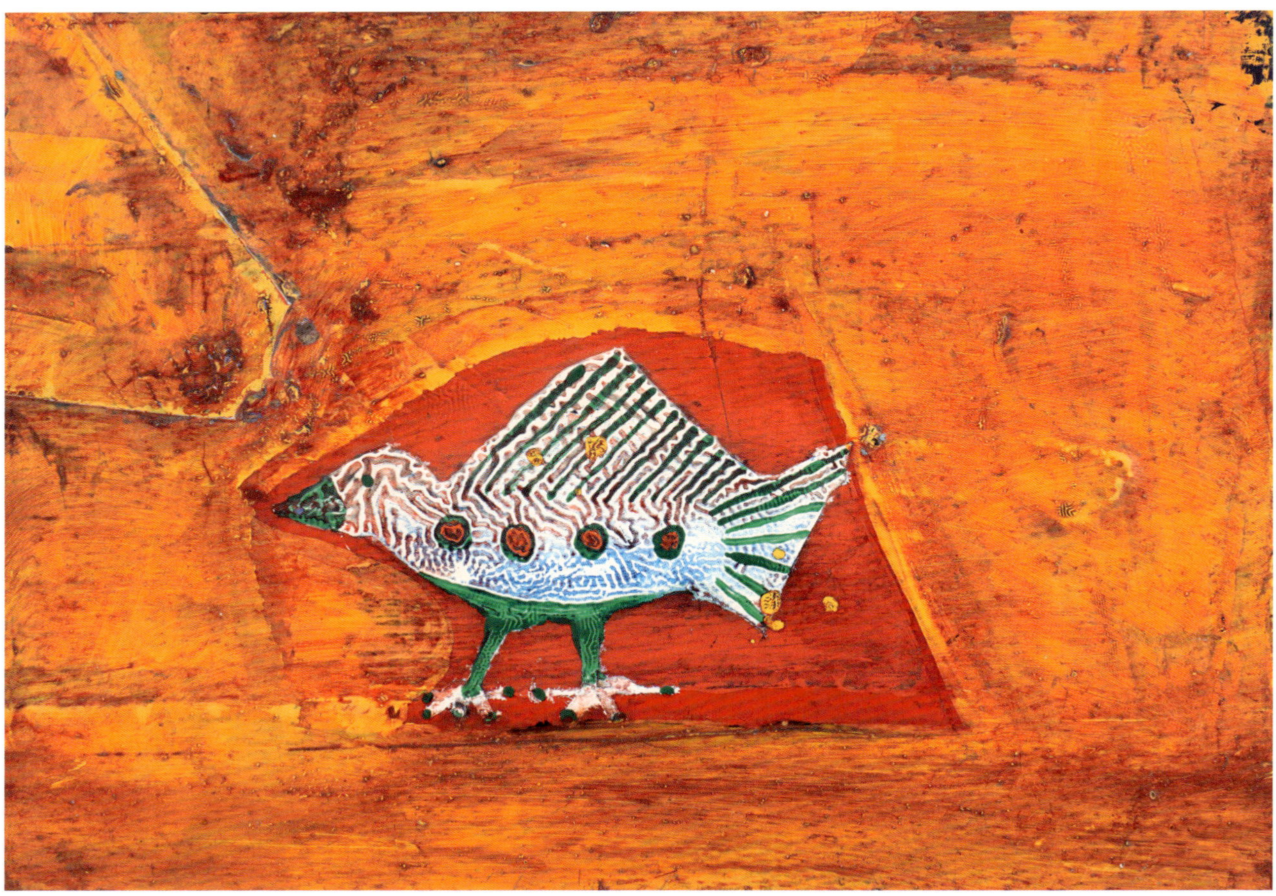

Herman shares a close affinity with German artist Julius Bissier (1893–1965), whose work he admires. Like Bissier, Herman seeks a synthesis between spirituality and abstraction, an integration of the two. On another level, Herman's often dream-like paintings combine mordant humour with enigmatic, naive simplicity.

A word must be said about Herman's working methods and the materials and implements he uses. Just as his art aims at transcendence, so too is it based on the habit of perpetual transformation. He is a naturally gifted improviser at every level of the creative process. He takes an almost holistic approach in his use of tools, inventing or adapting tools that encompass all media and techniques. Many of these are homemade, and the equipment that he stocks and uses in his studios is almost always the fruit of inspired scavenging.

Highly imaginative towards traditional techniques, Herman is able to coax new and inventive methods to further his artistic intent. He is blessed with a transforming genius and the ability to fuse sculpture, glass and painting into a single, fluid process. Herman wishes to push the boundaries of conventional materials and methods in the work he produces. In fact, breaking through traditional boundaries of medium and genre is his forte, working with a sense of liberation, experimenting with the play between the 2D and the 3D and between the personal and the universal.

Herman is fond of quoting American cartoonist and writer Scott Adams (b.1957): 'Creativity is allowing yourself to make mistakes. Art is knowing which ones to keep.' With sensitivity, sophistication and humour, Herman has continued to elaborate on a succession of themes and his own art retains a singleness of purpose and direction from which he has never wavered.

Mexican Dinosaur, 1991
oil on canvas, 18 x 25.5cm
(7 x 10 in), Private Collection

Opposite
Victory Celebration, 2011
oil on canvas, 51.5 x 40cm
(20¼ x 15¾ in), Private
Collection

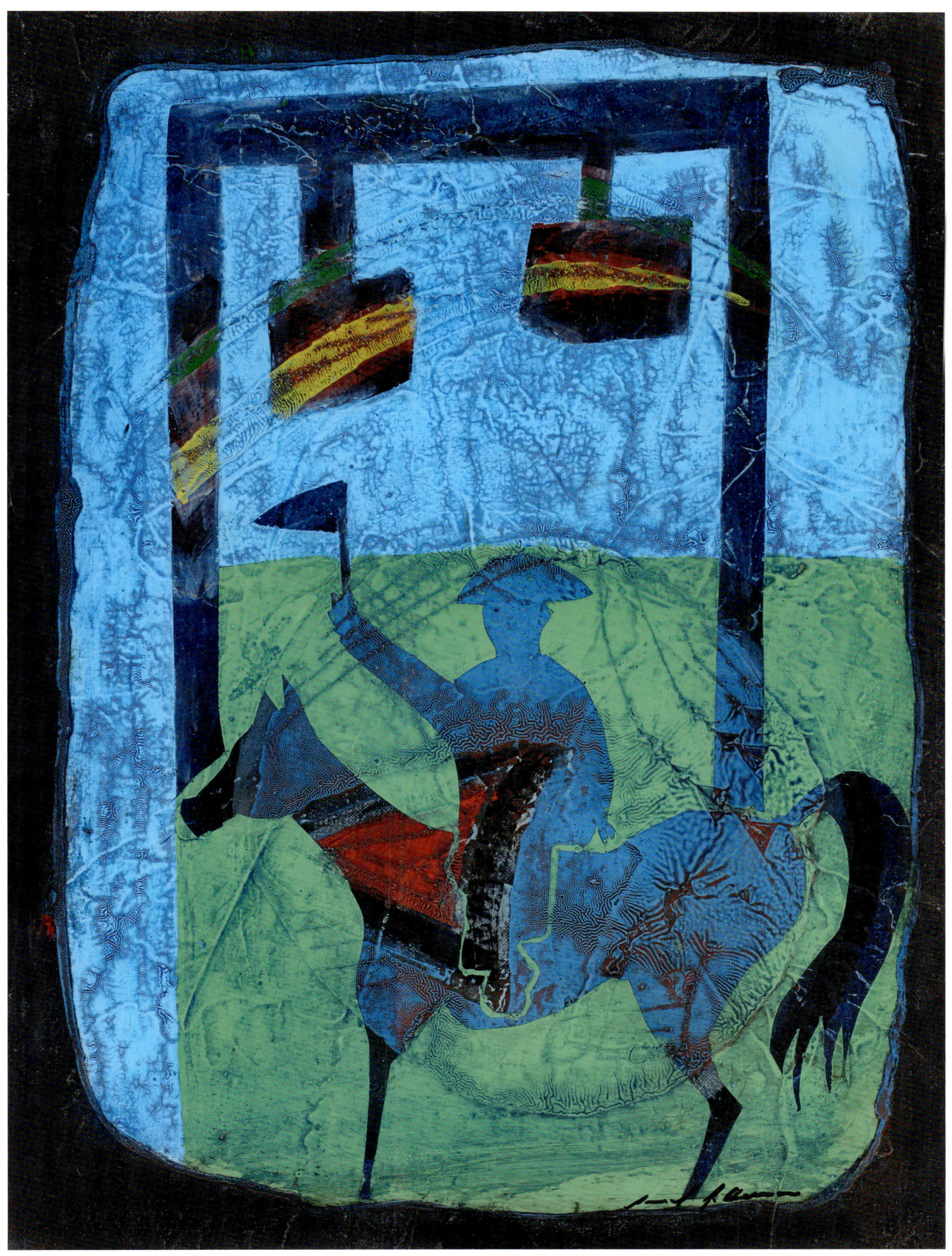

Ladies Who Luncheon, 2017
oil on canvas, 38.5 x 54cm
(15¼ x 21¼ in), Private Collection

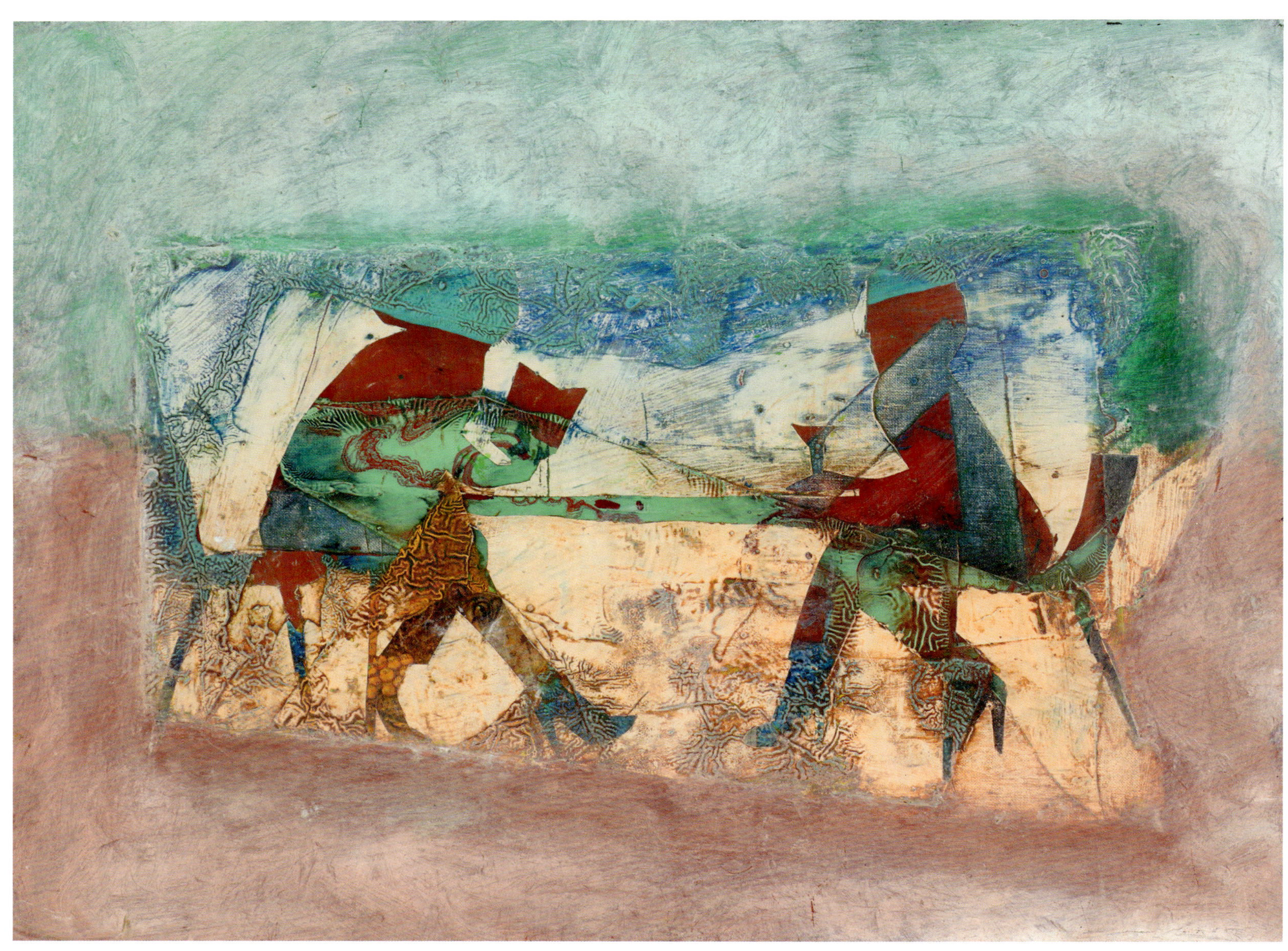

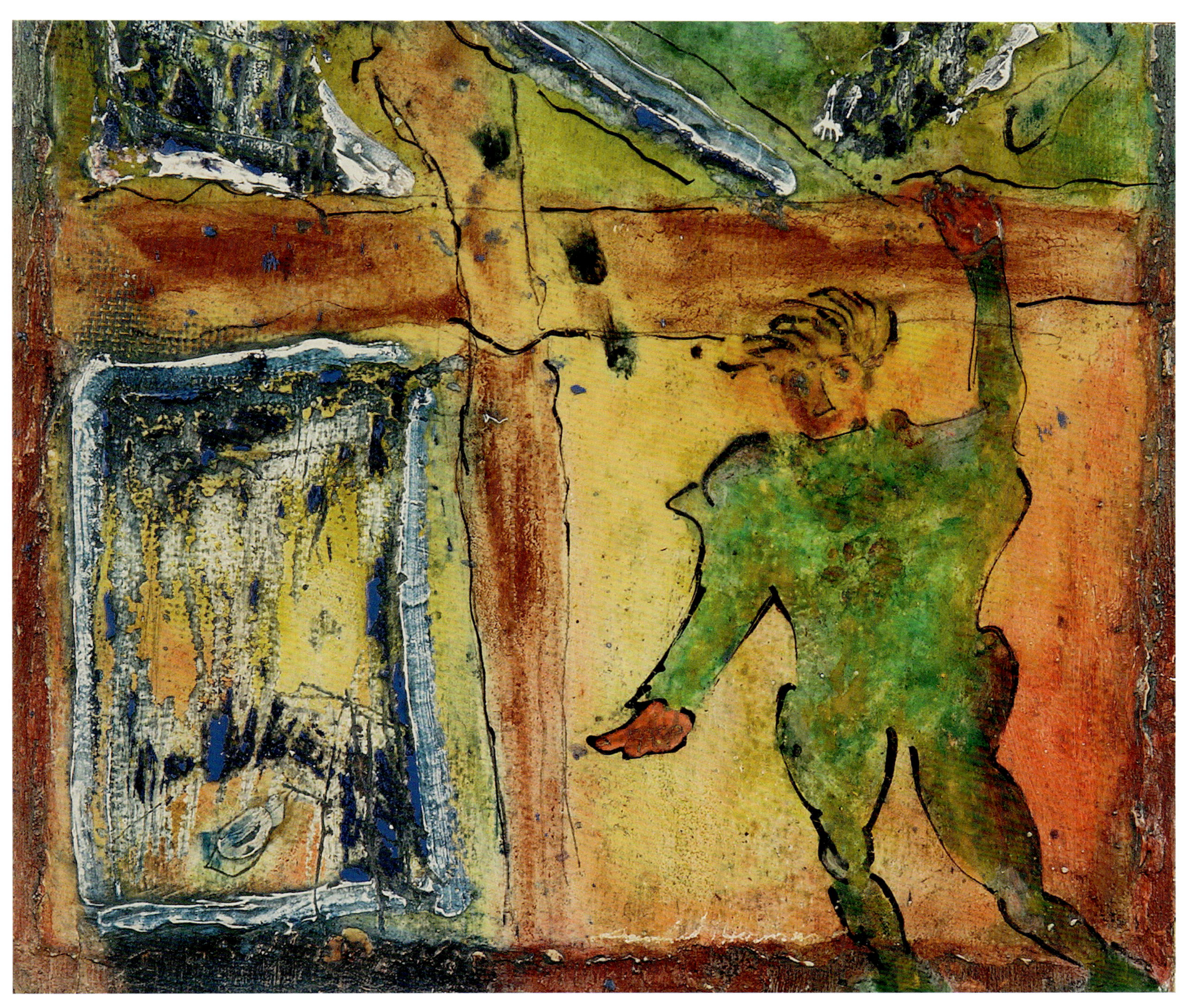

Coming Home, 1987
oil on canvas, 61 x 91cm
(24 x 35¾ in), Private Collection

Out of the Window, 2016
oil on canvas, 70 x 8˝cm
(27½ x 31¼ in), Private Collection

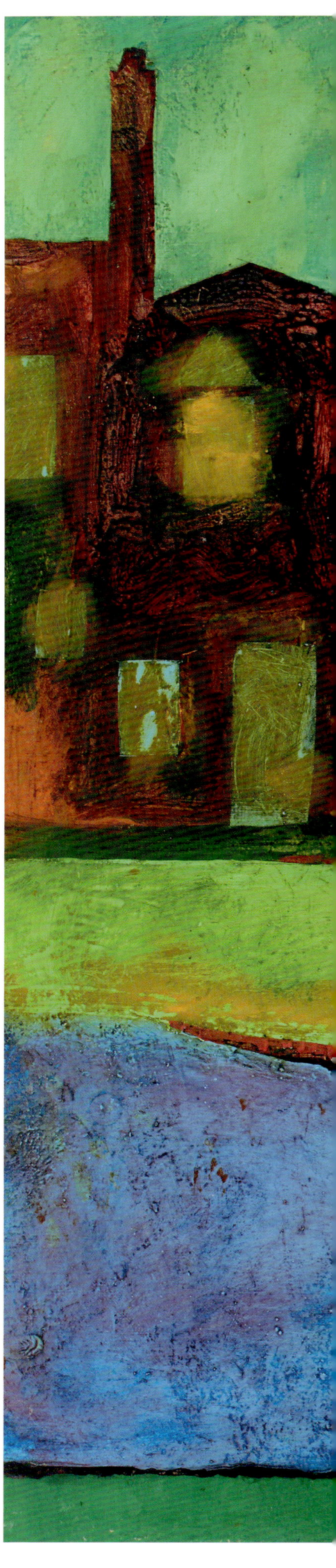

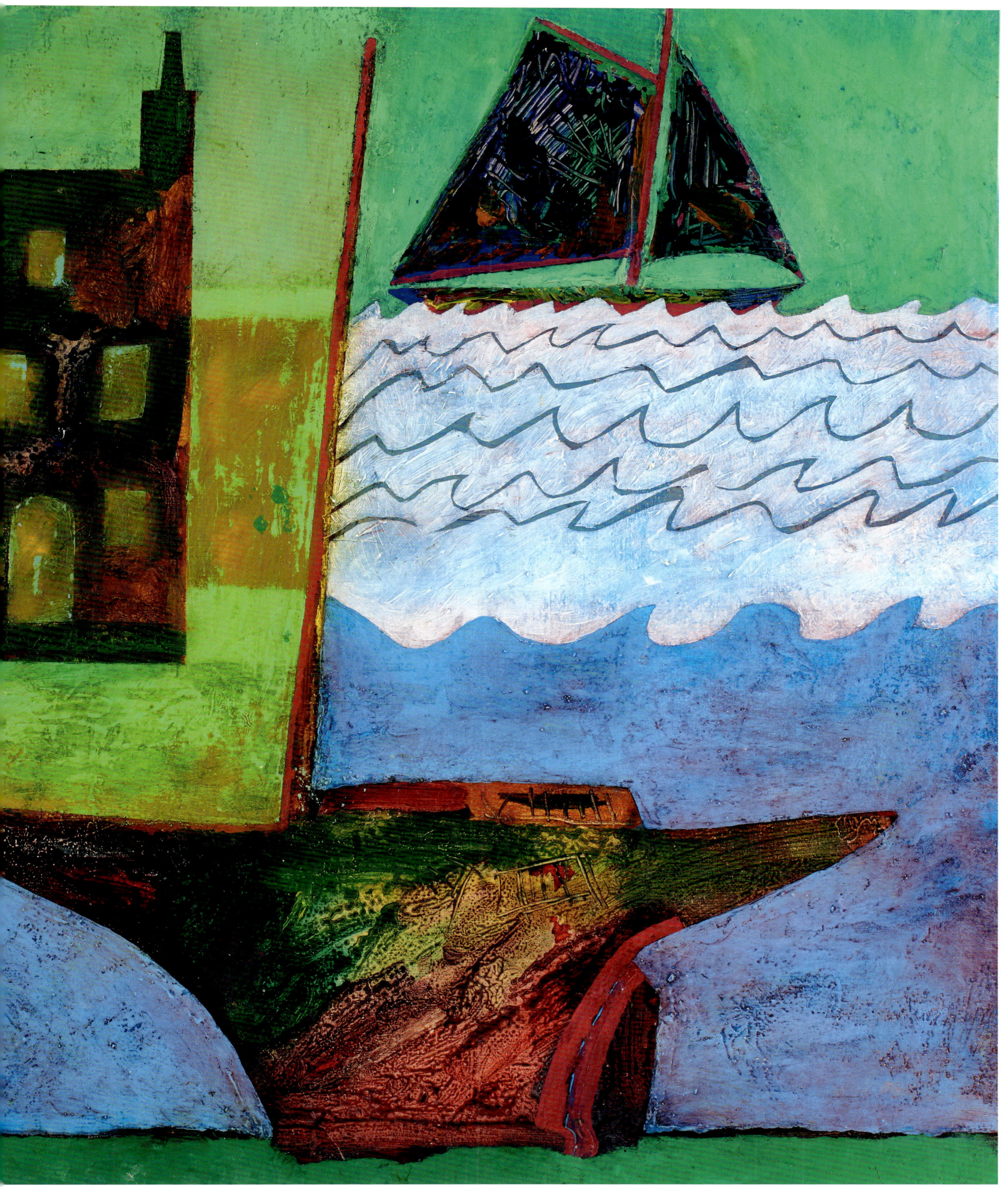

Notes

1   Alan Irvine in conversation with Lucy Abel Smith, 2018

2   *Flöckinger/Herman*, exh. cat., Victoria and Albert Museum, London, Her Majesty's Stationery Office, 1971, page unknown

3   Margot Coatts in conversation with Lucy Abel Smith, 2018

4   Sam Herman in conversation with Lucy Abel Smith, 2018

5   Sam Herman in conversation with Mark Hill, 2018

6   Sam Herman in conversation with Mark Hill, 2018

7   Sam Herman in conversation with Mark Hill, 2018

8   Sam Herman in conversation with Mark Hill, 2018

9   Sam Herman in conversation with Mark Hill, 2018

10 Sam Herman in conversation with Mark Hill, 2018

11 Sam Herman in conversation with Mark Hill, 2018

12 Sam Herman in conversation with Mark Hill, 2018

13 Woods, Paul, *A Potted Autobiographical History of the Growth of the Glass Department over the last Twenty Years*, 1984: p.10

14 Sam Herman in conversation with Mark Hill, 2018

15 Woods, Paul, *A Potted Autobiographical History of the Growth of the Glass Department over the last Twenty Years*, 1984, p.10

16 Sam Herman in conversation with Mark Hill, 2018

17 Sam Herman in conversation with Mark Hill, 2018

18 Sam Herman in conversation with Mark Hill, 2018

19 Sam Herman in conversation with Mark Hill, 2018

20 Sam Herman in conversation with Mark Hill, 2018

21 Sam Herman in conversation with Mark Hill, 2018

22 Sam Herman in conversation with Mark Hill, 2018

23 Sam Herman in conversation with Mark Hill, 2018

24 Sam Herman in conversation with Mark Hill, 2018

25 *Flöckinger/Herman*, exh. cat., Victoria and Albert Museum, London, Her Majesty's Stationery Office, 1971, page unknown

26 Sam Herman in conversation with Mark Hill, 2018

27 Sam Herman in conversation with Mark Hill, 2018

28 *The Design Journal*, 1970, p.42.

29 Sam Herman in conversation with Mark Hill, 2018

30 Sam Herman in conversation with Mark Hill, 2018

31 Sam Herman in conversation with Mark Hill, 2018

32 Sam Herman in conversation with Mark Hill, 2018

33 Sam Herman in conversation with Mark Hill, 2018

34 Sam Herman in conversation with Mark Hill, 2018

35 Sam Herman in conversation with Mark Hill, 2018

36 Sam Herman in conversation with Mark Hill, 2018

37 Sam Herman in conversation with Mark Hill, 2018

38 Sam Herman in conversation with Mark Hill, 2018

39 Sam Herman in conversation with Mark Hill, 2018

40 Wings are formed by adding glass to the sides of a piece. A trail is the addition of trails of glass to the surface of a piece. Straps are flat pieces of glass that are trailed all the way around a piece. Prunts are the result of the addition of hot glass to the colder body, which is then blown out causing the hot glass to expand while the cooler glass remains the same shape. Powder and/or chip enamels are rolled in the surface of the glass.

41 Sam Herman in conversation with Mark Hill, 2018

42 Sam Herman in conversation with Mark Hill, 2018

43 Sam Herman in conversation with Mark Hill, 2018

44 Sam Herman in conversation with Mark Hill, 2018

45 Sam Herman in conversation with Mark Hill, 2018

46 Sam Herman in conversation with Mark Hill, 2018

47 Sam Herman in conversation with Mark Hill, 2018

48 A lehr is a temperature-controlled kiln for annealing glass.

49 Sam Herman in conversation with Mark Hill, 2018

50 Scraps of broken or waste glass for remelting.

51 Sam Herman in conversation with Mark Hill, 2018

52 Sam Herman in conversation with Mark Hill, 2018

53 Sam Herman in conversation with Mark Hill, 2018

54 Personal written memories by Clifford Rainey

55 Personal written memories by Peter Aldridge

56 Personal written memories by Pauline Solven

57 Personal written memories by Peter Aldridge

58 The term 'kitchen sink' was first coined by art critic David Sylvester in 1954, when he applied it to a group of British artists working in the 1950s who painted ordinary people in scenes of everyday life.

59 The term 'Geometry of Fear' was coined by art critic Herbert Read in 1952 to describe the work of a group of young British sculptors that was characterised by tortured, battered or blasted looking human, or sometimes animal, figures. These works were executed in pitted bronze or welded metal and expressed a range of emotions related to the anxieties and fears of the post-war period.

60 Sylvester, David, 'The Foundations of Moore's Art', *Sculpture and Drawings by Henry Moore,* exh. cat., Tate Gallery, London, 1951, p.4

Chronology

1936	Born in Mexico City
1944	Moved to the United States of America
1947	Became a Citizen of the United States of America
1955–9	Served in the US Navy
1959–63	Attended Western Washington State College in Bellingham, Washington Graduated with a BA degree in Anthropology and Sociology
1963–5	Studied art at the University of Wisconsin MFA degree: sculpture and glass
1965	Received a Fulbright scholarship to study for one year at the Edinburgh College of Art, Scotland
1966	Invited to become a Research Fellow at the RCA, London, by David Queensberry Taught at Stourbridge College of Art, Gloucestershire
1967	Became Head of the Glass Department at the RCA, London
1968	Official invitation by the Czech Government to visit Czechoslovakia on a cultural exchange
1969	Conceived and established The Glasshouse in Covent Garden, London
1970	Held workshop and teaching sessions at Haystack Summer School, USA
1971	Major exhibition in London at the Victoria and Albert Museum Held workshop and teaching sessions at the University of California, Berkeley
1972–3	Participated in visit to Japan Workshops at California College of Arts and Crafts, Oakland, California Working visit to Erwin Eisch's studio in Germany
1974	Left the RCA, London, to take up a position at The Jam Factory in Adelaide, Australia, at the invitation of the South Australian Government
1975–9	Many exhibitions and workshops in Australia
1979–84	Returned to the UK to set up and run his own studio in Lots Road, London
1979–90	Took up position as Head of the Glass Department at Buckinghamshire College of Higher Education, High Wycombe, later becoming Head of the Ceramics and Glass Department in the mid 1980s
1983	Became an Honorary Fellow of the RCA, London
1986–2018	Concentrated on painting, architectural glass commissions, sculpture and stained-glass lighting pieces in studios in London and Spain
1990	Worked as a consultant and designer at Cristalleries, Val St Lambert in Belgium
1992	Established a studio in Mallorca, Spain
1994	Became a British citizen
2007	Returned to glass blowing at the studio of Aaronson Noon, making a body of work for an exhibition at the Zest Gallery, London
2010	Opened painting studio in Gloucestershire to complement the studios in Spain and London
2012	Had glass-working sessions at London Glassblowing
2015–17	Worked in blown glass at the Loco Glass studio of Colin Hawkins, Gloucestershire Continued painting and sculpture
2016	Moved his London studio to Gloucestershire

Selected exhibitions
since 1966

1967 Primavera Gallery, London, UK
1968 PUB Stockholm, Sweden
Museum of Glass and Jewellery, Jablonec,
  Czechoslovakia
Roselius-Haus, Bremen, Germany
1969 Heal's, London, UK
Crafts Centre of Great Britain, London, UK
Seibu, Tokyo, Japan
Gemeentemuseum, Arnhem, the Netherlands
Groninger Museum voor Stad en Lande,
  Groningen, the Netherlands
Museum Boijmans von Beuningen, Rotterdam,
  the Netherlands
1970 Design Centre, London, UK
Röhsska Konstslöjdmuseet, Gothenburg,
  Sweden
Pace Gallery, London, UK
Galerie L'Ecuyer, Brussels, Belgium
1971 Archer Gallery, London, UK
Victoria and Albert Museum, London, UK
Pilkington Museum, St Helens,
  Merseyside, UK
Oxford Gallery, Oxford, UK
Camden Arts Centre, London, UK
1974 Fine Art Society, London, UK
1975 Galerie L'Ecuyer, Brussels, Belgium
Narek Gallery, Canberra, Australia
Bonython Gallery, Sydney, Australia
The Jam Factory, Adelaide, Australia
1976 Greenhill Gallery, Adelaide, Australia
Collectors Gallery, Perth, Australia
Festival Centre Gallery, Adelaide, Australia
The Craft Centre, Melbourne, Australia
The Craftsman's Market, Brisbane,
  Australia
Western Australian Institute of Technology,
  Perth, Australia
British Crafts Centre, London, UK

Ararat Gallery, Ararat, Australia
The Fine Art Society, Edinburgh, Scotland
1977 Galerie L'Ecuyer, Brussels, Belgium
Gallery L, Hamburg, Germany
Narek Gallery, Canberra, Australia
1978 Downs Gallery, Brisbane, Australia
Galerie Skandinaviske Mobler, Frankfurt,
  Germany
The Crafts Centre, London, UK
1979 Galerie L'Ecuyer, Brussels, Belgium
International Glaskunst, Stuttgart, Germany
1980 Atkinson Art Gallery, Southport, Merseyside, UK
The Fine Art Society, Glasgow, Scotland
The Fine Art Society, Edinburgh, Scotland
Aberdeen Art Gallery, Scotland
Silverbergs, Malmö, Sweden
Liberty, London, UK
1981 Pilkington Museum, St Helens, Merseyside, UK
Century Galleries, Henley-on-Thames,
  Oxfordshire, UK
The Higgins Art Gallery & Museum, Bedford,
  Bedfordshire, UK
Glas-Galerie Lucerne, Switzerland
Oxford Gallery, Oxford, UK
Westminster Gallery, Boston, USA
Studio '40, The Hague, the Netherlands
1982 Galerie Mensendiek, Dusseldorf, Germany
Galerie D. M. Sarver, Paris, France
Galerie Monica Trujen, Bremen, Germany
Galerie Thiel, Luxembourg
Galerie Veltheim, Veltheim, Germany
1983 Galerie Nanky de Vreeze, Amsterdam,
  the Netherlands
Galerie Métiers Mormiron, Biot, France
Société Générale Galerie, Hong Kong
Galerie en Groß St Martin, Cologne,
  Germany
Glass Gallery, Toronto, Canada

La Galerie, Frankfurt, Germany
National Museum of Wales, Cardiff, UK
1984 Devon Guild of Craftsmen Gallery, Bovey
  Tracey, Devon, UK
Guildford House Gallery, Guildford, UK
1985 Kunstsammlungen der Veste Coburg,
  Bavaria, Germany
Coleridge, London, UK
1987 Générale de Banque, Liège, Belgium
Fitzwilliam Museum, Cambridge, UK
1988 Terranga Gallery, Dornbirn, Austria
1989 Tom Caldwell Galleries, Dublin and Belfast,
  Ireland
Transparence Gallery, Brussels, Belgium
Galerie L'Ecuyer, Brussels, Belgium
1991 Boundary Gallery, London, UK
Eastern Rooms, Rye, East Sussex, UK
1995 Pump House Gallery, London, UK
1996 The Royal College of Pathologists, London, UK
2000 Gallery 27, London, UK
2007 Zest Gallery, London, UK
2017 Peterborough Museum, Peterborough, UK
The Frestonian Gallery, London, UK

Selected work in public collections

UK

Victoria and Albert Museum, London
    Greater London Council
Derby Museum and Art Gallery, Derbyshire
New Walk Museum & Art Gallery, Leicester,
    Leicestershire
Fitzwilliam Museum, Cambridge, Cambridgeshire
Hove Museum & Art Gallery, East Sussex
Haworth Art Gallery, Accrington, Lancashire
The Higgins Art Gallery & Museum, Bedford,
    Bedfordshire
The White House Cone – Museum of Glass,
    Stourbridge, West Midlands
St Cross College, Oxford, Oxfordshire
Nottingham Castle Museum & Art Gallery,
    Nottinghamshire
National Museum of Scotland, Edinburgh
Aberdeen Art Gallery, Aberdeen, Aberdeenshire

USA

The Metropolitan Museum of Art, New York
Corning Museum of Glass, New York
Smithsonian Institution, Washington D.C.
Art Institute of Chicago, Illinois
University of Wisconsin–Madison, Wisconsin

Europe

J. & L. Lobmeyr, Vienna, Austria
Palais Stoclet, Brussels, Belgium
Musée du Verre, Charleroi, Belgium
Royal Family of Belgium
Museum of Glass and Jewellery, Jablonec,
    Czech Republic
Museum Kunstpalast, Dusseldorf, Germany
Glasmuseum, Frauenau, Germany
Calouste Gulbenkian Museum, Lisbon, Portugal
Röhsska Konstslöjdmuseet, Gothenburg, Sweden
Kunstindustrimuseet, Oslo, Norway

Australia

National Gallery of Victoria, Melbourne
Art Gallery of South Australia, Adelaide
Art Gallery of Western Australia, Perth
Queensland Art Gallery, Brisbane
Melbourne State College, Melbourne
Queen Victoria Museum and Art Gallery, Tasmania

Selected bibliography

Beard, Geoffrey, *International Modern Glass*, Barrie & Jenkins, London, 1976

Beard, Geoffrey, *Modern Glass*, Studio Vista, London, 1968

Eisch-Angus, Katharina, Kohl, Ines and Schrott, Karin (eds.), *Erwin Eisch – Clouds Have Been My Foothold All Along*, Hirmer Verlag, Munich, 2012

Falconer Byrd, Joan, *Harvey K. Littleton – A Life in Glass*, Skira Rizzoli Publishing, New York, 2012

Frantz, Susanne K., *Contemporary Glass*, Harry N. Abrams Inc., New York, 1989

Garner, Philippe, *The Contemporary Decorative Arts from 1940 to the Present Day*, Phaidon Press, London, 1980

Grover, Ray, and Grover, Lee, *Contemporary Art Glass*, Crown Publishers, New York, 1975

Hajdamach, Charles R., *20th Century British Glass*, Antique Collectors' Club, Woodbridge, Suffolk, 2009

Klein, Dan, *Glass: A Contemporary Art*, Collins, London, 1989

Klein, Dan, and Lloyd, Ward (eds.), *The History of Glass*, Orbis Publishing Ltd, London, 1984

Lutzeier, Sabine, *Modernes Glas von 1920 bis 1990*, Battenberg Verlag, Augsburg, Germany, 1997

Lynggaard, Finn (ed.), *The Story of Studio Glass: The Early Years. A Historic Documentation Told by the Pioneers*, Rhodos, Copenhagen, 1998

Neiswander, Judith, and Swash, Caroline, *Stained & Art Glass: A Unique History of Glass Design & Making*, The Intelligent Layman Publishers Ltd, Kingston upon Thames, Surrey, 2005

The making, signing and numbering of glass pieces
Sam Herman Studio

Working with hot glass requires such immediate decisions and such harmony between the material and the maker that Herman has always liked to work alone so he could control each piece. Due to certain physical constraints, the larger pieces, especially those made at the Val St Lambert factory, were in collaboration with the gaffers at the factory. Since returning to glass in the 21st century, Herman has always worked with an assistant due to the physical nature of the work and the toll that age takes. However, every piece signed by him has either been made entirely by him or, if he was unable to do some of the physical work, he was present for the entire making of the piece.

All unique glass pieces made by Herman are signed on the base with the signature 'Samuel J. Herman' and are nearly always signed by him with a diamond-point pen or burr. The signature appears as below:

The work is not always dated, but the distinctive style and colour of the different periods often clearly show when the work was made.

A numbering system was loosely used. The early work, between 1966 and 1974, was given a number with no initials. The Australian work, between 1974 and 1979, has a number prefixed by 'SA' for South Australia. The unique work made at Val St Lambert in the late 1970s has a number with the prefix 'VAL'. The work made at the Lots Road studio, between 1979 and 1984, shows a number with the prefix 'SJH' or 'CA to CZ' or 'CAC'. Production work made at Lots Road is unsigned but has 'Sam Herman Studio' written on the base. The few pieces made while Herman was teaching at High Wycombe have the prefix 'HW'. The work made in the 21st century is not numbered.

When Herman was assisted by another glass artist or craftsperson, he always tried to ensure that their initials appeared on the piece. The following are some of the people with whom Herman has worked and to whom he is extremely grateful for their understanding of his wishes and style and, of course, their physical strength and skill:

The teams at Val St Lambert
Eddie King at Aaronson Noon
Layne Rowe at London Glassblowing
Richie Alli at Loco Glass
Colin Hawkins at Loco Glass

The authors

The Marquess of Queensberry

David Queensberry was Professor of Ceramics at the Royal College of Art in London from 1959 until 1983. He belongs to the Crafts Council, is a Fellow of the Chartered Society of Designers (and recipient of the Minerva Medal, the Society's highest award), was President of the Design & Industries Association from 1976 until 1978 and was Senior Fellow of the Royal College of Art.

Lucy Abel Smith

Lucy Abel Smith is an art historian and Fellow of the Society of Antiquaries. She is also President of the Gloucestershire Guild of Craftsmen. She lectures and writes on a wide range of subjects, specialising in the Balkans and Eastern Europe, and also runs her own tour company, Reality and Beyond. With her husband, she founded the biennial Fresh Air Sculpture Show, as a charitable trust, in 1992. It is held in the grounds of their home in Gloucestershire. She has also founded the Transylvanian Book Festival, which is now on its third edition.

Michael Boylen

Michael Boylen was a fellow student of Sam Herman's at the University of Wisconsin and went on to become a well-known ceramic and glass artist. For many years he was President of the Vermont Council of the Arts and Professor of Ceramics at Marlboro College in Vermont. He has been a regular contributor to *American Craft Magazine* and lectured and given workshops in Canada, the UK, Germany, the Netherlands, Czechoslovakia and Scandinavia.

Mark Hill

Mark Hill was a specialist in the collectors departments at Bonhams and Sotheby's in London. He is now an author, publisher, television presenter and leading dealer in 20th-century decorative glass. Clients include international publishers, museums, educational institutions and private collectors. Mark is the co-author of the biennial international *Miller's Collectables Price Guides* and is also an expert on the BBC's *Antiques Roadshow*. He has published books on Mdina glass, Dartington glass, West German Ceramics and Czech glass design.

Dr Greg Votolato

Greg Votolato studied art history at Boston University, Massachusetts, and took degrees in fine art and architecture at Rhode Island School of Design, Providence, a Master of Fine Arts at Pratt Institute, New York, and a PhD in design history at Teesside University, Middlesbrough. Formerly Professor of Design at Buckinghamshire New University, he is now a lecturer in the Learning Department at the Victoria and Albert Museum, London. Greg is also a contributor to the Master of Studies programme in the history of design at Kellogg College, University of Oxford. His books include *American Design in the Twentieth Century* (Manchester University Press, 1998), *Transport Design: A Travel History* (Reaktion Books, 2007) and *Ship* (Reaktion Books, 2011).

Michael Regan

Michael Regan has a long career as an art curator and exhibition organiser having worked for a number of public institutions in the UK, including the Victoria and Albert Museum in London, the Whitworth Art Gallery in Manchester, the Arts Council of Great Britain and Canada House in London. He currently works in a part-time capacity as Curator of the Cultural Institute at King's College London, Curator of the Royal College of General Practioners in Guildford and Associate Curator of The Lightbox gallery, Woking.

Index

Aaronson, Adam 109

Aaronson Noon Studio and Gallery 109

Abstract Bull 137

abstraction, and spirituality 160

Adams, Scott 160

Adelaide 47–9, 81–93

Aldridge, Peter 128, 129, 131

Archer Gallery 46

Armitage, Kenneth 134

Australia 47–9, 81–93

Bailey, Dennis 19

Bellingham 23–4, 134

Billeter, Dr Erica 31

Bird 136

Bissier, Julius 160

Boat on Beach 153

bowl, three-cornered 131

Boylen, Michael 30

Brandt, Åsa 131

Braque, Georges 159

bronze sculptures 148

Bruce, Jane 47, 131

Bull bronze 150

Bull welded steel 136

Butler, Reg 134

California, Berkeley, university 31

Campbell, John 50

Chadwick, Lynn 134

Christiansen, Judith (later Herman) 24, 49

Civilization 159

Clarke, Dillon 131

Clarke, Geoffrey 134

Coatts, Margot 20

collage 153

Coming Home 163

Committee of Artists in Glass 31

Cook, John 42

Corner of Playground 152

Cosmos Containers 154

Crafts Centre of Great Britain 42

Crooks, Bob 47

Daden, Fred 81, 127, 128

Dartington's cullet 63

David 135

Don Quixote 156–7

Dorf, Rose (later Farber) 20, 20, 21, 22, 22

Echoe (Aldridge) 129

Edinburgh College of Art 31, 34–5, 37

Edsor, Simon 46

Eisch, Erwin 24, 31, 38, 42, 50, 50, 51

Eisch-Angus, Katharina 50–1

'El Dorado' range 44

Erwin Eisch – Clouds Have Been My Foothold All Along (Eisch) 51

Farber, Philip 22, 23

Farber, Rose (née Dorf) 20, 20, 21, 22, 22

Fine Art Society 46

Fischer, Heinrich (Harry) 46

Fischer Fine Art 46

Fishbein, Abrahm 20, 21

Fishbein, Efrain 20, 21

Fishbein, Miriam 20, 21

Flöckinger, Gerda 19, 45

found objects 137, 143

Fritz, Robert 31

Fulbright scholarship 31

Galerie L'Ecuyer 44

Gallé, Emile 44

Gemeentemuseum 46

The Glasshouse 46–7, 60–5, 130; frontage 46

Gossiping Neighbours 151

Hackett, Dr Earle 47

Hamada, Yoshio 131

Harcuba, Jiří 42

Harris, Michael 37, 38

Hawkins, Colin 109

Haystack Mountain School of Crafts in Deer Isle,

Maine 31

Heal's 42

Heaton, Bill 37, 38, 127

Herman, Joanna 94

Herman, Judith (née Christiansen) 24, 49

Herman, Sam: pictured in Mexican family portrait, 1938 20; pictured astride his 'bronco,' 1940 21; pictured in fancy dress with cousin Melke, Mexico City, 1941 21; pictured in New York family portrait, 1945 22; pictured in the US Navy 23; pictured in US Navy visiting Nara Park, Japan, 1957 23; pictured hiking in the mountains near Bellingham, 1962 25; pictured at Dominick Labino's studio in Toledo, Ohio, 1964 30; pictured working in the studio at Wisconsin, 1964 28; pictured with sculpture made for his degree show, 1965 26; pictured working at Stourbridge College of Art, 1966 35; pictured working at the Royal College of Art, c.1966 36; pictured with Fred Daden, Royal College of Art 128; pictured with Eisch, 1967 50; pictured at the studio at the Royal College of Art, 1970 39; pictured working at the Royal College of Art, 1974 49; pictured working in Australia 126; pictured working at London Glassblowing, 2012 108

High Wycombe 128

Hlava, Pavel 42

Hough, Catherine 47

Hughes, Graham 46, 47

Irvine, Alan 19

Jam Factory 47–9, 81–93

Kolman, Ivan 131

Labino, Dominick ('Nick') 27, 29, 29, 30, 31, 127; studio in Toledo, Ohio, 1964 30

Ladies Who Luncheon 162

Lang, Rodger 24, 30

Layton, Peter 109

Leloup, Louis 44

Libenský, Stanislav 24, 42

light, use of 139, 143

Lipofsky, Marvin 30, 31

Littleton, Harvey 24, 27, 29, 30, 31, 34, 35, 127, 137
Loco Glass 109
logo for Sam Herman Studio 49
London Glassblowing 109
Lots Road studio 50, 94–107

Marini, Marino 136
Marlborough Fine Art 46
Mdina Glass 38
Meech, Annette 47, 131
melting tanks 29
Meurrens, Hubert 44
Mexican Dinosaur 160
Millard, Helen 47
Moore, Henry 136
Moore, Simon 47
Museum Boijmans von Beuningen 46
Myers, Joel 29

Navy, US 23
Newell, Steven 47, 131

O'Looney, Betty 19
Open Handkerchief 138
Orup, Bengt 42
Out of the Window 164–5
Oxford Gallery 46

Pace Gallery 46
painting 152–64
Paolozzi, Eduardo 134, 136
Patrick, Andrew McIntosh 46
Playground, corner of 152
Pop Concert 158
Primavera Gallery 42

Queensberry, David, marquess 37, 38, 127

Rainey, Clifford 127–8, 131
Read, Herbert 134
Richards, Dick 47
Robins, Susannah 47
Röhsska Konstslöjdmuseet 46
Rosenthal 71–80
Royal College of Art (RCA) 36, 37–8, 60–5, 127–8

San José State University 31
Sarpaneva, Timo 81
Seibu 42
Shulman, Norman 31
Shy Boy (Rainey) 131
silver chloride 63, 71
Smith, David 136
Solven, Pauline 47, 130, 131
space, treatment of 152, 153, 159
spirituality and abstraction 160
Steppat, Leo 24, 134, 136, 139
Still Life 155
still-life paintings 153, 159
Stone, Jonathan 49–50
Stourbridge College of Art 35, 37, 128
Studio Glass Movement 31, 34
Šuhájek, Jiří 42, 131
Sydney College of the Arts 49

teaching 127–31
Toledo Museum School of Design, Ohio 27, 29
Tookey, Fleur 47
Turner, Helen Monro 34–5, 35, 37

Valkema, Sybren 31, 42, 51
Val St Lambert 44, 66–71
Victoria and Albert Museum (V&A) 19, 44–6;
entrance to Sam Herman's exhibition, 1971 18, 45
Victory Celebration 161
'Vrij Glas' 51

Wakefield, Hugh 19
waste materials 137
welding 134, 136
Western Washington State College 23–4, 134
'wet stick' technique 81–2
Weynans, Gilbert 44
Where are we? 152
Wilks, Helen 153
Wisconsin, university 24, 27, 134
Wiseman, Bella 22, 22
Wiseman, Nathan 22, 22
Woods, Paul 37
World Congress of Craftsmen 31

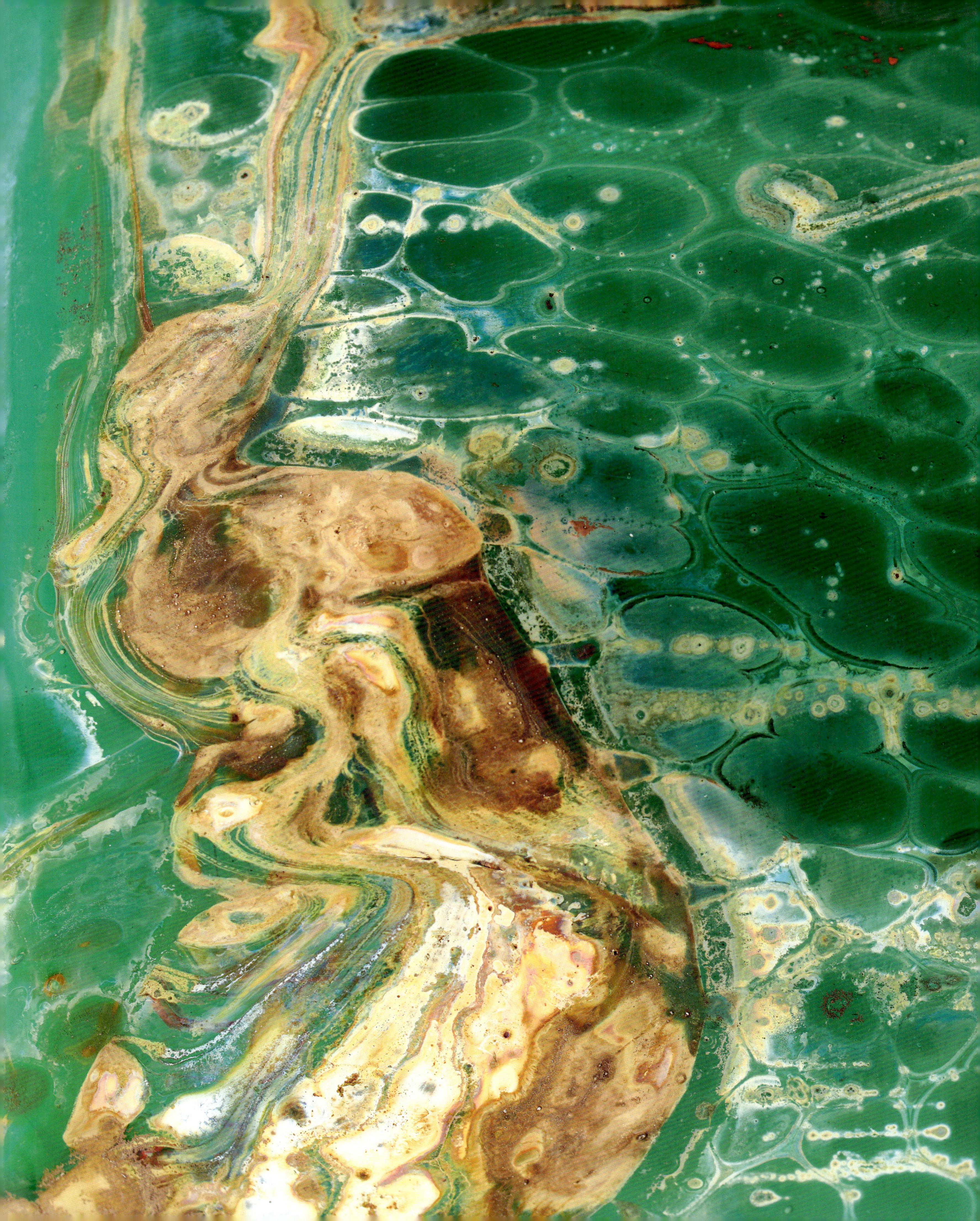

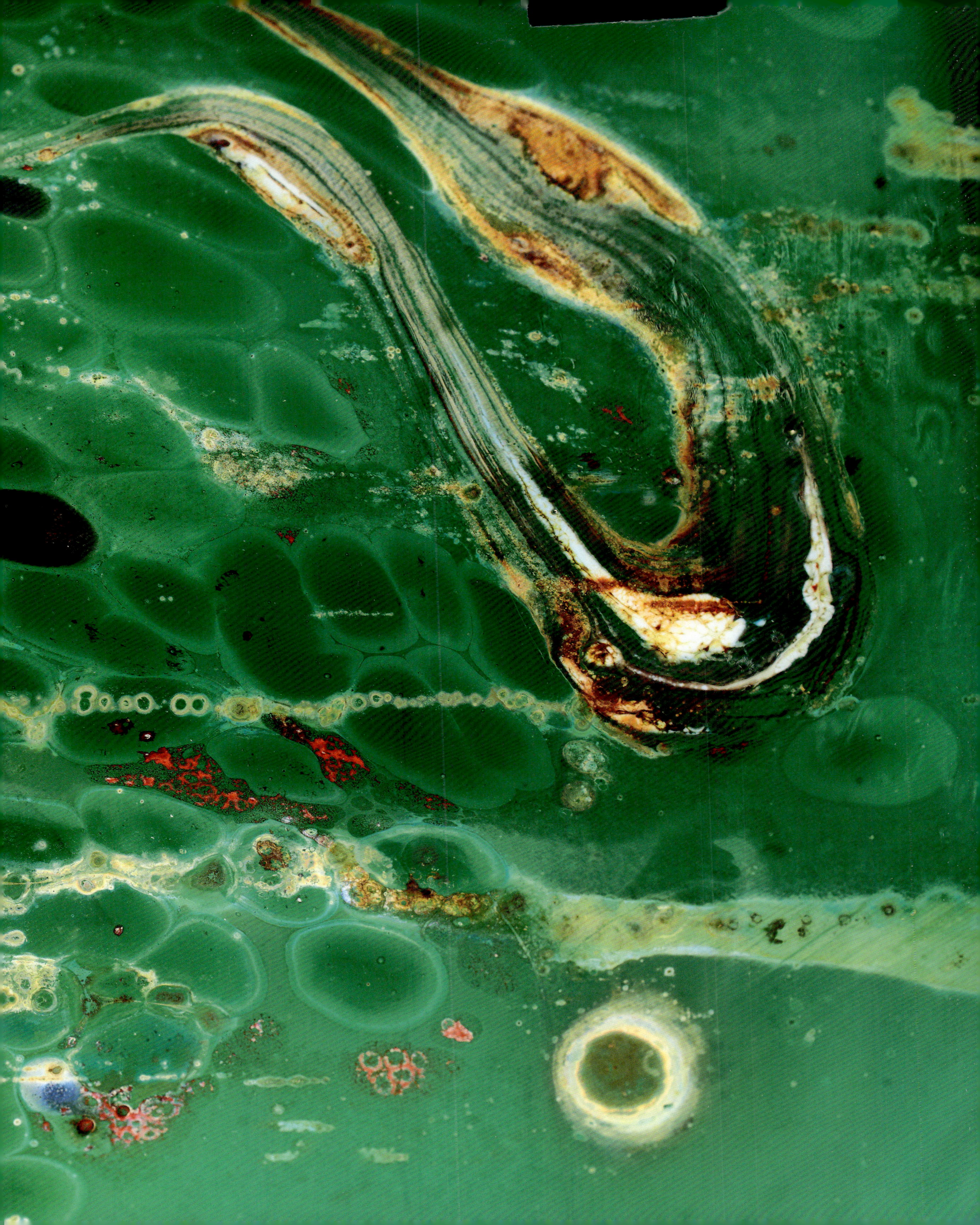

First published in 2019 by Lund Humphries

Lund Humphries
Office 3, Book House
261A City Road
London EC1V 1JX
UK

www.lundhumphries.com

ISBN: 978–1–84822–325–7

A Cataloguing-in-Publication record for this book
is available from the British Library

Designed by Myfanwy Vernon-Hunt, this-side.co.uk
Set in Calibre
Printed in Slovenia

Image credits
Photography by Sylvain Deleu with the exception of: Jane
Bruce page 46; Dalman and Smith pty.ltd page 49; Gretel
Eisch page 50; Martin Storey page 108; Tim Mercer page
128; Ester Segarra pages 141, 144, 147, 148, 149, 153, 163; Sam
Herman pages 135, 136, 137.
© Peter Aldridge page 129; © Pauline Solven page 131 (top);
© Clifford Rainey page 131 (bottom).

Front cover
Untitled, 2013
blown glass, 37cm (14½in),
Private Collection

Back cover
Untitled, 1971
blown glass, 32cm (12½in),
Private Collection

Pages 2–3
Untitled, 2009
blown glass, detail,
Private Collection

Page 4
Untitled, 1970
blown glass, 36cm (14in),
Private Collection

Page 6
Untitled, 2015
blown glass, 35cm (13¾in),
Private Collection

Pages 8–9
Untitled, 1982
blown glass, detail, Private
Collection

Page 11
Untitled, 1971
blown glass, 23cm (9in),
Private Collection

Pages 12–13
Untitled, 2012, 2008, 2013
blown glass, 36cm (14in),
46cm (18in) and 35cm (13¾in),
Private Collection

Page 14
Untitled, 2013
blown glass, 45cm (17¾in),
Private Collection

Pages 16–17
Untitled, 1971
blown glass, 14cm (5½in),
Private Collection

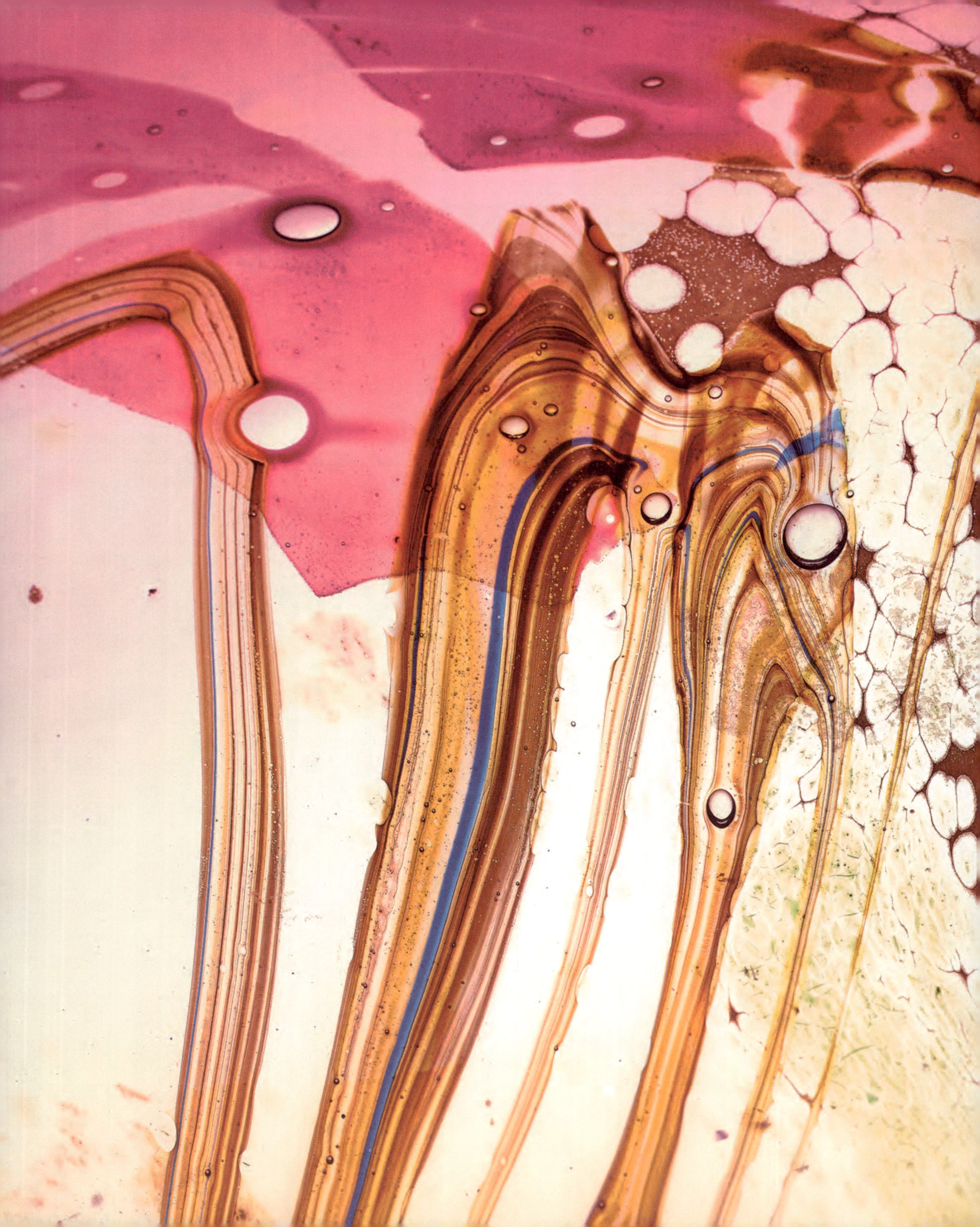